The competitive organization

THE HENLEY MANAGEMENT SERIES

Series Adviser: Professor Bernard Taylor

Also available in the McGraw-Hill/Henley Management Series:

MANAGING INFORMATION
Information systems for today's general manager
A V Knight and D J Silk   ISBN 0-07-707086-0

THE NEW GENERAL MANAGER
Confronting the key challenge of today's organizations
Paul Thorne   ISBN 0-07-707083-6

TOTAL CAREER MANAGEMENT
Strategies for creating management careers
Frances A Clark   ISBN 0-07-707558-7

Forthcoming

THE HANDBOOK OF PROJECT-BASED MANAGEMENT
Improving the processes for achieving strategic objectives
J Rodney Turner   ISBN 0-07-707656-7

CREATING THE GLOBAL COMPANY
Successful internationalization
Colin Coulson-Thomas   ISBN 0-07-707599-4

Details of these and other titles in the series are available from:

The Product Manager, Professional Books, McGraw-Hill Book Company Europe, Shoppenhangers Road, Maidenhead, Berkshire SL6 2QL
Telephone 0628 23432 Fax 0628 770224

The competitive organization
Managing for organizational excellence

Gordon Pearson

McGRAW-HILL BOOK COMPANY

London · New York · St Louis · San Francisco · Auckland
Bogotá · Caracas · Hamburg · Lisbon · Madrid · Mexico · Milan
Montreal · New Delhi · Panama · Paris · San Juan · São Paulo
Singapore · Sydney · Tokyo · Toronto

Published by
McGRAW-HILL Book Company Europe
Shoppenhangers Road, Maidenhead, Berkshire, SL6 2QL, England
Telephone 0628 23432
Fax 0628 770224

British Library Cataloguing in Publication Data

Pearson, G. J. (Gordon J)
  The competitive organization: managing for organizational
  excellence. – (The Henley management series)
  I. Title II. Series
  658
ISBN 0-07-707480-7

Library of Congress Cataloging-in-Publication Data

Pearson, Gordon J.
  The competitive organization: managing for organizational
  excellence / Gordon Pearson.
      p.   cm. – (The Henley management series)
  Includes bibliographical references and index.
  ISBN 0-07-707480-7
  1. Organizational effectiveness. 2. Organizational change.
  3. Strategic planning. 4. Corporate culture. I. Title.
  II. Series.
  HD58.9.P43 1992
  658.4 – dc20   91-42432

Copyright © 1992 McGraw-Hill International (UK) Limited. All rights reserved. No part of this publication may be reproduced, stored in a retrieval system, or transmitted, in any form or by any means, electronic, mechanical, photocopying, recording, or otherwise, without the prior permission of McGraw-Hill International (UK) Limited.

Typeset by Cambridge Composing (UK) Limited
and printed and bound in Great Britain at the University Press, Cambridge

For Eileen

Contents

Preface	xi
Acknowledgements	xv

PART ONE	**INNOVATION AND WHY IT MATTERS**	**1**
1	**The competitive model**	**3**
	1.1 Introduction	3
	1.2 Strategic approaches	3
	1.3 Entrepreneurs and entrepreneurialism	12
	1.4 The competitive model	15
	1.5 Summary	18
2	**The effects of innovation**	**20**
	2.1 Introduction	20
	2.2 Innovation and growth	21
	2.3 Innovation and competitive advantage	24
	2.4 Summary	27
3	**The process of innovation**	**29**
	3.1 Introduction	29
	3.2 Phases in the innovation process	30
	3.3 Roles in the innovation process	31
	3.4 Initiating change	33
	3.5 Evaluating change	34
	3.6 Implementing change	37
	3.7 Summary	37
4	**Innovation successes and failures**	**39**
	4.1 Introduction	39
	4.2 Characteristics of innovations	40
	4.3 Successful innovators	42
	4.4 Mechanistic and organismic organizations	45
	4.5 Reasons for failure	46
	4.6 Summary	48
5	**Business maturity**	**51**
	5.1 Introduction	51
	5.2 The business life cycle	52

5.3	The characteristics of maturity	54
5.4	Innovation and business evolution	58
5.5	Summary	61
6	**Industry assessment**	**63**
6.1	Industry assessment questionnaire	67

PART TWO   THE STRATEGY DIMENSION — 69

7	**Setting strategic direction**	**71**
7.1	Introduction	71
7.2	Strategic responsibility	72
7.3	Purpose of strategy	74
7.4	Outcomes from strategy	75
7.5	Strategic direction	77
7.6	Strategic position	79
7.7	Summary	80
8	**Developing external communications**	**81**
8.1	Introduction	81
8.2	Direct relationships	82
8.3	The broader context	84
8.4	Communications networks	86
8.5	Secondary sources of information	87
8.6	Summary	89
9	**Maintaining a long-term orientation**	**91**
9.1	Introduction	91
9.2	Strategic objectives	92
9.3	Long-term investment	95
9.4	Short-term pressures	96
9.5	Summary	98
10	**Exploiting core competences**	**99**
10.1	Introduction	99
10.2	Globalization	100
10.3	Identifying core competences	100
10.4	Acquiring core competences	102
10.5	Using core competences	105
10.6	Competitive challenges and competence gaps	107
10.7	Summary	108
11	**Focusing on the customer**	**110**
11.1	Introduction	110
11.2	Defining value	111
11.3	Identifying customer needs	115
11.4	Delivering value	119

	11.5 Analysing the competitor	119
	11.6 Summary	121
12	**Plotting the strategy profile**	**123**
	12.1 Introduction	123
	12.2 The components of strategy	123
	12.3 The strategy profile	125
	12.4 Assessing the strategy profile of your business	128
	12.5 Strategy profile questionnaire	130

PART THREE	**THE CULTURE DIMENSION**	**135**
13	**Empowering people**	**137**
	13.1 Introduction	137
	13.2 Progressive and traditional management	138
	13.3 The learning organization	141
	13.4 Control through structure and culture	143
	13.5 Psychological contracts	145
	13.6 Summary	147
14	**Building corporate integrity**	**149**
	14.1 Introduction	149
	14.2 The scope of integrity	150
	14.3 Business ethics	155
	14.4 Openness	157
	14.5 Summary	158
15	**Involving people in leadership**	**160**
	15.1 Introduction	160
	15.2 A pluralist view	160
	15.3 Participation in decision making	164
	15.4 Leadership	166
	15.5 Organization through teams	170
	15.6 Summary	172
16	**Motivating commitment**	**175**
	16.1 Introduction	175
	16.2 The mechanics of motivation	176
	16.3 Intrinsic human needs	178
	16.4 Rewards for work	181
	16.5 Ownership	182
	16.6 Summary	183
17	**Plotting the culture profile**	**185**
	17.1 Introduction	185
	17.2 The components of culture	186
	17.3 Assessing the culture profile of your business	187
	17.4 Culture profile questionnaire	189

PART FOUR ACHIEVING THE COMPETITIVE ORGANIZATION   193

18 The competitive matrix   195
   18.1 Introduction   195
   18.2 Caveats and limitations   196
   18.3 The two dimensions   197
   18.4 The matrix   198
   18.5 Natural tendencies and management responses   202
   18.6 Conclusion   203

19 Repositioning your business   206
   19.1 Introduction   206
   19.2 Repositioning 'butterflies'   207
   19.3 Repositioning liquidators   209
   19.4 Repositioning autocrats, bureaucrats and strong cultures   211
   19.5 Conclusion   219

Appendices
I A note on the original research project   221
II A note on using the questionnaires   226

Bibliography   229
Index   235

Preface

Innovations come in waves and the current wave is much bigger than most. It is sinking many well-established businesses, but those that ride on its crest could achieve fantastic success. By 2000, this particular high in technological innovation may have subsided and the innovative businesses – some of them now very small, some not even born – will be among the great and the good, established industry leaders. They will look back over the 1990s and see the wreckage of businesses that never learned to ride the waves.

If a business is successful it will grow. As it grows and matures it tends to standardize on certain ways of doing things that seem to be effective, it becomes set in these ways and loses some of its inclination to innovate; it becomes slower and less responsive to change. During a technological revolution, such as we are now enjoying, these tendencies seem to become decisive. Maturity seems to be bad news. It seems to be synonymous with ossification, hardening of the corporate arteries, bureaucracy, inflexibility and a complete inability to compete and respond to the real needs of customers and employees or the opportunities provided by technology.

This is the problem. It is management's job to ensure that while the business continues to enjoy the fruits of its own success, it avoids all these negative aspects of maturity and retains the ability to compete with the best. The difficulty is that the fruits of success often appear to be harvested mainly through effective control, while the entrepreneurialism required to compete, on the contrary, appears to require great freedom in order to prosper. The dilemma has prompted many solutions.

There are two broad approaches. The first is to leave the existing organization in place to *control* the existing business, and at the same time to find an alternative, a way round that controlling organization, in order to develop the entrepreneurial project. This can be done, for example, by setting up a new department, a separate division, or even a subsidiary company, where different rules apply. Or the innovatory project can be adopted by a 'champion' who personally sees it through or round existing systems. Or possibly, the company may settle on some form of matrix organization where individuals divide their time between the line tasks of controlling the existing business and the less formal, developmental, project work. In some cases it has even been advocated that management turns a blind eye to the covert hi-jacking of company resources by small informal teams, 'skunkworks', working on the entrepreneurial project.

All these techniques have been widely advocated. They are all ways round the existing, control-oriented organization. They do not seek to change the organization, merely to circumvent it.

The second approach is rather more radical. This approach seeks to change the whole organization so that it competes effectively by being entrepreneurial and innovative in its approach to the existing business as well as the new. In normal times, working round the existing organization may be good enough but, when faced with a technological revolution, the root and branch approach has more going for it.

As in everything to do with business management, there is no one best way. How best to make your business entrepreneurial will depend on its particular circumstances in relation to its customers, competitors and technologies. Having identified these circumstances, you will need to decide the most appropriate way for your business, in your industry, to be innovative without losing control; to grasp the new without losing the established position you have with the old; to continue giving customers what they need and at the same time satisfy the needs of other stakeholders like employees and shareholders; *to beat tomorrow's competitors as well as yesterday's*.

This is no simple task. In the first place it requires an ability to diagnose the existing structures and broad processes currently in place. It requires a knowledge of the available techniques and initiatives and how they might best be applied to your particular situation. This is the subject matter of this book.

Part One outlines a model of competitive management and looks at innovation and entrepreneurship and why they matter in an increasingly competitive and volatile world.

Part Two identifies the key characteristics of the strategic dimension of competitive management.

Part Three identifies the key characteristics of the cultural dimension.

Part Four integrates both dimensions of the competitive model and shows you how to identify your organization's position; more importantly, it suggests the sort of management actions that could reposition the organization to improve its competitive performance.

At the end of Part One there is a short questionnaire to help you assess the position of your industry and how it is likely to affect constituent businesses. At the end of Parts Two and Three there are further short questionnaires to help you assess the position of your business in terms of strategy and culture. The questions are presented in a simple structured format so that you can identify a profile of your own business which can then be applied in the competitive model described in Part Four. The application of this model will not provide all the answers, but it will highlight areas for consideration of further action, and it will enable managers to initiate a representative survey in their own businesses.

British companies are not often held up as paragons of entrepreneurial virtue. From a technical point of view the British may be highly inventive, but when it comes to the commercial exploitation of those inventions we have often been labelled as laggards. The international marketeers of new technology have learned that 'no need to change the organization' is a strong selling point in British markets, whereas in other markets the same product may be sold as providing the opportunity to break down rigid structures. We are conservative, prudent and naturally averse to risk; we love peace and harmony and we risk being trampled on by foreign competitors; and it seems likely to go on while ever the revolution in technology lasts.

This book is an invitation to consider somewhat un-British managerial behaviour. The main ingredients of competitive organization and successful entrepreneurship are to do with energy and activity levels, understanding the customer, knowing the technology and being willing to take avoidable risks. The lessons that have been learned during the various studies on which this book is based provide some indicators for entrepreneurial management action.

Finally, it should be noted that the subject matter of this book, like the job of general management, is extremely broad. It is not within the scope of a single volume to cover each topic in operational detail. The approach is therefore holistic and broad brush. References to further reading are provided for those wishing to go into any topic in greater depth.

Acknowledgements

This book is based on a great number of research programmes, carried out mainly in the UK and America, which are referred to in the text, and my debt to these more illustrious predecessors is heartily acknowledged. The shape of the competitive model itself was derived from some work carried out in the UK warp knitting industry identified in Appendix I. The success of that research depended on the help and cooperation of many people in the industry, from those who served the tea to top management who didn't. Without exception this was given generously and I am grateful to all those who participated. Many other individuals also provided assistance in various different ways, but particular thanks are due to my doctoral supervisors, Professors Alan Pearson and Derrick Ball of the R&D Research Unit at Manchester Business School, to Dr Subbash Annand of Bolton Institute of Higher Education, Mr John Smith, Managing Director of Karl Mayer Textile Machinery Ltd, Dr Bob Wheatley of Leicester Polytechnic and the late Professor Malcolm Burnip of Huddersfield Polytechnic.

PART ONE
INNOVATION AND WHY IT MATTERS

This book is about making your organization more competitive. It has never before been so important for organizations to be responsive to the changes in what their customers want and to be creative and innovative in delivering a product or service that satisfies those wants in a particular, distinctive way.

So much writing about innovation and change is really about how to cope with it, how to respond to it and take advantage of it. The obsession with the Japanese approach to business and management stems mainly from this defensive position. But our organizations need to do more than merely cope with Japanese competition and the effects of change. They need to create the changes that will enable them to beat their competitors and enjoy a brighter future.

Rather than follow the Japanese in their new technology or approach to managing people, we need to be creative and inject our own ingredients of change and become the leaders in our chosen arena.

This is not easy. Being creative demands a great deal of knowledge and experience. Before we can inject our own distinctive elements of creativity we need to understand the existing competitors, customers and technology and how they are changing and what they will be like in the future. Without this knowledge base, competitive creativity and change will be no more than stabs in the dark – some may be lucky, but the vast majority will fail.

So it is with this book. These first five chapters are largely concerned with laying the foundations for future development. They set out some of the relevant knowledge about the entrepreneurial competitive process that is needed before we can ourselves be creative.

The opening chapter gives an outline of the competitive model which is subsequently described in greater depth in Parts Two and Three and finally used in Part Four. This model is a tool for diagnosing the entrepreneurial status of any organization, whether in manufacturing or services. The diagnosis can be used as the basis for taking further detailed management decisions about both the organization's strategy and its culture. The shape of this model is introduced at the beginning so that subsequent sections can all be related back to the basic model as they are discussed.

Chapters 2 to 5 then review specific aspects of innovation and change in order to relate a particular sector or organization to the competitive model. One sector may be more immediately, or fundamentally, affected by the current wave of new technology and the opportunities for distinctive innovation may be different from those in another sector. Similarly, the basic processes of innovation may be accommodated more readily in one type of organization than another and are certainly accorded different priorities in different firms.

Chapter 4 reviews some of the most commonly found characteristics associated with innovative success and failure and suggests ways in which the individual business may assess itself in terms of these various characteristics.

A business, like any other social system or biological organism, strives to succeed and the fruits of that success are the attainment of maturity. In maturity the power and strength of the organization is at its height. Maturity is the goal of every new business. Chapter 5 assesses some of the orthodox wisdom about mature business. Most of us work for mature businesses and most of us will continue to do so. Western economies are crucially dependent on mature businesses for their future growth and prosperity. There is no natural law which dictates that mature businesses should be non-innovative, bureaucratic and poor financial performers. Many are quite the reverse. If you work for a mature business, you can assess how it lines up and the many management actions that can be taken to make it more entrepreneurial and competitive.

Following Chapter 5 there is a short industry assessment questionnaire. This deals with some of the issues raised in the previous chapters and is intended to guide readers towards an assessment of how things are in their industry. The questions raised are not intended to comprise a thoroughgoing industry analysis, but are simply to be used as guidance for the definition and interpretation of the entrepreneurial model outlined in Chapter 1, developed in Parts Two and Three and finally used in Part Four.

Answers to the industry assessment questions are intended to give some indication of the probable status and importance of innovation in your industry. This can then be used to highlight some aspects of strategy and culture as they may be expected to impact your business.

1
The competitive model

1.1 Introduction

Business management is a sufficiently complex process for those involved to feel some need for simplifying tools that will help them concentrate their efforts on the things that really matter, whether it be competitors, employees, customers, quality, technology or anything else. MBO, TQM, AMT, JIT, HRM and many others have from time to time achieved widespread application, but the same rules do not apply in every organization or in every situation – there simply is not one best way of doing things.

There is no substitute for knowing what it is you are trying to achieve before you set out to achieve it. You have to know what your competitors are doing before you can be distinctive. You must know what your customers want before you can make and sell a product at a profit. You must know what you are seeking to achieve from new investment before you commit the funds. You must be quite clear what you are to gain from a collaborative arrangement before you agree to any form of alliance.

Too often, important management initiatives are taken without a clear strategic intent. Technology is bought in on a bandwagon basis; investments are made because their internal rate of return is calculated as sufficient; long-term alliances are made for short-term gains. Fundamental errors like these are usually made because there is no clear business strategy.

This opening chapter looks very briefly at widely used approaches to strategy and then outlines the competitive model that is developed in detail in Parts Two to Four. The competitive model shows how a firm may identify practical steps to becoming more competitive, entrepreneurial and innovative and so take advantage of the increasing number of opportunities.

1.2 Strategic approaches

The problem with strategy is its intrinsic complexity. In even the smallest single-product business, strategy has to take account of many different factors: competitive activity, customer needs, production capability, financial strength, market structure and growth, and many more. In order to get a handle on these, managements have tended to make use of simplifying models. Since the days when corporate strategy was synonymous with long-range planning, and in most cases amounted to little more than cranking the annual budget over an extra four years, there have been just two strategic models of real consequence.

The Boston matrix

The first of these was Boston's business portfolio and its derivatives (Boston Consulting Group 1968a). Business portfolios were based on the empirically tested idea that total costs fall as experience is gained in making and selling a product. Boston's own work centred on an analysis of 24 different commodities (e.g. germanium transistors, silicon diodes, crude oil, ethylene, polystyrene, titanium sponge, refined cane sugar, Japanese beer, etc.) and it has been replicated many times. In 1957, for example, Western Digital's plant in Allentown, Pennsylvania, used 4000 workers to produce 5 transistors per worker per day at a unit cost of $2.50. By 1983 the same plant, using the same number of workers, was producing 5.3 million transistors per worker per day at a unit cost of thousandths of a penny each (Gilder 1986:202).

If costs fall with experience, simple logic suggests that the business that gains the most experience will enjoy the lowest costs. Thus, assuming a general market price, such a business would also enjoy the highest profits. Therefore, increasing market share in order to achieve a rapid increase in experience would be highly profitable. In a young and rapidly growing market, experience will be quickly doubled, thus multiplying the cost-reduction benefits.

Boston's portfolio thus had two dimensions: market growth rate and relative market share. From this the four Boston categories were derived: stars, cash cows, dogs and problem children, and the three strategic prescriptions: invest, ration investment, and withdraw. Boston's analysis was mainly based on manufactured goods, rather than services, and it is clear that the model is not so relevant to service industries where there is less potential for the automation of experience.

Boston originally emphasized that the cost-reducing effects of experience were only of significance in situations of high growth rates and originally presented the matrix with the cut-off point between high and low growth at the 10 per cent p.a. mark. Below this level it was acknowledged that the effects of experience were less material and by implication, therefore, the model itself would not be relevant. This suggested that the model would not be pertinent to the vast majority of

American or European businesses, but may well be relevant to firms enjoying the growth rates than widely experienced in Japan.

Paradoxically, American and European (especially British) businesses adopted the Boston portfolio very widely in trying to achieve strategic control (if that term is not a contradiction in terms), while the Japanese resolutely refused to submit.

A firm's relative market share was measured as share relative to its largest competitor and the split between high and low share was usually drawn at between 1 and 1.5 (i.e. market share between equality with, and 1.5 times, that of the largest competitor). Thus in any industry there could only be one business with a high relative market share. In industries experiencing low growth this could have been somewhat catastrophic because the Boston prescription for low growth/low share businesses was simply 'divest'.

On this basis, Boston suggested that the vast majority of British industry should be divested and, in fact, it seems this process has gone some way over the past two decades. Fortunately, many managers were too shrewd, or optimistic, to follow through the Boston prescription. They used the Boston model very widely, but apparently did not take its prescriptions too seriously if they did not accord with what they were going to do anyway.

The Boston model has been widely criticized (e.g. Alberts 1989; Pearson 1990), but the essential point at issue here is the fundamental proposition that the strategic success of a business could be determined by just two quantifiable factors. This seems too simplistic and could only be true if it was assumed that management itself could not make a difference. But management, for whom the Boston portfolio was created, only exist to make a difference – if they don't make a difference they may as well be replaced by robots.

The Boston prescriptions too were limited. So far as managing the business was concerned they were more or less silent, but restricted their outputs to versions of the 'buy', 'sell' or 'hold' type of decision illustrated in Figure 1.1. There is little of qualitative substance in these statements and little to assist strategic management apart from investment. The Boston decisions are those of the manager of an investment trust, or perhaps the HQ staff at a financial conglomerate such as Hanson Trust. They are not very helpful to someone managing a business.

Other matrices

Boston's simple growth–share matrix was variously enhanced, the two best known being General Electric's Business Assessment Array (BAA) and

6 THE COMPETITIVE ORGANIZATION

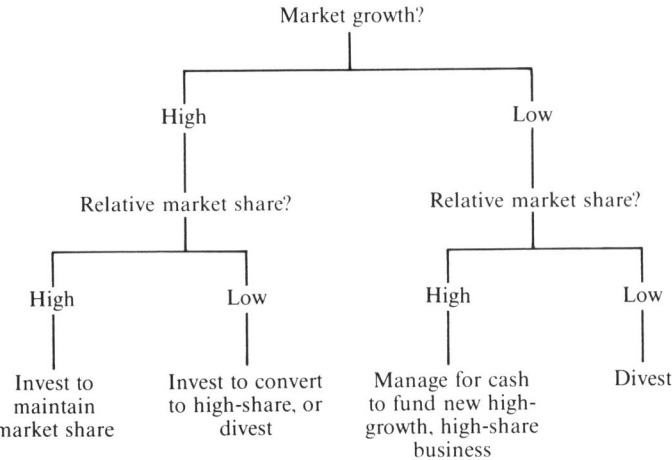

Figure 1.1 Boston portfolio prescriptions

Shell's Directional Policy Matrix (DPM) (Gluck 1985). These enhancements related to both the inputs and outputs of the model.

On the input side, the two quantitative measures of share and growth were replaced by much more detailed analyses of both the market and the business. For example, instead of market growth, the BAA model sought to measure *market attractiveness* indicated by such factors as size and growth of the market, cyclicality of growth, product life cycle position, industry profitability, ease of entry, business environment (e.g. government regulation, industrial relations, etc.), degree of competition and concentration of competitors, investment intensity, availability of labour and materials, marketing intensity and customer concentration. Similarly, instead of relative market share the BAA sought to measure *business strength* indicated by such factors as market share and change in relative market share, profitability, technological competence, brand loyalty, managerial calibre, product differentiation, production economics (age/absolescence of plant), plant capacity, company reputation and image.

The outputs of these enhanced models retained the simple buy, hold or sell prescriptions with only minor sophistications. The matrix was generally divided into nine cells rather than four and, in the case of the BAA, the prescriptions were 'invest/grow', 'improve/defend' and 'harvest/divest'.

Clearly, these models were less simplistic than Boston and required far more detailed analysis that would itself result in greater understanding of the business situation. Despite this, the prescriptions remain essentially limited to the options of an investment trust manager. If 'buy', 'sell' or 'hold' are the only strategic options, then business strategy is a relatively trivial pursuit, which it may not be.

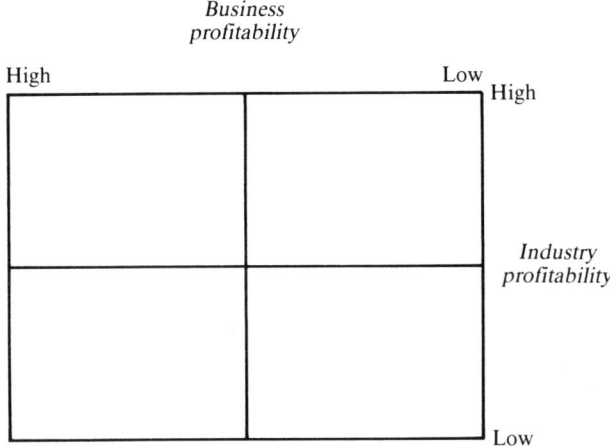

Figure 1.2 Porter's implied matrix

Portfolios addressed the 1960s problem of continuous market growth, and they were widely adopted throughout the 1970s, having a clear run as the dominant strategic model for about a decade.

Porter's generic strategies

Porter's approach focused on essentially the same two dimensions. Though he did not overtly define a portfolio matrix, one is nevertheless implicit in his analysis, as indicated in Figure 1.2. Instead of relative market share or business strength Porter goes directly to the simple measure of business profitability that he uses as a test of competitive advantage. This is discussed later in more detail.

Instead of market growth or industry attractiveness Porter simply uses the idea of industry profitability and then focuses on the factors that determine it. The factors he identifies are a further development of the measures of industry attractiveness described above. He divides them into five categories which he describes as the 'forces driving industry competition'. These are used as a check-list and include most of the industry attractiveness factors, divided according to economics categories: competitors, substitutes, new entrants and the transactional power of suppliers and buyers.

Enumerating *five* forces is somewhat arbitrary, especially when a sixth force, government regulation, is often the most important factor in determining the profitability of an industry. Porter himself investigated the pharmaceuticals and airline industries and found that government

8 THE COMPETITIVE ORGANIZATION

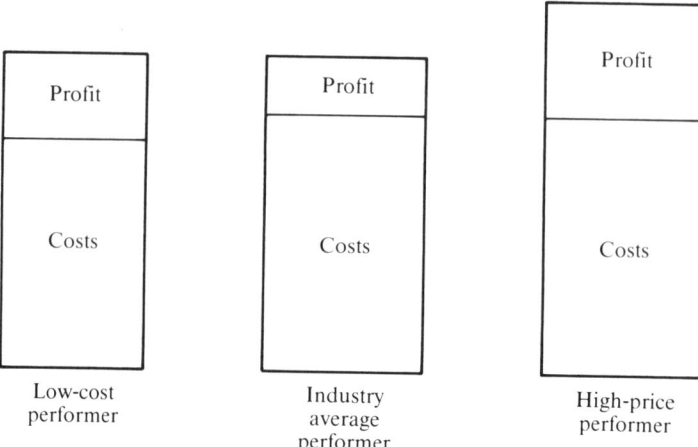

Figure 1.3 Profitability of industry participants

regulation and deregulation was the key to profitability in both (Porter 1988).

The detailed industry analysis commended by Porter leads, in one sense, to a dead-end. In the former models the purpose of assessing industry attractiveness was quite clear – it was to answer 'shall we buy into this industry, get out of it, or stay put?' But Porter is more concerned with what goes on inside a business and how it can be improved, rather than the simple 'buy', 'sell' or 'hold' decision set.

Industry analysis does not play a major role in the subsequent definition of strategy. However, the assessment of business profitability, the other dimension of Porter's implied matrix, is developed much further. The analysis of profitability starts from the very basic assertion that

$$\text{Profit} = \text{Revenue} - \text{Costs}$$

This relationship is both a statement of the obvious and also the starting point for the profit-maximizing model of classicial microeconomics which only requires the assumptions of perfect competition for it to be amenable to solution by calculus. It may not look too promising as the foundation of a practically useful strategic model but that is how Porter used it.

The question is: 'How can a business maximize its profitability, or at least become the most profitable performer in its industry?' Figure 1.3 illustrates the two different approaches suggested by Porter compared against the industry average performer. Maximum profitability can, *in principle*, only be achieved in one of two ways: either by minimizing costs or by maximizing prices. Thus any effective business strategy must aim to pursue one or other of these aims: to be the lowest cost producer or the highest price seller. It would be convenient to refer to these two strategies as cost leadership and price leadership except that 'price leadership' is used by economists to mean something rather different. Consequently, the terms initially used by Porter were 'cost leadership' and 'differentiation', referring to the means by which a premium price is earned. These two were referred to as 'generic' strategies because they are the only two ways, in this model, in which profitability can be maximized, i.e. the only two sources of competitive advantage.

Porter is emphatic that 'failure to make the choice (between cost leadership and differentiation) means that a company is *stuck in the middle*, with no advantage. The result is poor performance' (Porter 1988). This is undoubtedly a great danger as has been highlighted by many other writers; for example, Drucker asserted that 'concentration is the key to real economic results' (Drucker 1964).

Moreover, the basic concept of strategic direction seems to imply much the same thing. Many companies which have a clear direction and a distinct position are also demonstrably *either* cost leaders or differentiators, but not both. Names like Porsche, Bic, Yves St Laurent and KwikSave, for example, immediately classify themselves in one camp or the other.

However, there is nothing in the model that suggests a firm cannot successfully combine aspects of both cost leadership and differentiation. The most profitable firm in an industry could well be both a cost leader and a differentiator. Cases have been reported of firms that appear to be successful in combining low-cost strategies with differentiation – for example, Philip Morris cigarettes combine lowest cost production with a differentiated brand position (Hall 1980). Some researchers have even suggested that the most effective strategies for some situations comprise systematic oscillation between cost leadership and differentiation (Gilbert and Strebel 1988).

Thus, 'stuck in the middle' is not an intrinsic rule of the model, but a pragmatic enhancement to warn of the dangers, a rule of thumb which may be *knowingly* broken with advantage.

In the first exposition of the model Porter showed a diagram similar to that shown in Figure 1.4. It is clear that focus is different in kind from the other two generic strategies. It does not derive from the basic cost and price relationship and thus is not a generic strategy intrinsic to the model, but an added dimension that must sensibly also be taken into account, as any marketeer would insist. This is acknowledged to some extent by the changes made subsequently by Porter himself, shown in Figure 1.5.

In the revised version the anomaly of referring to focus as a 'generic' strategy has been removed. Also the emphasis on cost *leadership*, arising from the maximization aspects of the source model, has been relaxed and

10 THE COMPETITIVE ORGANIZATION

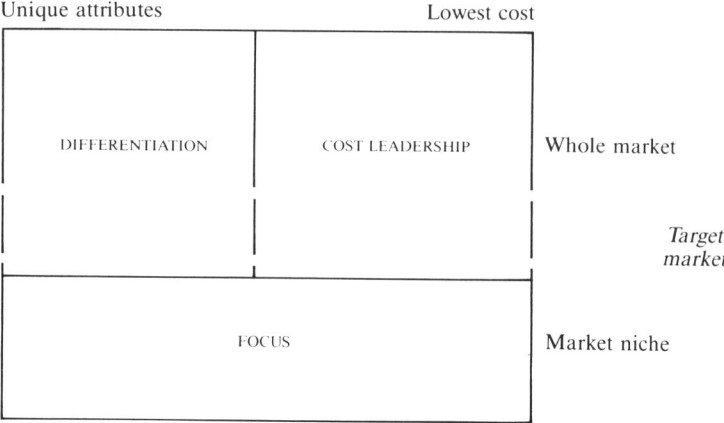

Figure 1.4 Three generic strategies (adapted with permission of The Free Press, a division of Macmillan Inc., from *Competitive Strategy: Techniques for Analyzing Industries and Competitors* by Michael E. Porter Copyright © 1980 by The Free Press)

he now refers to 'low-cost strategies'. Clearly, in any industry there can only be one cost leader – all other would-be cost leaders would necessarily fail and their fate, according to the model, would necessarily be the same as if they were 'stuck in the middle'.

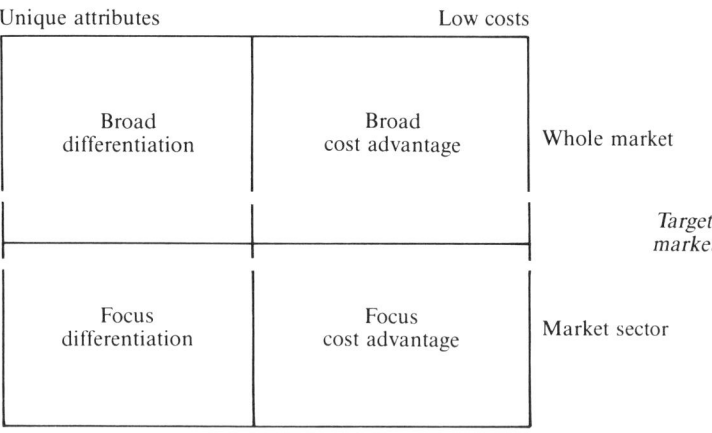

Figure 1.5 Generic strategies (adapted with permission of The Free Press, a division of Macmillan Inc., from *Competitive Advantage: Creating and Sustaining Superior Performance* by Michael E. Porter Copyright © 1985 by Michael E. Porter)

The original introduction of focus as a generic strategy obscured the simple basis of the whole model – that profits could be maximized either by achieving lowest costs or highest prices. Competition erodes profits by the various means indicated in Porter's analysis of industries (i.e. substitutes, new entrants, etc.) and perfect competition erodes profitability perfectly. A way of minimizing this erosion would be to minimize competition. This can be done by focusing on areas of the market where there are the fewest competitors. Hence the *focus* strategy. But focus is not a strategy as such, more a question of degree – at the end of the day all strategies are focused to some extent. Even Ivory Soap (Porter 1988), which has a very broad appeal, is carefully positioned as a multidimensional brand aimed at a fully researched customer profile. Focus, like 'stuck in the middle', is a pragmatic addition to the model. Its consideration may be important, but it is not itself a generic strategy.

Porter's model of generic strategies was the leading orthodoxy of the 1980s and, like the portfolio model, enjoyed about a decade of dominance. However, neither of these models has been fully effective, being attended as they have by the continuous relative decline of Western business where they have been most widely used. Moreover, neither model has much to offer in terms of the main issues confronting businesses today.

A model for technological competition

Today's problems are to do with the rapid global spread of new technology for both manufacturing and service industries and the self-evident fact that so many Western companies are being so often beaten by the Japanese and other Far Eastern countries. This is happening not just on the world scene, but also in our own back yards.

The stakes are extremely high. The new technologies may require massive investment, but in return provide reduced unit costs, radically improved quality, and increased variety, flexibility and ability to respond to customer desires. Such high investment makes it essential to achieve rapid market penetration in order to amortize the capital costs involved. To achieve this there has been an emphasis on global marketing and, as a consequence, a progressive convergence in consumer tastes across national markets. These have been largely satisfied by the businesses that have led the investment in new technology, mainly the Japanese manufacturers. Previously we had a relatively peaceful, if competitive, global coexistence. Now we have a form of warfare, where the stakes are often too high for a single company and campaigns are fought through technological collaborations and strategic alliances.

Now, just as many Western businesses are gearing themselves up to fight back on the global front, so the technology leaders are starting to set up production and design centres on a regional basis to cater for national tastes. Thus, having cracked the global market, they are now rapidly deglobalizing so that the essential rapid sales growth will not be available to their competitors. They are trying to close the door firmly behind them. It is not just the Honeywells, Chryslers and Caterpillars that are losing out: every small and medium-sized niche business is vulnerable.

This global competitive war has spurred new thinking about how to compete on the world stage and a new strategic model is emerging that seeks to respond to these problems. Most firms are not, and will never be, global leaders, but the lessons learned from the global arena are relevant to every business. Technology is global and affects every business. Even a business with only local market aspirations must be aware of, and exploit, the new technology in ways that are appropriate to their strategic intentions. It is not necessary to be a global leader to exploit leading-edge technology, as exemplified by the producers of Carter's Gold Medal Soft Drinks.

Carter is a medium-sized UK producer of soft drinks with sales confined largely to the Midlands region. The firm has no plans to achieve global leadership in its product markets. It does not seek to emulate Coca-Cola and would no doubt regard any comparable business which did have such aspirations as naive and unrealistic. Nevertheless, Carter regards it as vital to make full use of the latest technology in the industry from wherever it comes, and through its use to deliver value to their customers.

They recently opened a new factory described as the 'world's most advanced automated soft drink bottling plant' which permits it to respond flexibly to changes in demand. In the press release announcing the opening of this new facility, chairman Tony Marchmont said:

> In this industry, flexibility means tripling production because of a heat-wave. It means a special promotion for a single retail store wanting, say, pink bottles with a special label. It means producing ten lines of 1000 bottles as cheaply and quickly as one line of 10 000 bottles.

Carter is not a global leader, but recognizes the need to exploit global technology to achieve their strategic aims.

The entrepreneurial model suggests ways for a business to achieve its strategic intentions through the appropriate use of innovation and change.

1.3 Entrepreneurs and entrepreneurialism

The entrepreneurial approach is open to many interpretations. With the retreat of socialism, entrepreneurialism has become almost a political credo and, in Britain, government bureaucracies, such as the DTI and the Training Agency, have become heavily involved in its promulgation. Such approaches depend for their inspiration on agreed definitions such as those given below. However, while it may not be difficult to recognize an entrepreneur when we meet one, it seems that attempts to define them inevitably fail to capture the essential ingredients:

– *Entrepreneur*
The standard dictionary definition emphasizes organization and management and does not capture the full implications of the term. For example:

> 'One who organizes, manages and assumes the risks of a business or enterprise in the hope of profit'   (Dictionary of the English Language, Longman, 1984)

A more appropriate definition might be:

> 'One who creates, or quickly identifies, new and risky (i.e. not risk-free) opportunities to satisfy customer needs or desires and organizes their satisfaction at a profit'

– *Innovation*
> 'The technical, industrial and commercial steps which lead to the marketing of new manufactured products and to commercial use of new technical processes and equipment'   (HMSO 1968)

> 'An idea, practice or object, that is perceived as new by an individual or other unit of adoption'   (Rogers 1983)

– *Intrapreneur*
> 'An entrepreneur operating inside the corporation'   (Pinchot 1985)

The entrepreneurial idea is very old and is being replicated every day of the year. Most would agree that the true entrepreneur beats the competition to market, rather than following it. The idea is also based on the satisfaction of some well understood customer need. The original entrepreneur, when he set up his business, must have known exactly what the need was. Otherwise he would not have survived for long. But most businesses, as they develop over the years, introduce so many 'new' products and digress down so many diversificationary paths, that they completely lose sight of the original purpose of the business. The original entrepreneur not only knew the purpose of the business, i.e. the customer need it satisfied, but also knew what distinctive competence was brought to it in order to make the business different from its competitors. To be successful every business must possess some competitive specialism that customers regard as important, though it need not be the lowest costs or the highest prices.

As well as knowing the purpose of the business and understanding the competitive specialism, the original entrepreneur enjoyed a natural small company strength of being fleet of foot and able to concentrate all efforts on delivering the competitive specialism to the customer, and also of being able to communicate this focus to the other members of the business. These entrepreneurial strengths tend to get lost as a business grows and becomes more diversified. The problems of managing a large organization often appear to be as important as ensuring its real business purpose is being fulfilled. The niceties of organizational structures start to receive more management attention than ensuring efforts are concentrated on exploiting the competitive specialism. Sophisticated financial control systems may become the main form of internal communication and hitting budget the most important message, rather than the original message about business purpose and competitive specialism.

These few ideas encapsulate something of what entrepreneurialism is about. The concept is simple enough, but there is an infinite variety of forms in which it can be realized. George Gilder described entrepreneurs in the following terms:

> Entrepreneurs understand the inexorable reality of risk and change. They begin by saving, foregoing consumption, not to create ersatz security but to gain the wherewithal for a life of productive risks and opportunities. Their chief desire is not money to waste on consumption but the freedom and power to consummate their entrepreneurial ideas. (Gilder 1986:254)

The most important ingredients of entrepreneurialism are the early (i.e. earlier than the competition) recognition of new customer wants, the identification of opportunities to innovate in order to create new business, the foregoing of current consumption in order to build a long-term business, and the preparedness to embrace the personal risks involved. Putting these ingredients together is a creative process and is what makes an entrepreneur.

The motivation for entrepreneurialism is essentially personal, but it is unlikely to be simply the creation of personal wealth – there are easier ways to achieve that end. More important is the creative desire to build a business of substance that will long outlast its creator. Personal ownership is an important underpinning.

> Lease a man a garden
> And in time he will leave you
> A patch of sand.
> Make a man a full owner
> Of a patch of sand
> And in time he will grow there
> A garden on the land.
> (Gilder 1986:23)

The problem is how to recreate this personal 'ownership', which is embedded in the entrepreneurial situation, within a multi-product business or multi-business company. It is not easy. Not only is there no possibility of real ownership, but also the essentially simple entrepreneurial concepts such as business purpose and competitive specialism will have been obscured and perverted in most medium-sized and large firms. Nevertheless, in an era of rapid change, when competitive structures are in flux, being truly entrepreneurial is the key to real business success.

1.4 The competitive model

The competitive approach outlined in this book identifies what appear to be the key characteristics that enable a business to be competitive and entrepreneurial. These characteristics are relevant to businesses of any size and in any industry, whether manufacturing, service or even public sector, though their implementation will differ according to individual circumstances. In suggesting how to be more effective this model responds to the business problems of the current decade – unlike portfolios and generic strategies, which contribute little to the development of entrepreneurialism.

The detailed basis of the model and its practical application are described in subsequent chapters. The outline description contained in this section indicates only the bare structure of the model and is based on literally thousands of studies of how businesses succeeded or failed at being competitive, innovative, flexible and entrepreneurial.

> Since the Second World War there has been an increasing interest in the problems of industrial innovation. In 1956 a British government sponsored report was published based on investigations in 269 different firms and four separate industries. By 1962, Everett Rogers was able to refer to 405 innovation studies in his book 'Diffusion of Innovations'. In the second edition published in 1971 this number had quadrupled to 1500, and by the third edition in 1983 the number had more than doubled again. Some of these studies were obscure and of little practical use, but there were also 2297 empirical studies and these, plus many more since, have generated a much deeper understanding of the processes of innovation and the prerequisites for success. (Rogers 1983)

Not surprisingly, these studies do not all agree as to the critical components, but there is an emerging consensus on which the approach described here is based.

The competitive approach is largely concerned with two groups of organizational characteristics that can, to a great extent, be managed and controlled. They are:

- *strategy*, which is about knowing what you want to achieve and how to achieve it, and
- *culture*, which is about engaging the intelligence, expertise and commitment of people in achieving the strategy.

Before they can be of practical use these characteristics must be capable of measurement so that a firm can see how it appears to perform. This is what the competitive model does. The assessment of strategy is achieved in terms of being focused or dispersed. A focused strategy is where a business is very clear about its intent and all the members of the business know and understand what that strategy is and how it is to be achieved.

The measurement of culture is made in terms of being progressive or traditional. A progressive culture is one where the people are not only aware of the aims of the business, understand them and have the freedom to take initiatives, but also are personally involved in, and committed to, their achievement.

Both culture and strategy are composite characteristics that comprise a number of factors. For example, in this model strategy comprises a clear strategic direction and position, an openness to external communications, an orientation to long-term development, awareness of customer needs and desires, knowledge and use of appropriate technology, acquisition and development of core organizational competences, understanding of competitive products and competences and the ability to put all these together in order to deliver real value in the business product or service. Similarly, culture is defined for this model as comprising a particular philosophy about people in business organizations, a consistently upheld corporate integrity, the participation of people in decision making, their involvement in leading the organization, and their proactive commitment to the strategic aims of the business.

A successfully competitive organization needs both a focused strategy and a progressive culture.

The model can be drawn as a simple two-dimensional matrix as shown in Figure 1.6. The four quadrants of the matrix exhibit quite distinct types of organization and the labels annotated on the matrix – 'autocrats', 'bureaucrats', 'butterflies', etc. – serve to describe the types of business that fit each quadrant. These labels are borrowed from the study referred to in Appendix I where the model was first used and the terms were suggested by various employees to describe the firms in which they worked.

Organizations in the progressive–focused quadrant were found to be the most effective innovators and the 'innovative teams' label aptly describes them. Such firms have a clear stategy that is well known and understood by members of the organization as well as a culture that not only gives members the freedom to use their intelligence, skill and expertise in pursuit of the strategy, but has also successfully engaged their commitment. Such organizations are structured flexibly with an emphasis on

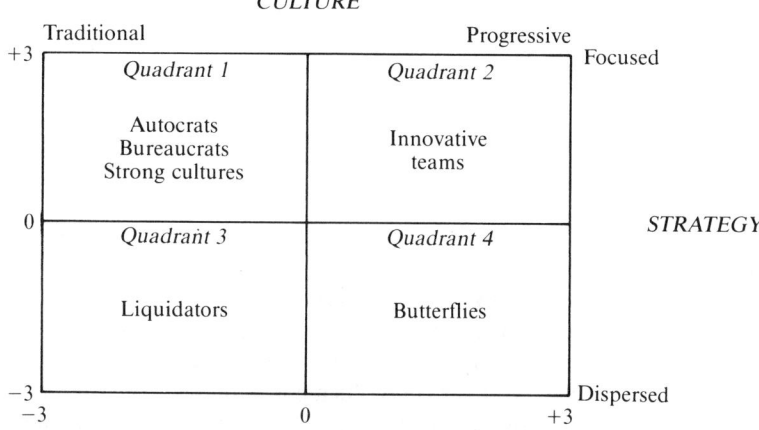

Figure 1.6 The competitive matrix

development through project teams rather than preserving the status quo through rigid hierarchies.

Organizations in the traditional–focused quadrant also enjoyed a clear strategic focus, but lacked the progressive culture. These organizations would be well suited to a stable environment if one still existed, but in today's rapidly changing circumstances they were vulnerable and their competitive strengths fragile. Three distinctive organization types were identified in this quadrant: 'autocrats', 'bureaucrats' and 'strong cultures'. 'Autocrats' were those organizations that were led by a dominant individual and consequently reflected the strengths and weaknesses of his or her personality. Some 'autocrats' were highly effective competitors, flexible, innovative and responsive to customer desires, while others completely lacked these characteristics. However, even those that were successful often failed to attract and retain high-calibre members or to gain the commitment of those they did manage to attract. In all cases, the organization was wholly dependant on the leader and consequently vulnerable to his or her demise, departure or failing energy.

'Bureaucrats' were rigidly structured, often large, mature organizations that had mostly lost the ability to flex with changing circumstances. They were often efficient in their core operations, but may have accumulated sufficient non-core and institutional activities and characteristics to nullify their fundamental efficiency completely. Again, they were often incapable of attracting and retaining the commitment of high-calibre members. 'Strong cultures' were organizations that had deliberately sought to avoid the pitfalls of bureaucracy by the adoption of more subtle forms of control to replace old-fashioned rule and regulation. However, to the extent that their new methods were successful, so they also tended to lose the essential characteristics of entrepreneurialism and flexibility that they tried to develop.

'Liquidators' tended to be organizations that had lost sight of their strategic focus. Their previous responses to environmental change and turbulence had not been effective and so, in the face of mounting financial difficulties, they had been driven to focus entirely on short-term financial criteria, predominantly cost reduction and the elimination of any long-term investment. 'Butterflies' also lacked strategic focus, but enjoyed a progressive culture that gave organizational members the opportunity to be creative and innovative. Without any strategic direction, however, initiatives tended to lack any concentration of effort across the organization and were inconsistent over time. As a consequence, the organizations flitted from one interesting project to another without achieving any solid competitive success. Such organizations appeared to be able to recruit high-calibre members, but not to exploit their strengths and in the end not to be able to retain them.

By identifying the strategic and cultural characteristics of these various organizational forms, the model makes it possible to define the programmes of management action needed to achieve a more competitive repositioning on the matrix. The questionnaires in Chapters 12 and 17 show you how to position your organization on the matrix and, the remaining text, how to identify the action programme to achieve a repositioning.

This skeletal description of the model clearly raises far more questions than it answers. The more detailed description and demonstration of the model in subsequent chapters (Parts Two, Three and Four) will provide most of the answers but, for the time being, it is sufficient to identify just the bare bones of the approach.

1.5 Summary

- There are no simple answers to achieving business success that apply equally to all firms and every situation.
- The two most widely applied approaches to strategy – business portfolios and competitive strategy – provide few answers relevant to the current decade.
- Competitive success appears to depend on knowing exactly what it is you are trying to achieve before you try to achieve it.
- The competitive model sets out a structure for assessing the position of any business in relation to the key organizational characteristics. These are divided into two groups – strategy and culture.
- Strategy is about knowing what you want to do and how to do it, while

culture is about harnessing the intelligence, expertise and commitment of people in achieving the strategic intent.
- These two groups of characteristics define the two dimensions of a matrix that is described in operational detail in subsequent chapters.

References

Alberts, W. W., 'The experience curve doctrine revisited', *Journal of Marketing*, July 1989.
Boston Consulting Group, 'Perspectives on Experience', Boston Consulting Group, Boston, 1968a.
Drucker, P. F., *Managing for Results*, Harper & Row, New York, 1964. (Currently available from Heinemann Professional Publishing, Oxford, 1989.)
Gilbert, X. and P. Strebel, 'Developing Competitive Advantage' in J. B. Quinn, H. Mintzberg and R. M. James, *The Strategic Process*, Prentice Hall, Englewood Cliffs, 1988.
Gilder, G., *The Spirit of Enterprise*, Penguin Books, Harmondsworth, 1986.
Gluck, F. W., 'A fresh look at strategic management', *The Journal of Business Strategy*, Fall 1985.
Hall, W. K., 'Survival strategies in a hostile environment', *Harvard Business Review*, Sept–Oct 1980.
Pearson, G. J., *Strategic Thinking*, Prentice-Hall, Hemel Hempstead, 1990.
Pinchot, G., *Intrapreneuring*, Harper & Row, New York, 1985.
Porter, M. E., *Competitive Strategy: techniques for analyzing industries and competitors*, Free Press, New York, 1980.
Porter, M. E., Video film and pamphlet: 'Michael Porter on Competitive Strategy', Harvard Business School Video Series, 1988.
Rogers, E. M., *Diffusion of Innovations* 3rd edn, Free Press, New York, 1983.

2
The effects of innovation

2.1 Introduction

No single approach to management can be successfully applied in exactly the same way in all situations. Effectiveness depends on circumstances. This applies to the competitive model just as much as to any other approach. Circumstances vary from business to business, from industry to industry and from country to country and the circumstance which, at the moment, affects every business crucially, whether manufacturing or service based, is technological innovation.

The central role of technological innovation is the only plausible explanation of economic history (Baumol 1986). Until the industrial revolution of the eighteenth century the story of economic development was one of continuous ups and downs of plagues, wars and peace, famines and years of plenty. The formation of great empires tended to concentrate existing wealth in geographical areas rather than result in the creation of new wealth. Then, in the eighteenth century, this irregular pattern was suddenly broken by the application of new technology.

As late as 1800, no European country had yet reattained the living standards of Imperial Rome 15 centuries earlier. But in the following 50 years real income per head in Britain, for example, trebled and over the past 100 years has risen more than sevenfold. In the last 100 years or so, it has been calculated, real per capita income in the 16 leading industrialized nations rose on average by 700 per cent, labour productivity rose by 1200 per cent and exports by 6000 per cent (Maddison 1982). The contrast between this explosion of economic growth and the previous 15 centuries can only be explained as a result of technological innovation.

Whether all change and development has its source in new technology may never be finally resolved, though many argue that all significant social and organizational changes have their origins in technological developments. On the grand scale this is very apparent. The technological developments of the eighteenth century clearly produced epochal social changes:

population explosion, mass migration to urban areas, large-scale factory organization, etc. On a small scale, it is also a persuasive argument. For example, the networking of computers makes it feasible for many workers to operate from home with substantial impacts on their quality of life.

Technological innovation generates all these effects and is a crucial factor in the global economy, the state of nations, the well-being of industries, the competitive strength of individual businesses and thus the effective entrepreneur.

2.2 Innovation and growth

Natural resources are strictly finite and cannot (under normal circumstances) be either created or destroyed, but can, of course, be converted into other forms. The processes of their conversion, distribution and consumption are what economics is all about. If the cost of the resource plus its conversion and distribution is less than the value placed on it by its ultimate consumer, then a surplus value, or wealth, will have been generated. These processes have been improved and developed over time so that ever-increasing amounts of wealth have been accrued and in turn invested in further improvements. The development of conversion, distribution and consumption all stem from technological innovations and their long-term effects have been all pervasive.

Conversion

Innovation in the conversion process is illustrated by the Nottingham twist lace industry, which grew up in the early nineteenth century. It was based on the Leavers machine, patented in 1813, some of which are still in use today. Patterning information for this machine was stored on metal cards joined together in chains which, for elaborate patterns, could weigh many tons and take several weeks to set up on a decommissioned machine. Modern warp knit lace equipment stores patterning data electronically, weighs a few grammes and is down-loaded to the machine in a matter of seconds.

This is typical of the substitution of intellect for manual dexterity being made in most manufacturing and service industries today.

The skills, knowledge, numbers and calibre of people required by the new situation are quite different from the old. This change has fundamental implications for recruitment, training and style of management.

Distribution

The distribution of newspapers was previously achieved by printing centrally and physically transporting printed paper to the customer. The technology has long been available to distribute news information without the use of paper. However, the newspaper industry recognizes that it is not simply in the business of news dissemination, but also entertainment, leisure, non-news information dissemination, etc.

Consequently it makes careful use of the technology to reduce costs while delivering a high-quality hard copy product to the consumer. Thus, data are distributed electronically to regional printing centres in order to reduce distribution costs.

This reduces costs and makes completely new products feasible – such as the first European-wide newspaper and the first national daily paper to be distributed across the whole of the United States.

Consumption

Innovations in the provision of sound recordings have been accompanied by changes in the process of consumption as ever-increasing quality both creates and satisfies consumer demand and continually improves consumers' quality of life.

Technology has progressed from low-quality breakable 78 rpm discs, through soft plastic LPs, read-and-write magnetic tapes, optical compact discs, read-and-write optical media, and plug-in programmable chips. This progression is being mirrored by innovation in consumption. Progress is being developed with care so that applications of software technology coincide with the consumers' acquisition of the necessary hardware.

The cross-fertilization of electronic information technologies continues to spawn new forms of consumption. The distinction between audio and video equipment will progressively disappear and merge with other domestic computer technologies, to generate cheap interactive entertainment.

The industrial revolution itself was based on many fundamental innovations including the application of coal energy, steel and the steam engine. These in turn gave rise to the mechanization of textiles and other manufacturing industries as well as the development of rapid railway transportation on a massive scale and the subsequent launching of inorganic chemistry.

All these innovations gave birth to industries that grew up and grew old more or less together. Their eventual decline was marked by the great depression of the 1930s and the demise of many old industrial enterprises or the migration of old industries from the advanced economies to the Third World (Piatier 1984).

A second coincidence of fundamental innovations took place around the 1930s and created a further dramatic explosion in terms of economic growth. These were centred on the discovery and application of oil, mass exploitation of electric power, the internal combustion engine, motor vehicles, sheet steel, aircraft, organic chemistry and synthetic materials. The growth created by these innovations was interrupted by the Second World War, but was finally realized in the post-war reconstruction of the 1950s and 1960s – the period to which Boston's business portfolio was particularly relevant.

Most of the industries of this second wave of innovations are now in the mature or decline phases. As with the first industrial revolution, much of the business that grew up in those industries has ceased or migrated to the less advanced economies, leaving only specialist, relatively high-technology segments to be serviced by the original firms. This decline phase, where businesses were forced to compete for bigger slices of a dwindling cake, is the period to which Porter's competitive strategy model was particularly relevant.

All this is history, but it guides our understanding of what is happening at present. The current technological revolution is another coincidence of fundamental innovations. This time the main thrusts are in electronics and information technology, biotechnology and molecular engineering and a myriad other applications of quantum mechanics.

In all three waves of innovation, the core technologies all had generalized applicability. For example, the steam engine was used first for pumping out mines and then as a means of transport and also for driving large-scale factory machinery. Similarly, the internal combustion engine and the electric motor became almost universal replacements for older forms of motive power. Currently, the computer or electronic chip exhibits similar universal application, providing many sources of product or service differentiation, at the same time as achieving higher quality and greater flexibility than ever before.

The potential for economic growth from these new technologies surpasses anything the world has previously experienced, but the form this will take is substantially different from the earlier revolutions. The previous technologies multiplied mankind's strength, whereas the new technologies multiply our intellectual power. The old technologies generated tremendous demand for additional low-skill manual labour, whereas the new technologies require far greater skill and technical knowledge and expertise. The old brought large numbers of people together in large-scale production units, while the new make it possible to produce effectively in units employing only small numbers of specialist staff with little requirement for unskilled or semi-skilled labour. In addition, the old technologies produced relatively inefficient industries that generated huge amounts of unwanted and damaging by-products to the extent that global ecology was endangered. The new technologies, which in many cases contain even

24 THE COMPETITIVE ORGANIZATION

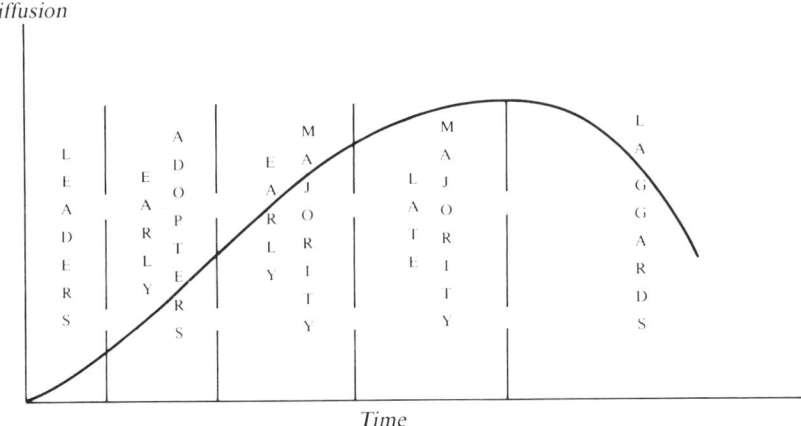

Figure 2.1 Leaders and laggards

greater adverse potential, are consequently accompanied by a new awareness of the fragility of the ecosystem.

All these technological developments serve to increase the scale and effectiveness with which we use resources, whether it is in conversion, distribution or consumption. The effects of economic growth are seen in ever-increasing standards of living and quality of life of those in the industrialized economies. These trends are apparent at national level, but their impacts are made at the level of industries and individual businesses.

2.3 Innovation and competitive advantage

Innovation is the key weapon in achieving a sustainable competitive advantage. To compete successfully it is vital to use the most appropriate technology to produce and distribute your product or service. Generally, this means using the latest technology, which will incorporate more features, higher performance, greater quality or lower costs. In some cases this may involve invention as well as innovation. Innovations may be based on inventions or discoveries, but their importance rests on their commercial exploitation. Rogers' definition of innovation (see Section 1.3) implies that anything that is new to the person or business adopting it is an innovation. This suggests there is no distinct split between the original inventors and the subsequent adopters or imitators, but rather a continuum of shades of innovativeness between the initiators of an innovation (i.e. the leaders), early adopters, the majority and the laggards (see Figure 2.1).

In normal times the leading innovator may achieve a competitive

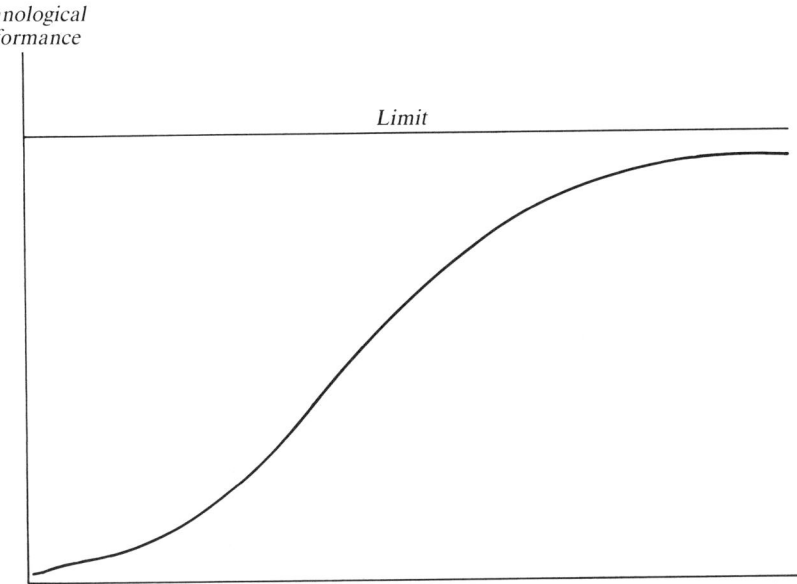

Figure 2.2 The S-curve and limit

advantage that he is able to sustain for a considerable period. Similarly, the laggard innovators may also be able to survive for a long period, albeit with a reducing market. However, during a period of great technological change, the differences in a product achieved through innovation may be so decisive as to make it essential for any would-be survivors to adopt the innovation quickly themselves. For example, manufacturers of vacuum valves had to move quickly to transistor technology or get out of the industry. Thus the time delay between leaders and laggards has closed up and the competitive advantage from being a leading innovator becomes sustainable for shorter periods of time.

As Drucker said, 'any leadership position is transitory and likely to be short-lived' (Drucker 1964:7). Moreover, 'what exists is getting old' and is doing so now much faster than before. One of the most difficult decisions confronting management in these circumstances is knowing *when* to ditch an old technology in which a leadership position is enjoyed. Make the change too soon and not only will the business forfeit a lot of profit, but it may also cede its leadership position to a less powerful competitor. On the other hand, making the move too late will almost certainly lead to a permanent loss of position and an inexorable decline into mediocrity.

There is a pattern in the development of technologies (see Figure 2.2) that may be helpful in timing a change in technology. A new technology usually only emerges slowly. At the research and development phase there is relatively little resource made available and only a small number of people involved. But as the necessary scientific knowledge and engineering expertise is developed so the performance of the technology is developed. Technologies that survive these early stages then win wider acceptance and investment gathers pace. Competition during this rapid growth phase also acts as a spur to further rapid development and substantial improvements in its technological performance are achieved. Then in due course the rate of improvement slows down as it approaches its limit, which may be technological (e.g. some physical limit on performance), economic (e.g. diminishing returns from further research and development) or social (e.g. production of undesirable by-products). At this point there will be considerable economic and competitive benefit in changing to an alternative technology to which the limit does not apply, and consequently in due course a new technology will emerge and be adopted.

There are many examples where this model appears to hold good, from computer technologies to tyre cord, from metal machining to electric light bulbs. The S-shaped curves of technological development – slow start followed by rapid growth followed by slow growth tending to a limit – seems to have an almost universal application. Nevertheless, there are exceptions and yours may be one. The process of changing from one technology to another that seems likely to be the next, remains dangerous and potentially traumatic.

However, competitive innovation is not simply about the major changes where one technology is replaced by another. It is also very much concerned with continuous incremental innovation. It may be imitative, or it may be original, but in the main it is evolutionary rather than revolutionary. The S-curve does not adequately model this process. The sustainability of competitive advantage seems unlikely to depend on achieving major break-throughs but rather more on continuous innovation, unless (as is unusual) the break-through developments are adequately protected by patent (e.g. Xerography).

Sustainability is more likely to be achieved by building layers of advantage, no single layer being long sustainable, but the multi-layered structure being less pervious. Thus, simply being the lowest cost producer would not be sufficient, especially if the source of low costs was based on a single thrust. Low costs in conjunction with another layer of advantage would be much more sustainable. For example, Philip Morris combine at least two layers of advantage by using new technology to achieve low-cost cigarette manufacture, but combining this with a strongly differentiated product brand through investment in marketing.

Sustainability may be achieved through attacking a competitor's weak points and then developing other layers of advantage from there on. Honda originally penetrated the British motor cycle market with small low-cost machines. They achieved volume sales with these products and then developed other layers of advantage with larger, more sophisticated products. Sustainability can be achieved by using other people's resources through collaborative arrangements, joint ventures, licensing, outsourcing, etc. The Japanese attack on American domestic TV, video and hi-fi markets was based on this thrust; they supplied manufactured products to American firms who, while they saved on R&D, eliminated themselves from the next-generation technology.

Clearly, there are many ways of using competitive innovation to achieve a sustainable competitive advantage, but they all depend on the organization adopting innovation and change as its equilibrium position, rather than something to be coped with when necessary and avoided when not. Innovation is the principal tool of the competitive organization.

2.4 Summary

- Technology developments are the only plausible explanation for the explosion of wealth that has taken place since industrialization. It is at least arguable that *all* change, including social and organizational change, has its roots in technological developments.
- The innovative process that can be seen at the macro level of the world economy is actually implemented at the level of the individual organization.
- Key innovations may take place at any stage of the economic process, i.e. in the conversion, distribution or consumption processes.
- There are two major effects of innovation: growth and competitive advantage.
- The individual business, whether it is in manufacturing or a service industry, will achieve its main competitive advantages through the application of technological innovation. It can be done through once-and-for-all changes in basic technologies, or more frequently through the continuous application of evolutionary innovations.
- Competitive advantage is not easily sustainable, especially if based on single technological developments. Competitive advantage based on layers of different innovations is much less pervious to competition.
- Layers of advantage can only be achieved by an organization that regards continuous change as a desirable and much sought-after state of affairs.

References

Baumol, W. J., 'Entrepreneurship and a century of economic growth', *Journal of Business Venturing*, No. 1, 1986.

Drucker, P. F., *Managing for Results*, Harper & Row, New York, 1964. (Currently available from Heinemann Professional Publishing, Oxford, 1989.)

Maddison, A., *Phases of Capitalist Development*, Oxford University Press, Oxford, 1982.

Piatier, A., *Barriers to Innovation* (a study carried out for the Commission of the European Communities Directorate), Francis Pinter, London, 1984.

3
The process of innovation

3.1 Introduction

The previous chapter concluded that a successfully competitive organization would regard continuous innovation as highly desirable rather than as something the organization must, reluctantly, cope with. To see what an organization would need in order to flourish, with innovation and change as its equilibrium state, we need to look more closely at innovation itself. Clearly, it is not a single-step change event but a process with a number of distinctive phases.

Moreover, according to many researchers on the topic, each phase in the innovative process demands different organizational characteristics. Initiating change requires an organization that is open and flexible; evaluating change requires the ability to take the long-term view and a willingness to ascribe value that may not be quantifiable by orthodox financial methods; to implement change requires efficiency and tight control. Thus, according to the orthodox wisdom, the innovative organization needs to embody contradictory characteristics. Hence the preoccupation with creating alternative organizations within the main organization, or informalizing ways round the main organization with project champions, skunkworks, etc.

Providing an innovative route round the organization may be appropriate where innovation and change are not the norm, but in the face of technological revolution the whole organization is affected, and if the organization adopts continuous change and innovation as its desired way of building competitive advantage then the whole organization must be made innovative and entrepreneurial. The innovation process may involve a wide variety of different roles according to the stage of the process and the situation in which it is carried out. This chapter briefly looks at the process itself and identifies the different roles involved, some of which may be recognizable in the reader's own organization. Then it looks at the organizational requirements of the three main stages of the innovative process.

3.2 Phases in the innovation process

The process of innovation is often idealized as a logical and relatively simple process along the following lines:

1. identification of a problem or need
2. initial review of feasible solutions
3. identification of preferred solution
4. research and development
5. evaluation and decision to proceed
6. commercial development
7. implementation

This process presumes that innovation results from the deliberate and systematic identification of needs and possible solutions, that there is a rational decision process that results in identifying the best solution, and that implementation is also carried out in a similar methodical, rational and efficient way. If this is how the process actually happens, it will be fairly straightforward to define the ideal conditions in which each of these logical steps might be carried out. However, innovation doesn't often happen like this. Many empirical studies of the process show that it is more often an opportunistic, haphazard and reactive process that rarely follows a simple linear sequence of events.

An alternative model was proposed by Myers and Marquis (1969) as outlined in Figure 3.1. This indicates a series of activities through which the process proceeds with any number of repeats and reversals. It could be a preplanned, rational, linear sequence, or it could be entirely haphazard. In this model the initiating stimulus is seen as coming from either the recognition of technological feasibility or of potential demand. The model thus incorporates both the 'discovery–push' and 'demand–pull' stimuli to innovation. Discovery–push includes stimuli that spring both from the discoveries of pure science and the developments of technology. Demand–pull includes stimuli that spring both from an analysis of customer needs and from internal organizational needs that may be identified through the operation of systems such as management by objectives.

The Myers and Marquis model is interesting because of the emphasis it gives to the availability of technological knowledge from within the organization, through its research and development and other technical personnel, and also resulting from information already available from external sources. The simple linear model is clearly idealized and unreal-

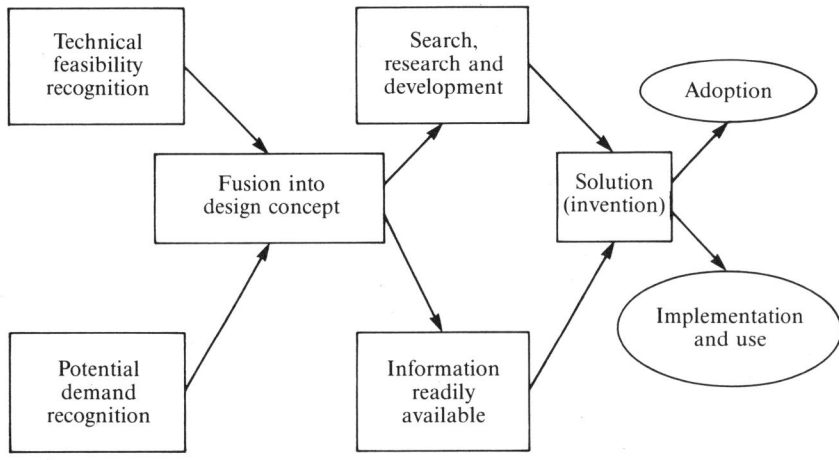

Figure 3.1 The innovation process (based on Myers and Marquis 1969)

istic, but nevertheless serves to capture the main stages of the innovative process:

- *initiation phase*: idea generation – screening out unsuitable ideas – testing and development of concept
- *evaluation phase*: strategic and financial evaluation of alternative new product concepts
- *implementation phase*: product development – test market – launch – post-implementation monitoring

Although these models were developed from research concerned primarily with new product innovation, process innovation follows similar stages: ideas are generated, screened, tested in concept, financially appraised, engineered, tested and commissioned. While the activities of the people engaged in them may differ, both forms of innovation share the three main phases of initiation, evaluation and implementation. Equally, the same basic stages are involved in non-technological changes. Major organizational changes, or changes in marketing or financial strategy are also likely to follow a similar process.

3.3 Roles in the innovation process

The innovation process depends on the knowledge, skills and enthusiasm of people in the innovating organization. It is an intensely personal process and the personal involvement can be seen in a slightly different view of the sequential process:

KNOWLEDGE → PERSUASION → DECISION → CONFIRMATION

The individuals concerned in the process may be involved in one or more of the following aspects:

- *stimulation* of interest in the new idea among members of the organization who may be relevant to its possible adoption;
- *initiation* of the new idea, expressing it in more operational detail and emphasizing its potential benefits to organization members who may be influential on its future adoption;
- *Legitimation* by powerholders in the organization of the idea as a valid project in order to overcome the potential apathy or obstruction of established members of the organization;
- *Decision* to act;
- *Action*.

This view of innovation treats it as a social or political process. The significance of this form of analysis will depend on the particular organization. In some firms innovation may be simply a matter of 'authority decisions' where a single individual may be responsible for all stages, merely enforcing the decision on others. This is sometimes the case in small organizations or 'autocrats' as referred to in Chapter 1. At the other extreme are the rational–legal decision processes of large, rigidly structured, highly formalized bureaucratic organizations. Most innovation decisions are taken in circumstances between these two extremes, by teams or groups of individuals, or at least with the participation by various system members.

There are two key functions that have been frequently identified in relation to collective innovation decisions: the opinion leader and the change agent. Opinion leaders, sometimes referred to as fashion leaders, gatekeepers, key communicators or tastemakers, informally influence other individuals' attitudes or behaviour. Rogers' survey of diffusion research (Rogers 1983) indicated that opinion leaders enjoy active social participation and high social status. In addition they conform more to the social system's norms so that, when system norms favour change, opinion leaders are innovative but, note, the reverse may be equally true.

The change agent performs a similar role to the opinion leader but does so overtly and is the professional changer. Rogers identified seven roles in the change process that change agents fulfil:

1. develop the need for change on the part of their clients
2. establish a change relationship with them
3. diagnose their problems
4. create intent to change in their clients
5. translate their intent into action

6. stabilize change and prevent discontinuance
7. achieve terminal relationship with clients

The success of change agents is positively related to their effort and the degree to which their programme is compatible with client needs, their empathy with clients and the extent to which they work through opinion leaders. The significance of any of these roles depends on the situation in which they operate. For example, in many rigid, stable, long-established businesses change may only be expected to occur if stimulated from outside by a change agent. In other situations the stimulus may arise internally but still require the active support of a high level 'project champion' or opinion leader.

Almost without exception the purpose served by these various roles is to overcome the inertia and change avoidance which is assumed to be the norm in business organizations. The roles would be somewhat different if an entrepreneurial organization were assumed, i.e. an organization for which continuous innovation and change is the norm and desired state of affairs.

3.4 Initiating change

This first stage of the process is the essentially creative phase of innovation where the requirement is for freedom, openness and flexibility. These characteristic requirements for successful initiation are held to be those which typically are artificially created for creative problem-solving sessions (e.g. brainstorming, synectics). All parties are encouraged to participate without inhibition of any kind, to suspend disbelief, to avoid closed or negative behaviours that might be suggested by experience or prior knowledge. Status and formal job roles and titles are, as far as possible, deliberately neutralized. Open-mindedness, mutual encouragement and a positive attitude are the intended norms for the duration of the session in order to encourage the delicate creative process into life.

Imagine such a session attended by Newton, Fleming, Watt, Einstein, Stephenson, Whickham Skinner and two other less eminent individuals. Having agreed, in some cases possibly after a moment's hesitation, to participate in the process, they would adopt positive attitudes, suspend disbelief and successfully reject any negative remarks they may be tempted to make when their knowledge and experience told them the ideas being discussed were stupid. Would that be the most effective way of exploiting those talents in the innovation process? Or would it be more likely that better progress would be made by exploiting their knowledge and experience to the fullest extent possible?

Simon (1986) says that creativity itself depends on knowledge; the greater the knowledge, the greater the potential for creativity. Freedom, openness and flexibility are enabling factors, but knowledge is the foundation of creativity. Creativity is not dependant on 'sparks of genius' and is not the result of some chance conjunction, but is 'thinking writ large'. Newton and Leibnitz invented the calculus because they had more than ten years of relevant mathematical experience and had absorbed more than 50 000 bits of relevant data. Fleming's discovery of penicillin was achieved as a result of his previous knowledge and experience rather than the popular fable about his chance encounter with mould. Watt's invention of the external condenser sprang from his previous relevant experience and '50 000 bits of relevant data', rather than the chance acquaintance with a boiling kettle.

Creativity in management arises similarly from experience and knowledge in two main areas:

– 1. Knowledge about the content of the organization's work, i.e. industry-specific knowledge about technology, customers and competitors.
– 2. Knowledge about human behaviour in organizations and how organizations work.

The managerial knowledge necessary for the organization to succeed is about the organization's competitive advantage in satisfying the customer's needs, and knowledge about how this competitive advantage can be established, e.g. through innovation in product, process, system and organization.

Thus, openness does not simply refer to open communications within an organization, but openness to information on customers, competitors and technologies. This means not simply that channels of communication are available but that they are used and in a purposive way that increases the relevant information base from which to be creative. Flexibility to be creative does not simply mean that there is freedom to do anything, but that the freedom is itself purposive, directed to the particular aims of the business organization.

These issues are developed in greater detail in later chapters – all that is intended here is to highlight the fallacy that open structures that allow individuals to be creative are in themselves sufficient. Freedom is a hygiene factor which permits of creativity, but the driving force for initiating innovation is relevant knowledge and expertise.

3.5 Evaluating change

Britain and America both suffer from the dominance of financial institutions that control their equity markets and, particularly in Britain, the dominance of accounting mores that control internal management. Both

THE PROCESS OF INNOVATION   35

> A technology gap has opened up between the US and the UK on the one hand and Japan on the other, caused to a significant extent by the way financial appraisal methods are used in the US/UK.
>
> - In US/UK, a typical new project is required to achieve 15–25 per cent Internal Rate of Return (IRR). For risky projects (e.g. innovations) a risk premium is added of up to 10 per cent. Thus for risky projects a total required IRR may be as high as 35 per cent.
> - In Japan, a similar project would be required to achieve around 10 per cent IRR equivalent and they do not use a risk premium.
> - In US/UK, a typical new project will be conservatively forecast to achieve sales growth in line with previous experience, i.e. around 2–2½ per cent p.a. If the project is accepted this forecast becomes self-fulfilling.
> - In Japan, a typical new project will be conservatively forecast to achieve sales growth in line with previous experience, i.e. around 10 per cent p.a. If the project is accepted this forecast becomes self-fulfilling.
>
> The result of these differences is that many projects that are accepted in Japan are rejected in the US/UK. Consequently, US/UK do not gain experience of increments in new technology. In many cases US/UK have missed out on whole generations of technology and then find it impossible to regain their former position.

Figure 3.2 Evaluation and the technology gap (based on Hodder 1986)

these influences tend to result in investment decisions being taken on the basis of a short-term rationale. This is particularly the case in decisions that involve significant risk, which is almost invariably the case in investments in innovation.

The evaluation phase is often overlooked, although there is a lot of evidence in the UK and the US that this is a crucial stage where the majority of potential innovations fall down and are not exploited commercially. The reason for this appears to be the accounting procedures and short-term orientation of Anglo-Saxon business (see Figure 3.2). The Japanese, and to a lesser extent, German, orientation appears more favourably disposed to evaluating new innovations positively. The reason for this anti-innovation investment bias does not lie with the appraisal methods themselves, but in the way they are used. The principle of conservatism exerts considerable influence over assessment and not always in a wholly rational way.

> DCF [Discounted cash flow] is a means of appraising the financial effects of alternative courses of action. In the case of a single project appraisal the alternatives considered are investing in the project or not investing in it. Both cases are equally important, because it is the difference in the cash flows of the two cases which are the basis for calculating the return. Accounting principles, however, tend, except in the most extreme circumstances, to lead to a concentration on the investment case. The idea of the 'going concern' covertly takes care of the non-investment case. Thus the fact that part of the business will die if the investment does not take place is not often reflected in the cash flow projection. The benefits of investment are therefore understated. This understatement is again supported by the principle of conservatism, and often further strengthened by artificially cutting off the 'project life' at, say, ten, seven or sometimes even five years.
>
> The only way round this is to include in the appraisal a realistic projection of the business which would otherwise 'die'. Of course, this creates great difficulty. It calls for a thorough and harshly realistic appraisal of the prospects for the existing business without the investment, in order to be realistically generous in the appraisal of the new spending. This may sound as though an artificial loading in favour of strategic investments is being advocated, but this is not quite the case. The proposition is that all germane factors be taken fully into account, including the element of corporate renewal.
>
> If this is difficult to quantify a more general adjustment can be made to offset the existing bias against such investments. This positive bias could be incorporated by reducing the required DCF cut off rate with a 'strategic discount'. Thus a company whose cost of capital might be 15%, and who might require word processors to achieve a minimum of 17% IRR, could reasonably require a strategic investment to achieve a return of say 12%. The arguments against such a device run parallel with those raised against the risk premium. It is purely a device to offset the existing bias against investment when there is insufficient quantitative information to make the full strategic case. In this context it is specific to DCF, but, of course, a strategic discount is more widely applicable. Any financial appraisal routine can be modified so that the returns required on a project which offers strategic benefits are reduced rather than increased, as is otherwise the norm.
>
> Similarly the strategic discount has a general application. The existing bias to short-term results is completely general. Both financial and behavioral factors produce a strong short-term bias. The behavioral bias arises when managers seek to achieve quick results in order to develop their careers more quickly, in time scales which are incompatible with those of a mature business. Under these circumstances, there is a powerful motivation to cut costs, reduce asset levels and so on. By comparison, the long-term strategic development of the business is of little interest. The strategic discount is the generalized reaction to these destructive short-term pressures and seeks to give proper weight to long-term considerations.
>
> (Pearson 1985:21-3)

While financial evaluation is the predominant formal method of appraising investments in innovation and change, its ill effects may to some extent be mitigated by the application of common sense or 'gut feel'. Nevertheless, a decision in favour of an investment in innovation (which is by definition risky), despite a negative financial appraisal, is rare. Such a decision leaves the decision taker in an exposed position. For this reason, the formal accounting methodologies are extremely influential and important to the innovation process.

3.6 Implementing change

Orthodox wisdom suggests that implementation of a project requires an emphasis on detailed planning, monitoring and tight control as against the openness and flexibility required at the initiation phase. Implementation is seen as the role of line management. They will have to take it over when the project is completed or commissioned, so implementation requires the same management approach as does running the existing business.

The emphasis on control may be right for a mature business in a stable environment. At least that has often been said, but there are no longer any stable environments so it can't be tested. The dominance of control, as opposed to the progressive culture outlined in Part Three, may once have been appropriate, but it has limited applicability in the 1990s.

The focus of implementation may be more concerned with internal organization issues like directing, motivating and managing people to achieve results. In a bureaucratic organization, the focus may be on getting round red tape, cutting corners and breaking rules wherever necessary to achieve rapid results. However, implementing innovations may require just as much flexibility and creativity as does the initiation phase. The organizational characteristics required for both initiation and implementation, and indeed for the vast majority of existing businesses in this period of rapid change, are thus essentially similar. The distinction between the two is more apparent than real.

3.7 Summary

- A successfully competitive organization regards continuous innovation as a highly desirable state rather than something it must learn to cope with.
- In order to identify what such an organization needs it is essential for it to understand the process of innovation.
- Various personal roles may help or hinder the innovation process. Particular emphasis is laid on the opinion leader and change agent roles,

an understanding of which may be helpful in achieving innovation in a fundamentally non-innovative organization.
- Orthodox wisdom suggests that an open, flexible organization is required for initiating innovations, whereas efficiency and tight control are required for implementation of innovative projects. This analysis is not supported.
- The process of innovation is not necessarily a linearly logical and straightforward process, but is often haphazard and irrational.
- The stimulus for innovation may come from the recognition of technological feasibility (i.e. technology–push) or the recognition of potential demand (demand–pull) which may be either customer demand for new products or internal demand for new processes.
- The organizational needs for effective initiation are not simply openness, flexibilty and freedom but, above all else, knowledge. This knowledge exists internally in the organization's staff in R&D and other functional areas, and can be obtained from other external sources.
- The intermediary stage of an innovation is its evaluation, which in the UK means predominantly financial evaluation. In orthodox appraisal methods there are pressures that lead to a concentration on readily quantifiable short-term results and the omission of less easily quantifiable long-term outcomes. This emphasis needs to be redressed (e.g. by use of a 'strategic discount').
- Implementation of innovations may well require the same organizational characteristics as managing an existing business. However, during a technological revolution these include the ability to be flexible and creative and are not simply to do with cost efficiency and tight control.

References

Hodder, J. E., 'Evaluation of manufacturing investments: a comparison of US and Japanese practices', *Financial Management*, Spring 1986:17–24.

Myers, S. and D. G. Marquis, 'Successful Industrial Innovations: a study of factors underlying innovations in selected firms', National Science Foundation, 1969.

Pearson, G. J., *The Strategic Discount*, Wiley, Chichester, 1985.

Rogers, E. M., *Diffusion of Innovations* 3rd edn, Free Press, New York, 1983.

Simon, H. A., 'How managers express their creativity', *Across the Board*, No. 3, 1986.

4
Innovation successes and failures

4.1 Introduction

British industrial decline relative to its major competitors has been more or less continuous throughout the present century and has been the concern of successive governments. The underlying weakness of the first industrial revolution industries was apparent in the inter-war years but their collapse was postponed by the imperatives of the Second World War. Since then their decline has quickened and in addition industries from the second revolution have also started to decline, thus multiplying the overall effect on the British economy.

While there may be a natural tendency for older industries to migrate to less developed economies, which can continue to exploit old technology, there is nothing inevitable about it. Machine tools, motor cycles, automobiles and many other industries were certainly mature when the Japanese manufacturers got hold of them. But the investments they made, which the British and others failed to make, in innovations resulted in both competitive restructuring and overall growth. Was there any intrinsic reason why the UK could not have achieved the same success, or was our failure inevitable? Figures 4.1 and 4.2 provide some clues.

It was to answer questions like this that the British government initiated a major investigation in the early 1950s 'in the belief that the full and speedy application of science in industry is necessary to economic progress and should . . . be one of the most important objects of national policy' (Carter and Williams 1956:1). This seminal study, led by Carter and Williams and jointly sponsored by the Royal Society of Arts, the British Association for the Advancement of Science and the Nuffield Foundation, investigated a total of 269 firms, developed 152 'usable general case studies', four industry-wide case studies and five innovation-specific case studies. The investigation was prompted by highly practical needs rather than as academic interest; its methods were practical and operational, rather than academic and abstruse; and its findings were also practical and down to earth rather than academic and elegant. It was a substantial piece of work and the first of many such practically oriented projects.

Since the Carter and Williams study there have been literally thousands of empirical investigations. Some have focused on individual innovators/ entrepreneurs, some on particular environments or industries, and some on the organizational characteristics that help and hinder firms in being innovative. This last category is the research that is most relevant to practising managers, because to a great extent they are able directly to control or influence organizational characteristics, whereas they are almost powerless to influence the nature of their whole industry or the personal characteristics of their chief executive. From all this research, a practical, useful and fairly coherent picture emerges of what an organization needs to be like if it is to be competitive and innovative.

4.2 Characteristics of innovations

Some types of innovative activity are easier to implement than others and it is important to distinguish between the types of innovation before trying to assess innovativeness. For example, evolutionary innovations are clearly more straightforward than revolutionary ones (White 1966; Rothwell 1979). Revolutionary product innovation is concerned with radically new products or services, typically incorporating one or more 'state of the art' technological inventions and often requiring significant organizational changes in order to exploit them fully. Evolutionary innovation is concerned with the improvement of existing products or services or the extension of a product line or range of services, typically by the exploitation of less advanced technology and requiring no organizational change.

An alternative categorization was identified by Robertson (1967) as 'continuous', 'dynamically continuous' and 'discontinuous'. Continuous innovations involved the modification of a product or service with no requirement for the consumer's behaviour to change. Dynamically continuous innovation involved greater change but still with no fundamental alteration in consumer behaviour. Discontinuous innovations resulted in fundamentally new products or services that required significant changes in consumer behaviour (e.g. CD records, antibiotics, phototypesetting).

Whichever categorization is used, various investigations have confirmed that the greater the chance implied by the innovation, the greater will be the risk and the slower the rate of adoption (Chisnall 1985a). Or, put another way, the more revolutionary the innovation the more difficult it will be to implement. This seems hardly revolutionary, but does point the way to some further analysis which is of practical use.

> The use of a computerized expert credit rating system by bank counter staff enables many small routing loan decisions to be taken without involving the bank management, who are thus freed to devote more time to developing new business. In Germany, the product was sold as an opportunity to free the manager from routine work so that he could concentrate on more important things.
>
> By contrast, in the UK the same product was sold as being suitable for operation by the bank manasger, so that it could help reinforce his or her power position in the branch.

Figure 4.1 Compatibility of a new product (based on Child *et al.* 1987)

The significant characteristics of the revolutionary–evolutionary categories have been identified in more detail by Rogers (1983) as:

- *Relative advantage* is the degree to which an innovation is perceived as better than the idea which it supersedes. For example, the introduction of CD records in place of LPs would best be done by emphasizing the relative advantages of sound quality, resistance to damage and longevity. The greater the perception of relative advantage by the end user, the greater the prospect of adoption.
- *Compatibility* is the degree to which an innovation is perceived as being consistent with existing values, past experiences and needs of the receivers. In the UK many innovative products are sold on the basis of compatibility with existing structures, whereas the same product may be sold in Germany on the basis of the opportunities the product provides for changing existing structures (see Figure 4.1).
- *Complexity* is the degree to which an innovation is perceived as relatively difficult to understand and use.
- *Trialability* is the degree to which an innovation can be experimented with on a limited basis. This implies an element of reversibility. An innovation in a manufacturing process that requires plant to be closed, removed and replaced is not readily reversible and has to have more counterbalancing benefits than innovations that can be simply 'bolted on' and if not satisfactory 'bolted off' again.
- *Observability* is the degree to which the results of an innovation are visible to others.

A number of researchers have also identified a bandwagon or *diffusion* effect, i.e. the cumulatively increasing degree of influence on an individual to adopt an innovation resulting from the increasing rate of knowledge and adoption of the innovation throughout the social system. The diffusion effect is probably greater in social systems with more effective interpersonal communication channels.

Another way of categorizing innovations is to distinguish them as defensive or offensive (Myers and Marquis 1969). Defensive innovations are aimed at preserving market share and the existing rate of corporate growth and could arise from changes in competition, change in market demand for quality, reliability, design or safety, increased costs of material, labour or money, price erosion of the product or changes in government regulation. Offensive innovation on the other hand is a proactive policy of opening up new markets, or enlarging existing markets by a planned series of new products or services. As would be expected, the defensive innovation is seen as substantially easier to implement than the offensive.

These various ways of categorizing innovations all seem to suggest that the less innovative a project, the easier it will be to implement, but the less will be its economic benefits. Conversely, the greater the innovative element, the more difficult it will be to implement, but the greater will be the ensuing benefits. It might be expected therefore that the more effective a firm is as an innovator, the more likely it is to achieve sustainable competitive advantages through innovation.

4.3 Successful innovators

The 1956 Carter and Williams research identified the characteristics of what they called 'the technically progressive firm', i.e. one that was 'keeping close to the best which could reasonably be achieved in the application of science and technology'. These characteristics are summarized as:

- Good external communications:
    high quality of incoming communications
    deliberate survey of potential ideas
    willingness to share knowledge
    willingness to take new knowledge on licence and to enter joint
        ventures
    readiness to look outside the firm
- Readiness to look ahead:
    effective selling policy
    good technical service to customers
- Good internal communications:
    effective internal communications and coordination
- Positive attitude to science and technology:
    high status of science and technology in the firm

use of scientists and technologists on board of directors
- Recruit and train high-quality people:
    sound policy of recruitment for management
    ability to attract talented people
    willingness to arrange effective staff training
- Professional management:
    high-quality chief executives
    good quality intermediate managers
    ability to bring the best out of managers
    consciousness of costs and profits in R&D
    ingenuity in getting round material and equipment shortages
    use of management techniques
    identify outcome of investment decisions
    rapid replacement of machines
- High rate of expansion

The list of factors found to be associated is long and confirmed the researchers' prior hypotheses, though the strength of association of the various factors is not indicated, nor is the technically progressive firm identified in any operational sense. Nevertheless, the broad findings have been replicated by subsequent researchers. For example, lack of external communications in the non-progressive firms, particularly in relation to market appraisal and marketing research, has been found repeatedly to be associated with innovation laggards. Burns and Stalker (1961) found that the most successful innovators paid closest attention to their market and did not concentrate exclusively on the research and development aspect. Similar findings were confirmed by Myers and Marquis (1969).

The Centre for the Study of Industrial Innovation (1971) also found that the 'most prevalent factors leading to shelving related to apparently unfavourable market characteristics which only arose, or were only identified by the firm, after development costs had been identified'.

Research carried out in 1972, called Project SAPPHO (Scientific Activity Predictor from Patterns with Heuristic Origins), also confirmed much of the Carter and Williams research. The SAPPHO research was conducted in two science-based industries, chemicals and instruments, and concentrated its attention on new product innovation; it identified the following factors as being associated with successful product innovation:

- understanding user needs
- more attention paid to marketing
- development work carried out more efficiently
- more effective use of outside technology and scientific advice
- individuals responsible for innovation were more senior and had more authority.

Robertson (1973) confirmed the SAPPHO findings and summarized the root causes of innovation failure as 'the neglect of marketing research and preconceived ideas about market needs'.

Similarly, successful innovations have been identified as depending on direct links between research and development and marketing, on planned programmes of innovation, and on management being both technically effective and market-oriented (Chisnall 1985b). Various other studies (e.g. Cooper 1980; Hopkins 1981) have broadly confirmed the SAPPHO findings in identifying key activities associated with successful innovation, including:

- good contact with the firm's product markets (to know accurately user's requirements) and its technological environment (to know the state of the art);
- good internal cooperation and coordination between engineering (R&D), production and marketing;
- careful planning and control;
- efficient development work;
- the will on the part of top management to innovate;
- provision of good after-sales service and user education;
- existence of key individual such as a product champion, business or technical innovator, etc.

Mansfield's econometric analysis (Mansfield 1969) of innovation in American coal, petrol and railway industries highlighted the significance of firm size and the expected profitability of the innovation. However, size was found to be less important in Ray's study of innovation diffusion in mature industries (Ray 1983). Ray's model of diffusion also identified the bandwagon effect whereby the probability of a firm adopting an innovation increased as the number of firms that had already adopted it grew. Mansfield also found that company profits, liquidity, profit trends, and age of the company president were all insignificant factors, but hypothesized that the personality attributes, interests and training of the top management may well be relevant.

Holloman (1967) identified what he found to be the essentials of innovativeness:

- technical staff knowledgeable about the state of science;
- technical staff fully understanding the strategy and objectives of the business;
- the innovator, or entrepreneur, being organizationally separated from the normal day-to-day business.

Holloman's first two points seem to synthesize much of what has been indicated before from Carter and Williams through SAPPHO and many other researches. His third point has a rather different ancestry stemming from the other early classic research on innovation by Burns and Stalker (1961).

4.4 Mechanistic and organismic organizations

A quarter of a century ago Burns and Stalker (1961) studied the attempts to implant the fledgling electronics industry in parts of Scotland that had only previously experienced the old heavy 'smoke-stack' industries of coal, steel and shipbuilding. The old industries were dying and it was hoped to take up some of the inevitable unemployment with the new high-growth high-tech industry. In carrying out their research they identified two types of organization which have since found their way into fairly common currency: mechanistic and organismic (or organic) organizations.

The mechanistic organization is suited only to stable conditions. In it the job of management is broken down into specialist functions, each with its precisely defined task. There is a clear hierarchy of control, with the reins firmly held at the top. Communications flow down the line and occasionally back up, but rarely across the organization. There is an emphasis on loyalty to the company and obedience to one's superior. The result of this bureaucratic system is that individuals in the organization are not committed to its fundamental business aims, only to obeying the rules, fulfilling their (strictly limited) employment contract and enjoying whatever perks such a regime may offer. Burns and Stalker found it ill-suited to handling innovation.

Croome describes mechanistic organizations as demanding that everyone shall have one job, clearly defined and delimited, with responsibility running up to a recognized limit and stopping there. Employees are not isolated, but are part of the organizational machine. In so far as they have to think at all about their relations with other parts of the machine, they see them as outside 'their' job. They are necessary to the job only as tools are necessary. 'For some data needs he can appeal to the slide rule, for others he may appeal to another individual; some tasks can be performed by a tool, others by an order to a subordinate' (Croome 1960). But the clear definition of 'the job' and the simple set of outside relationships break down when conditions change. New situations do not exactly match the traditional frontiers of responsibility. Individuals no longer know just what instructions are needed or where to seek them; they have to consult with, rather than merely give orders to, their subordinates.

The organismic organization is at the opposite end of the spectrum. It lacks rigid structure, and lives by a process of continual adaptation, often involving the redefinition of individual tasks. Communications occur in any direction as may be required at any particular time, and the commitment of employees is open-ended and generally dedicated to the achievement of organizational aims. As one might expect, organismic systems are well suited to handling the new and unfamiliar: they are highly effective innovators.

According to Burns and Stalker, the work of the manager under the organic system is much more exacting. 'He must give up his safe, cut and dried, contractual relationship with the firm – a relationship with an impersonal, immutable "they" – for membership of a body kept going by a shared creative activity; for the limited commitments of the "nine to fiver" he must substitute the general open-ended commitment of the professional.' Burns and Stalker do not suggest there is 'one best way' of organizing. If the mechanical system is adequate, then so much the better because it is the most efficient. However, as Croome suggested, 'when the firm is tackling new tasks, whether commercial or technical, this system of differentiated responsibilities must be elastically shared' (Croome 1960). Every effort must be made to encourage the sense of the business as a whole with objectives and goals common to all its members, rather than a complex of 'separate jobs'. The stronger this sense, the more there will be resource to lateral consultation. This should be recognized and facilitated, and not regarded as a mere semi-legitimate supplement to vertical channels of command.

Organismic and mechanistic are opposite ends of a continuum. Neither is likely to be met in its full glory, but most companies exhibit tendencies to be closer to one or the other. The more organismic a business organization is, the better suited it is likely to be to handle innovation and change. This is the basis of the orthodoxy that flexible systems with high levels of participation and open communications are essential for handling change, while rigid, mechanistic, bureaucratic systems are most efficient for handling routine and stable situations.

4.5 Reasons for failure

Firms fail to be innovative because they lack those characteristics identified above as being prerequisite for success. But, of course, that is not the whole story. The pressures against innovation and change are considerable.

To a greater or lesser extent we all experience a personal characteristic of behavioural inertia (Mohr 1987). What persuaded Jewish people to stay on in Hitler's Germany long after Nazi-led anti-Semitism had made their lives intolerable? Why do people continue to live in the lee of a live volcano? Why are unemployed people so reluctant to move from areas of high unemployment? Sticking with 'the devil you know', despite its manifest disadvantages, is a universal irrational tendency that probably underlies much of the apparent reluctance to change experienced in work situations.

Individual behavioural inertia undoubtedly impacts on larger groups

> One of the problems in staffing supermarket chains is how to recruit and retain high-quality branch managers when all the significant management decisions, apart from personnel supervision, are taken at headquarters.
>
> When electronic point of sale (EPOS) equipment became available it provided various opportunities for improving the efficiency and effectiveness of operating retail chains.
>
> In Germany, EPOS was used to relieve branch staff of routine work and allow them to get involved in buying and marketing.
>
> In Britain, EPOS was used to increase central control and reinforce the *status quo* and so further reduce branch management to the role of personnel supervision.

Figure 4.2 Organizational conservatism in retailing (based on Child *et al.* 1987)

and results in what is often termed organizational conservatism (see Figure 4.2). This manifests itself as a response to an external change stimulus that seeks to minimize the amount of change resulting from the stimulus. Typically, the opportunities for positive change, especially organizational structural change, are rejected and the stimulus perverted as far as is possible in order to reinforce the existing structures. The examples shown in Figures 4.1 and 4.2 are instances of this response.

It would be a mistake to assume that these responses are wholly irrational. There are good reasons why organizational change might be minimized. For example, it is usually expensive, its end results are essentially unknown, but may well result in job losses, and it will normally involve significant requirements for retraining. Moreover, existing power-holders may feel threatened by new technology, or other change stimulus and will naturally try to control the innovation's application so that it reinforces their existing power positions.

In most organizations the stimulus for innovation is also offset by the fact that existing ways of doing things – organization structures, strategic recipes, technologies, etc. – have clearly worked so far, so why change them? This is a particularly powerful basis for organizational conservatism in the case of the obviously successful organization. In addition, there may be a tremendous financial and psychological investment sunk in the existing way of doing things, which makes it very difficult to change. Finally, there may be three further reasons for failure to innovate:

– You don't know what to do.
– You don't know how to do it.
– You can't be bothered to do it.

Not knowing what to do is probably the most widespread difficulty. Lack of a clear strategic direction, perhaps being 'stuck in the middle', trying to head in two or more directions at the same time, inevitably results in lack of concentration of resources, efforts and enthusiasm, and inconsistency in investment decisions. Under these circumstances innovation will be haphazard and random and unlikely to succeed in the medium to long term.

Lack of capability may also be an apparent problem, perceived especially by smaller firms when considering competitive battles with global competitors. However, in many cases this difficulty is more apparent than real. Consider the position of Japanese camera maker, Canon, when it decided to 'Beat Xerox', with IBM and Kodak having already failed in this endeavour. Canon's technological capability and market knowledge were hopelessly inadequate, but they succeeded (as shown in Chapter 10).

Finally, lack of commitment and the will to succeed may also be a reason for failure. This is discussed further in Part Three.

4.6 Summary

- Britain's long-term industrial decline has been accompanied by a relatively poor performance in technological innovation. This has prompted a lot of research into the practical reasons why we have done so badly and what should be done about it.
- The more revolutionary, discontinuous or offensive an innovation is, the greater its economic impact and the more difficult it is to implement. Evolutionary, continuous and defensive innovations are easier to implement but make less impact.
- The first research study was initiated by government 'in the belief that the full and speedy application of science in industry is necessary to economic progress'. Its report, published in 1956, suggested that it was necessary for success at innovation to:
    have good external communications
    be ready to look ahead
    have good internal communications
    have a positive attitude to science and technology
    recruit and train high-quality people
    have professional management
- Subsequent research has confirmed these broad findings though sometimes with slightly different emphasis, tending especially to stress close customer relations as a crucial part of external communications.
- Burns and Stalker studied the early attempts to implant the electronics industry into dying smoke-stack areas of Scotland and identified two distinctive forms of organization: mechanistic and organismic.

- Organismic organizations are effective innovators. They lack rigid structure and live by a process of continual adaptation, continuous redefinition of individual tasks. Communications occur in any direction as required. Commitment of employees is open-ended and generally dedicated to the achievement of organizational aims.
- Mechanistic organizations are suited to stable conditions and are ineffective innovators. They are rigidly structured. The job of management is broken down into specialist functions with precisely defined tasks, a clear hierarchy of control from the top, communications flowing down the line, and an emphasis on loyalty to the company and obedience to one's superior.
- Organizations also fail to innovate because of:
    behavioural inertia of people
    Organizational conservatism
    Lack of strategic direction
    Lack of capability
    Lack of commitment and will.

References

Burns, T. and G. M. Stalker, *The Management of Innovation*, Tavistock Institute, London, 1961.

Carter, C. F. and B. R. Williams, *Industry and Technical Progress – factors governing the speed of application of science*, Oxford University Press, Oxford, 1956.

Centre for the Study of Industrial Innovation, survey of shelved R&D projects – 'On the Shelf', 1971.

Child, J., H.-D. Ganter and A. Lieser, 'Technological Innovation and Organizational Conservatism' in J. M. Pennings and D. Buitendam (eds) *New Technology as Organizational Innovation*, Ballinger, Cambridge, Mass., 1987.

Chisnall, P. M., *Strategic Industrial Marketing*, Prentice-Hall, Hemel Hempstead, 1985a.

Chisnall, P. M., *Marketing: a behavioural analysis* 2nd edn, McGraw-Hill, Maidenhead, 1985b.

Cooper, R. G., 'How to identify potential new product winners', *Research Management*, Vol. 23, No. 9, 1980.

Croome, H., 'Human Problems of Innovation', Department of Scientific and Industrial Research pamphlet, Problems of Progress in Industry, No. 5, 1960.

Holloman, J. H., 'Innovation and Profitability', Science of Science Foundation, 1967.

Hopkins, D. S., 'New product winners and losers', *R&D Management*, May 1981.

Mansfield, E., *Industrial Research and Technological Innovation: an econometric analysis*, Longman, London, 1969.

Mohr, L. B., 'Innovation Theory: an assessment from the vantage point of the new electronic technology in organizations' in J. M. Pennings and D. Buitendam (eds) *New Technology as Organizational Innovation*, Ballinger, Cambridge, Mass., 1987.

Myers, S. and D. G. Marquis, 'Successful Industrial Innovations: a study of factors underlying innovations in selected firms', National Science Foundation, 1969.

Project SAPPHO, 'Success and Failure in Industrial Innovation', Science Policy Research Unit, University of Sussex, 1972.

Ray, G. F., 'The diffusion of mature technologies', *National Institute Economic Review*, No. 106, November 1983.

Robertson, A., 'The marketing factor in successful industrial innovation', *Industrial Marketing Management*, Vol. 2, 1973.

Robertson, T. S., 'The process of innovation and the diffusion of innovations', *Journal of Marketing*, Vol. 3, January 1967.

Rogers, E. M., *Diffusion of Innovations* 3rd edn, Free Press, New York, 1983.

Rothwell, R., 'Successful and unsuccessful innovators', *Planned Innovation*, April 1979.

White, I., 'The Perception of Value in Products' in J. W. Newman (ed.) *On Knowing the Consumer*, Wiley, New York, 1966.

5
Business maturity

5.1 Introduction

The industries created by the current technological revolution seem to be the most exciting. The technology itself is extremely clever and is affecting all our lives in a myriad of ways. Not surprisingly the older industries seem pale and tired if not plain boring by comparison. Not surprising either that firms in these mature industries are often regarded as, by definition, examples of Burns and Stalker's mechanistic organizations. Nor is it therefore surprising that an orthodoxy has grown up and been widely accepted about mature businesses and what they can and can't do.

Despite all the excitement over the new technologies, most people still work in mature businesses. Moreover, despite all the change that is happening as a result of the technological revolution, in ten years time most people will still be working in mature businesses. This will be so even if the companies they work for bear names like Canon, Honda, Sony, Toshiba and Toyota. There need be nothing wrong with mature businesses. They can be innovative, as the above list of names may suggest. They can be efficient and effective. 'Mature' is not a euphemism for old-fashioned, out of date and generally incapable of competing in the modern world. The orthodoxy simply need not apply. There are some tendencies that managers in mature businesses must watch out for and take specific action to correct, but maturity also implies the existence of considerable strengths.

This chapter takes a brief look at business evolution and the goals of a business in its various phases. The characteristics of a mature organization are then discussed in more detail, including some that might appear to inhibit the business from being innovative. The changing emphasis of innovation as a business matures is then discussed and the conventional wisdom questioned. Finally, two opposite organizational forms are discussed and a method of assessing such organizational tendencies is presented.

System phase	System goal
Birth	Survival to achieve maturity
Adolescence	Growth, building strength to achieve successful maturity
Phase change volatility	
Maturity	Autonomy, longevity and control of environment, self-actualization
Phase change volatility	
Decline	Stability, peace and quiet, seeking to delay the return to focus on survival
Death	Survival

Figure 5.1 System goal cycle

5.2 The business life cycle

There is a natural cycle in the development of most systems, whether biological, technological or social. It seems to apply to systems as diverse as single cells, lighted candles, human beings, products and businesses, even nation states. They all appear to follow the familiar pattern of birth, adolescence, maturity, decline and death and at each stage they appear to be driven by certain common goals as summarized in Figure 5.1.

In infancy, most successful systems are dominated by the need to survive. This is entirely natural and appropriate because of inherently high infant mortality rates. High infant mortality among human beings has been reduced primarily by state provision in such areas as public hygiene, health and other social needs. Infant humans are also usually nurtured by loving parents in a generally benign adult population.

The infant business has few of these benefits. The doting parent or founder may lack the competence to ensure the fledgling survives. The wider population is by no means benign – if an infant business makes too much of a nuisance of itself it is likely to be squashed by its larger competitors. Moreover, state provision is extremely unreliable. From time to time governments may make welcoming noises about small business, enterprise and the like, but few coherent attempts are made to provide a healthy environment. There are no state midwives, hospitals, doctors and health visitors for the infant business. The UK government has invested substantial sums in publicizing its enterprise initiative, but its far more powerful policy on interest rates takes money away from the small high-growth cash-hungry business and gives it to the bureaucratic, cash-rich leviathans of industry, which often have no very good idea of what to do with the gratuitous wealth thrust upon them.

Under such circumstances, an obsession with survival seems entirely appropriate for the infant business. If it survives this first phase the adolescent will be able to turn its attention to growth and the development of functional strength. It progresses through adolescence being sharp, opportunistic and focused on satisfying customers' needs. It carries no spare weight, no passengers. It is lean and fit, quick on its feet and builds its strength through constant striving and exercise. This phase sees the business change from being a one-man band with a simple structure to employing an increasing number of professional specialists concerned either with the firm's technological development or the professionalization of its various management functions.

In a growing market the adolescent business has to run fast in order simply to maintain its market share. If it fails to do this then in all probability it will not survive the first shake-out when market growth starts to falter. In a static market there is not the same necessity to grow. Many businesses stay small, providing relatively stable employment for small numbers of people. Other businesses are more ambitious and grow rapidly in order to achieve the critical mass at which the new specialists can be profitably supported. Growth in static markets can only be achieved by increasing market share or by moving into new markets, both of which may be problematic in highly competitive situations. Just why some businesses go for this, while others stay put, can probably only be explained in terms of the personality and purpose of the founding entrepreneur. The purpose of the entrepreneur is not simply to make money, but to build for the future. The most successful entrepreneurs are all builders. Their aim is not simply to make a quick personal killing, but to build a business of substance that will survive and grow to full maturity.

To achieve maturity is the goal of all systems. Maturity is the phase when a successful system achieves maximum entropy, the most efficient process of energy conversion, the closest to self-actualization or fulfilment. In the case of a business, maturity is the phase when wealth creation is maximized, when the most surplus cash is generated and when the business achieves its position of greatest power and influence. Just how it uses this power and wealth is a matter of extreme importance that is discussed in the following section.

In most systems it appears that ultimate decline and extinction are certain. In most cases they are entirely predictable. A candle, for example, follows all these system stages. When first lighted, it may spit and sputter and possibly go out. If it stays lit, the flame quickly burns up to its full size. This is its mature phase when it burns the maximum wax and gives off the greatest light. In due course, it starts to putter and flicker and thereafter fairly quickly declines and goes out. Depending on the size of wick and the diameter and length of the candle, its longevity is fairly predictable. Likewise, the longevity of a human cell is also reasonably calculable. But social systems are less predictable. They are renewable in a way that physical systems are not. One of the aims of most social systems, and most managements, is to prolong the life of the system for as long as possible. Some succeed better than others.

For those that do not achieve continuous renewal, decline will ultimately set in. During decline the focus of attention moves once more back to a focus on survival, and this preoccupation becomes totally dominant up to the point of extinction.

5.3 The characteristics of maturity

Maturity is the result of successful infancy and adolescence. The success is usually based on doing the right things in the right way. The business progressively becomes more expert. It learns successful ways of doing things. It finds out what its customers like and gets good at delivering those things. It develops its technological expertise. It uses recipes that work and it becomes efficient. It becomes effective.

Wilf Penney, one time sales director of TAC Construction Materials Ltd, an archetypal mature business, once explained that in the early 1960s, when he was a 'humble rep', customers used to call him 'Sir' and plead for an increase in their allocation. 'But now the world has changed,' he added ruefully, but with a twinkle in his eye, 'now when I visit a customer, I throw my hat in first and if there's no sounds of gunfire, I go in!'

At the time Wilf was being called 'Sir', TAC was in its prime, with a maximum amount of power over its environment. It had around 80 per cent of the UK market with just one competitor manufacturing in the UK. There was very little interference from imported products largely because, it was presumed, of the punitive retaliatory possibilities if a European company tried to compete on TAC's home patch.

By the time Wilf was telling the anecdote, that power had dwindled and TAC was in decline. Its market share had fallen to less than 40 per cent. Two new competitors had set up manufacturing in the UK, encouraged by the high rates of profit previously earned by TAC. Finally, the major European producer had broken ranks and acquired a small UK competitor, thus changing for ever the *de facto* restrictions on competing in each other's home markets, which had been in place for half a century or more.

TAC survived to live again only after major surgery.

We have already seen how difficult it is for a successful business to make a fundamental change in the technology in which it has established its leading position. Such a business has major investments in the old technology. Getting into something new may mean writing off huge capital assets that will weaken the balance sheet and in the short term wreak havoc with profitability. Nor is it at all certain that leadership in the new technology will necessarily follow. Moreover, there are psychological investments in the old technology. One of the fruits of maturity is the ability to pay top salaries and thus attract top-calibre people. Many of these highly qualified professionals, managerial and technical, may have built their entire careers on the old technology and their very natural response to such a change is likely to be defensive and reactive. Nor is this necessarily a bad thing – giving up a leading position should certainly not be done lightly.

The successfully mature business generates substantial surplus funds that appear not to be required in order to maintain the status quo. How these funds get invested depends very much on the circumstances of the individual business. Very few such businesses give the funds back to the shareholders in their entirety, unless they happen to be wholly owned and tightly controlled subsidiary companies, in which case surplus cash may go back to the parent company for ultimate disbursement throughout the group. More typically, surplus funds are applied in the following three ways:

– diversification
– organizational slack
– managerial discretion

Diversification is usually the first choice home for surplus funds because this appears to reduce the reliance on the existing business, thereby reducing risk and exposure should the existing markets decline. Diversification can take many forms, from acquisition to the introduction of a relatively small new product, to a new, but associated, market. Whatever the form of diversification, and whatever its scale, the result is that the business starts to become more complicated. This may become apparent through the necessary organizational changes, or through some loss of clarity about the firm's strategic direction.

Organizational slack is often the second choice home for surplus funds. By slack is meant the investment in optional items which do not in themselves contribute directly to the value that is delivered to the customer, but may provide the business with some substance. In many ways, investment in organizational slack is simply a way of storing fat. The most obvious investments are made in people. Overmanning occurs, usually in indirect knowledge workers such as accountants, corporate planners, IT specialists, human resources managers and so forth. These investments, while reversible when necessary, have two adverse effects in themselves. First, hiring a corporate planner may give management the erroneous feeling that they have done something about corporate planning; hiring an IT specialist gives the feeling that something has been done about IT. Both are dangerous misconceptions – there is and can be no substitute for management themselves being directly involved with, and doing something about, corporate planning, IT, human resources and the other specialist areas. Second, such recruitments generally develop a self-sustaining momentum of secondary recruitments, so that whole new departments and functions grow up that contribute only peripherally, if at all, to the purpose of the business.

Other investments in organizational slack include inessential investment in items such as luxurious office buildings, irrelevant research facilities and unnecessary production plant; even whole new factories may, in reality, only be items of slack, built because the firm could afford it. Investments in organizational slack are also made in kind by, for example, permitting people time to invest in one of the government award schemes (training awards, Queen's awards, etc.) or in one of the increasing number of business games, or attending exotic, but hardly pertinent, conferences.

Investments in managerial discretion are company investments in their managers and other staff over and above what would be required to recruit and retain their services. These investments include higher than necessary salaries and all payments in lieu of salary, perks, etc. Many of the 'symbols of maturity' described in the personal account below represent items of managerial discretion that have been built up over the years. These and many others were condoned by intelligent people, often with charm and a sense of humour, as recently as 1985. They formed an intricate system of 'carrot and stick' socialization, comparable in many ways to the 'strong culture' process identified by Pascale (1985) used in such companies as IBM, ITT, Procter & Gamble and others. The word 'executive' has come to be synonymous with such items. An executive car is an up-market model priced at a level that attracts only the corporate purchaser who is, above all, sensitive to the status value of such investments. These investments are non-mandatory and reversible. The following account, by an interviewee in the research described in Appendix I, highlights some of the 'symbols of maturity'.

> The day I started work at Neals Ltd stays vividly in my mind. I turned into the car park and was guided to my designated place by a uniformed attendant. I was on the fifth row from the exit – the first row was for directors.
>
> I walked into the main entrance hall and was confronted by a choice of ways up to the first floor. There were two lifts side by side, differentiated only by the

fact that the one on the right had brightly polished brasswork whereas its sister was dull. There was a wide black marble, carpeted staircase and there was a small open side door which I later discovered led to an old uncarpeted 'servants' stairway. That morning I chose the marble stairs. It was a lonely ascent. I later discovered that the marble stairs were for directors, the polished lift for directors and executive managers, the unpolished lift for managers and the disabled and the back stairs for the able-bodied other ranks.

I had been recruited as an executive manager. This entitled me to a carpeted office and a tray of cut-glass tumblers and carafe of fresh water delivered each morning. I had a personal secretary rather than using the pool. I had my own initialled hand towel in the executive managers' cloakroom. I used the executive managers' dining room and from time to time was invited to lunch in the directors' suite. On those occasions it was customary for the most junior person there to cut the bread – lunch invariably started with soup accompanied by bread which was a small crusty loaf of very fresh brown bread. The cutting implement was a bread knife which, I suspect, was kept deliberately blunt so that it was impossible to do other than make an unholy mess of cutting. Work, politics, sex and religion were taboo topics of lunch-time conversation in the directors' suite, but current affairs, particularly financial matters and, curiously, South Africa, were regularly discussed – thus leaving the newcomer at a loss as to precisely where the line of acceptability was drawn. Lunch induced humility in the visitor.

In terms of goal orientation the mature business, like many other systems, seeks to control its environment in order to ensure its own future well-being. The one thing the mature business, with all its heavy investments sunk in the *status quo*, seeks to avoid is change and instability. It will find it advantageous to invest heavily in preserving the current state of affairs. First of all it will seek to control its own industry, preferably through the achievement of a monopoly position, or as near monopoly power as it is possible to achieve. In this way it can hope to control prices at a level that ensures its own profitability, and can control the level of business to set limits on the competitive activity that it would be profitable for any other business to embark on. For similar reasons it may well seek to achieve control over its sources of raw material supply if they are in any way insecure. It may seek to achieve this through the exercise of its purchasing muscle in tying up long-term supply arrangements. Or it may have to go so far as to acquire its key supplier(s) – such vertical acquisition is a common feature of many mature industries.

Other examples of mature businesses seeking to control their environment can be seen in the activities of organizations such as trade associations or industry research associations. Some such arrangements may be used purely for the interchange of technical information; others may reach covert agreements on what industry members will agree to pay for key raw materials; still others may agree precisely what prices will be charged and what price increases will be effected and when; some may explicitly agree in what proportion markets will be divided among industry members; others may even agree which jobs will be taken by which industry members. With varying degrees of legality, these approaches are all attempts to stabilize and control the environment. They may give the industry members concerned a feeling of security, but they are not to be relied on. At best such arrangements will serve only as temporary insulation against harsher competitive forces further afield.

Nevertheless, such restrictive environment-controlling approaches continue as they always have. The crude cartels and explicit agreements to restrict competition may have become illegal and unfashionable, but they are rapidly being replaced by 'strategic global alliances', whose format may be couched in terms of technology, but the underlying motivation, and the ultimate effect, is unchanged – to introduce stability and control over the environment.

The tendencies outlined in this section relate to what businesses actually do. It is, of course, not suggested that these are the optimal stratagems. On the contrary, diversification, unless done with great care, can have disastrous effects in reducing concentration and providing employees with confusing messages about the strategic direction of the business. Investments in organizational slack are, almost without exception, not merely a waste of money but counterproductive in the messages they give to members of the organization. Similarly with investments in managerial discretion. There are far more positive homes for the surplus funds generated by a mature business.

The same cautions apply to the various attempts to manipulate and control the environment. As soon as a business erects a protective barrier between itself and its competitors, it starts to relax. Its goose is cooked. Instead, businesses should go out and meet their competitors and potential competitors, not raise barriers or limit competition. Knowledge is the key to effective competition. Artificial constraints, above all else, constrain the truth.

5.4 Innovation and business evolution

A number of research studies have noted how firms change the emphasis of their innovative efforts as they become mature. The orthodox wisdom arising from this work comprises two main conclusions:

1. The emphasis is on product innovation during the early rapid growth phase and then moves on to process innovation as growth slows down.
2. The total amount of innovation declines as the firm grows more mature.

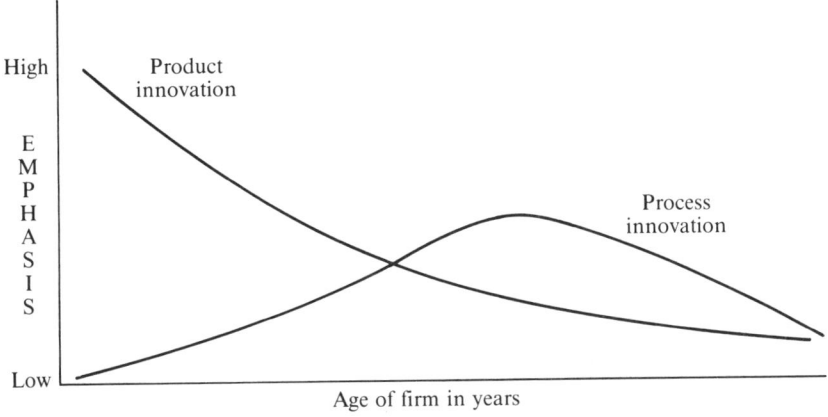

Figure 5.2 The emphasis of innovation (based on Utterback and Abernathy 1975)

Figure 5.2 summarizes this position. Moreover, as Skinner has demonstrated, it is also true that for most businesses the emphasis of process innovation is very much on short-term cost reduction through improvements in labour productivity (Skinner 1986). The results of this emphasis are both paradoxical and potentially disastrous, resulting in many businesses falling behind in the technology war and cutting away their ability to compete. It tends not to happen in Japan.

A familiar example of this pattern can be seen in the personal computer world. During the initial stage of very rapid growth there were literally hundreds of different firms competing with each other by providing highly innovative products, all different and all with their own unique selling points. As the market grew, certain standards of performance and agreed ways of doing things began to emerge. IBM came on the scene when the market was ready to harmonize behind a single operating system and from that point on competition began to focus more and more on providing a standard product at a competitive price. To achieve this, manufacturers turned their attention to making production economies through process innovations. Product innovations still occur, but new standards emerge very quickly. For example, when Intel introduced the 20386 processor, the standard set-up based on it comprised 1 mb RAM, 40 mb hard disk, 3½ in. floppy and a VGA monitor. All the clone manufacturers were counted in and competed on price and credibility; that is, the emphasis of innovation moved away from the product onto the process, concentrating on costs and marketing. The mortality rate among PC producers has been extremely high, and even now the situation among clone makers certainly remains interesting.

The pattern shown in Figure 5.2 is based on empirical work, i.e. it reports what actually appears to be the case. It is not necessarily suggesting that this is an ideal or desirable state of affairs, but simply that this is the way it is. It may in fact be highly undesirable, but is nevertheless a natural tendency that management may overcome only with considerable effort. Rather than assume that managers in mature businesses should focus their efforts on achieving process innovations it would be well to recognize that there may be situations when managers in a mature business might achieve tremendous success by focusing on product innovation.

The example of the UK warp knitting industry should give some cause for thought about this. There can be few industries that exhibit such unambiguous symptoms of maturity. Not only has it been around for a few hundred years, but it has also undergone most of the distinguishable phases in an industry's evolution, including the concentration on process innovation during its mature phase. And yet, at this eleventh hour, it produces a surprising number of new product developments which are the key to the profitable growth of its most innovative producers.

> Invention of the first machine knitting system is generally attributed to William Lee of Calverton in Nottingham, in 1598. The first warp knitting machine was introduced in 1769 and was used to produce fancy work such as laces, nets and tattings as well as cheap and simple fabrics for army uniforms and blankets. A warp knitting machine has many knitting needles operating simultaneously across the width of the machine.
>
> After the initial burst of innovation on products such as these attention turned to process innovations to reduce costs and improve efficiency. By the late nineteenth century machines were running at speeeds of around 100 courses per minute (cpm), a course being the completion of a completed stitch. By the 1920s, as a result of continuous development, machines were running at 240 cpm. By 1939, again as a result of continuous development, speeds had almost doubled again to 450 cpm. In 1939 the compound needle was introduced and halved the distance of travel of the knitting elements, thereby doubling the speed to almost 1000 cpm. This was further developed after the war until today it is possible to run machines at around 2500 cpm.
>
> Warp knitting is undoubtedly a mature industry that has focused a lot of attention on process innovations with considerable success. However, in the last few years, it has also developed many new products and even created completely new markets and the most successful firms in the industry are active in these new product areas, rather than in the traditional markets where highly efficient production of cheap standard product is the key to survival.
>
> The new products include: weft insertion lining fabrics, multi-axial insertion fabrics, terry towelling sheeting and gown fabric, sun and light protection nets, tile support and plaster nets, grass catcher bags, falling rock protection nets, high tensile polyester (htp) protection padding, reflective warning garments, kermel heat protection fabric, waffle fabric, glass and htp conveyor belting, pvc coated htp tubing, polyester geomembrane, water embankment fabric, new elastomeric fabrics, new top quality raschel lace fabrics, knitted lace pantyhose,

weft insertion coated flat roof covering and tarpaulin fabrics, secondary carpet backing, raschel fishing nets, floatable water protection nets, anti-dazzle nets, weft insertion tyre cord, Kevlar and epoxy reinforced fabrics for artificial arteries and bone structures. (Pearson 1989)

Drucker lists a few of the most innovative fast-growing companies in America and notes that the fastest growing is

> a chain of barbershops. And next to it, both in sales growth, and profitability . . . a chain of dentistry offices, followed by a manufacturer of hand tools and by a finance company that leases machinery to small businesses . . . . One of the best performers is a company making and selling living room furniture; another one is making and marketing doughnuts; a third, high quality chinaware; a fourth, writing instruments; a fifth, household paints; a sixth has expanded from printing and publishing local newspapers into consumer marketing services; a seventh produces yarns for the textile industry; and so forth.
> (Drucker 1985:8–9)

All these businesses are mature, all are innovative and all have innovated in the product that the customer buys. Process innovation may achieve reductions in cost, but if it makes no impact on the product or service the customer buys then its effect is likely to be strictly short-term. Strategic innovation affects the customers and the product they buy. This applies to mature business just as to those still enjoying the flush of adolescence.

5.5 Summary

- Mature businesses are important. Most people work in them and most people will continue to do so.
- Mature businesses can be innovative, and many are.
- The object of any business is to achieve a prolonged phase of maturity, when it will be at its most effective as a wealth producer and cash generator.
- Maturity is the reward for a successful infancy and adolescence. The problems of maturity are the problems of success, e.g. the difficulty of ditching an existing technology in which the business has a lead. The many financial, physical and psychological investments in the *status quo* are very difficult to write off.
- A major problem of mature business is what to do with the surplus cash generated. Most businesses appear to invest it in diversifications, organizational slack or managerial discretion. Each of these can be counterproductive to the maintenance of a successful, competitive business. There are more positive things to do with surplus cash.
- As businesses mature they tend to invest less and less in innovation, and what they do invest increasingly goes to process innovations, rather than

new product developments; increasingly it is focused on cost reduction and raising the productivity of direct labour (an increasingly irrelevant measure of efficiency). However, investment in innovation doesn't need to decline.
- A focus away from product innovations is not necessarily the best strategy. Many mature businesses have grown dramatically and profitably by exploiting opportunities for new product development within their mature industries.
- Concentration on direct labour cost reduction can be wholly counterproductive.
- Maturity tends to be associated with mechanistic organizations as opposed to organismic, but it is not necessarily so. Though there may be a natural tendency for organizations to become progressively more bureaucratic, management has the responsibility and power to counter this tendency.

References

Drucker, P. F., *Innovation and Entrepreneurship*, Heinemann, London, 1985.
Pascale, R., 'The paradox of "corporate culture": reconciling ourselves to socialization', *California Management Review*, Vol. xxvii, No. 2, 1985:26–41.
Pearson, G. J., 'Factors which facilitate and inhibit innovation in a mature industry', unpublished doctoral thesis, Manchester Business School, University of Manchester, 1989.
Skinner, W., 'The productivity paradox', *Harvard Business Review*, July-Aug 1986:55–9.
Utterback, J. M. and W. J. Abernathy, 'A dynamic model of process and product innovation', *OMEGA*, Vol. 3, No. 6, 1975:639–56.

6
Industry assessment

The material in these first few chapters has identified a number of issues that are useful for characterizing an industry or sector. Some of them serve to identify the competitive characteristics and performance of an industry. Others relate to the process of innovation relevant to particular industries. There are also several organizational characteristics common in particular industries which, research suggests, may help or hinder innovation.

The competitive matrix introduced in Chapter 1 and shown here in Figure 6.1 is divided into four equal parts, each accommodating particular kinds of organizations (shown in Figure 1.6 as autocrats, butterflies, liquidators, etc.). This static presentation hides the fact that there are some natural movements in the matrix representing forces that management has to combat. For example, as firms mature there is a natural tendency for them to become bureaucratic. It is by no means inevitable, but there is nevertheless a tendency for it to happen unless management takes explicit action to prevent it. In terms of the matrix this tendency is represented by a migration from quadrant 2 to quadrant 1, i.e. organizations that operate effectively as 'innovative teams' tend to formulate

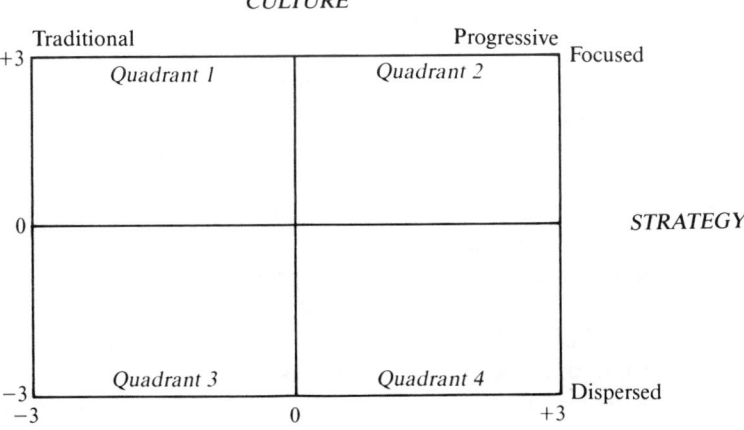

Figure 6.1 The competitive matrix

64 THE COMPETITIVE ORGANIZATION

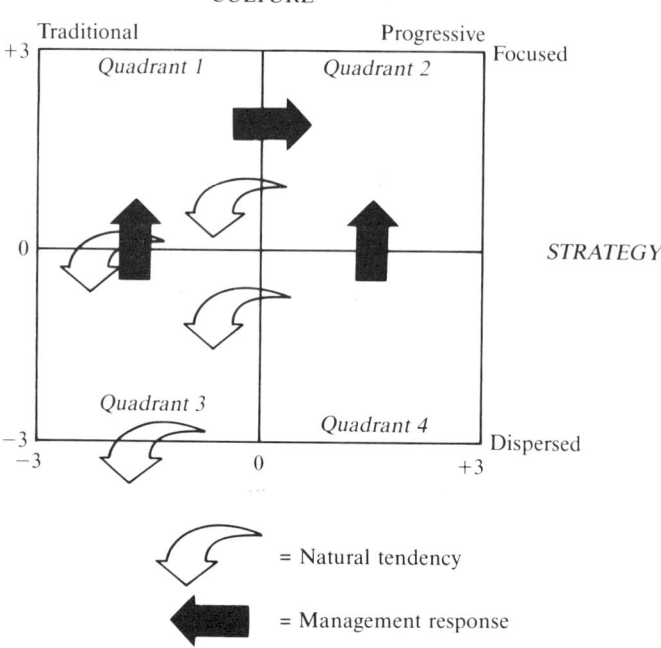

Figure 6.2 The competitive matrix: natural tendencies and management responses

successful recipes that become set rules of working; they tend, as they grow, to adopt standardized regulations, to invest in organizational slack and managerial discretion and gradually to build up the systems of the 'bureaucratic'. In some industries these tendencies may be more pronounced than in others.

There is also a further tendency for mature bureaucrat firms to diversify and lose their strategic focus and so, in due course, be pressed to focus on strict cash control and cost reduction – this is represented on the matrix by migration from quadrant 1 to quadrant 3. In addition, there is also a natural movement of quadrant 4 organizations, 'butterflies', which are never successful for long, towards quadrant 3, i.e. they become organizations that invest carelessly and inconsistently in projects selected randomly with respect to strategy, eventually run out of cash and are forced to adopt the strict cost control of the liquidator organization. Finally, there is a natural tendency for liquidators to go out of business altogether.

These tendencies are shown in Figure 6.2 together with the opposing managerial thrusts that would be required to maintain, or improve, an organization's position.

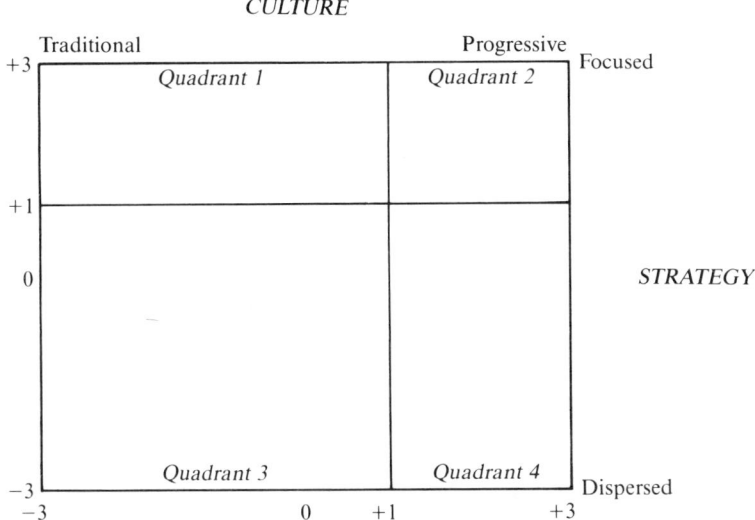

Figure 6.3 The competitive matrix (for an innovative sector)

In declining industries, the natural tendency for organizations to migrate to the liquidator quadrant and then to extinction may be very pronounced, while in others the pressures may be less strong. If the pressures in your industry are severe then you will have to take more decisive action to combat them. This means that, in terms of positioning your organization on the competitive matrix, you should aim to achieve a more focused strategy and progressive culture, i.e. a higher position in quadrant 2, than would otherwise be necessary. This requirement could be accommodated on the matrix by redrawing the axes to intersect at point 1,1, rather than 0,0, as shown in Figure 6.3. This makes the attainment of a quadrant 2 position more difficult to achieve by reducing it in size.

Achieving a high score in quadrant 2 would also be important in a high-growth, highly competitive and innovative industry where entrepreneurial behaviour is essential just for survival. For these very different reasons management in such an industry must aim to have their organization well up into the top right area of quadrant 2 of the matrix. Thus, under these circumstances, the amended matrix of Figure 6.3 would also be appropriate.

A preliminary assessment of your industry's position can be obtained by responding to the questionnaire at the end of this chapter. Your answers will help to define the parameters relevant to the competitive matrix. The questions are concerned with the probable importance of innovation and change to your industry, whether the industry appears to be well adapted to coping with a rapidly changing technological environment and whether it could be an effective change generator.

In general, very high and very low scores would indicate that a firm in that industry needs to position itself well up in quadrant 2. Thus, it is suggested that scores of below 25 per cent or above 75 per cent would seem to justify modifying the matrix as in Figure 6.3. Even more extreme scores may warrant even further modification. Scores from 25 per cent to 75 per cent imply that there is no requirement to modify the entrepreneurial matrix from that shown in Figure 6.1.

As far as possible, respond to these questions accurately. Give them reasonable consideration – it is the factual responses that count, not your immediate perceptions. Where accurate answers are not known and are difficult to obtain, make your best guess or approximation, preferably after conferring with colleagues. Where there is absolutely no feel for the answer, omit the question. However, if there are more than two or three of these unanswered questions, then you clearly do not know your industry well enough.

6.1 Industry assessment questionnaire

Answer the following questions about the industry in which your business operates by scoring it from 0 to 10 as indicated.

1. From which technological revolution does your industry stem?

    (NB Chapter 5 identifies three – the eighteenth century, the 1930s and the current technological revolution – and identifies several industries that grew up in each period.)
    0 for the first revolution, 5 for the second and 10 for the third

2. If your industry is from the first or second revolutions, would you say that its focus is mainly on specialist, high quality and relatively high technology parts of the market?
    0 = Not at all 1   2   3   4   5   6   7   8   9   10 = Completely

3. How has your industry been affected so far by the new technologies?
    0 = Not at all 1   2   3   4   5   6   7   8   9   10 = Comprehensively

4. To what extent do you envisage it will be affected over the next 5 years?
    0 = Not at all 1   2   3   4   5   6   7   8   9   10 = Comprehensively

5. At what stage of technological development (i.e. on its S-curve) is your industry?
    0 = Early stage 1   2   3   4   5   6   7   8   9   10 = At its limit

6. Does the current technology fully satisfy customer requirements?
    0 = Completely 1   2   3   4   5   6   7   8   9   10 = Not at all

7. Is continuous innovation the norm for participants in your industry?
    0 = Not at all 1   2   3   4   5   6   7   8   9   10 = Completely

8. Does your industry have open technological communications?

    (e.g. Does it have a research association that makes technical information and advice available to members? Does it have a trade association with a similar role?)
    0 = Not at all 1   2   3   4   5   6   7   8   9   10 = Comprehensive

9. Is your industry's basic technology developing fast?
    0 = Extremely slow 1   2   3   4   5   6   7   8   9   10 = Very fast

10. Are the leading firms in your industry managed by finance professionals?
    0 = Mainly 1   2   3   4   5   6   7   8   9   10 = None

11. Is technological competence more important than cost efficiency in your industry?
    0 = Definitely not 1   2   3   4   5   6   7   8   9   10 = Definitely

12. Does your industry have an active research organization?
    0 = No 1   2   3   4   5   6   7   8   9   10 = Yes, highly active

13. Does knowledge of new technological innovations spread quickly in your industry?
    0 = Yes 1   2   3   4   5   6   7   8   9   10 = No

68 THE COMPETITIVE ORGANIZATION

14. Is your industry heavily unionized?
    0 = Yes 1 2 3 4 5 6 7 8 9 10 = No
15. Do you believe typical junior managers in your industry frequently work long hours without overtime pay?
    0 = None 1 2 3 4 5 6 7 8 9 10 = Many
16. Has your industry seen much structural change as a result of new technology?
    0 = Not at all 1 2 3 4 5 6 7 8 9 10 = A great deal
17. Are the leading firms in your industry long established?
    0 = Yes 1 2 3 4 5 6 7 8 9 10 = No
18. Do the 'big three' firms in your industry have around 50 per cent or more market share?
    0 = Yes 1 2 3 4 5 6 7 8 9 10 = No
19. Is your industry subject to a lot of overseas competition?
    0 = No 1 2 3 4 5 6 7 8 9 10 = Yes
20. Is price the main competitive weapon?
    0 = Yes 1 2 3 4 5 6 7 8 9 10 = No

Total score = ... (Max = 200) = ... per cent

PART TWO
THE STRATEGY DIMENSION

Part One was concerned mainly with outlining the competitive model and the main concepts and research base of innovation and entrepreneurialism. The chapters in this part are concerned with the various components that make up the strategy dimension of the competitive matrix.

The strategy dimension is fundamentally about knowing what you want to achieve and how to achieve it. This is not as simple as it seems. Knowing your own business is not the result of cold analysis, but of experience and expertise in the core activities of the industry. Knowing what you want to achieve has to be based on that expertise, but also on the identification of a rousing and stimulating aim, which people can readily understand and wish to support. Nor is knowing how to achieve the strategic intent the result of analysis, so much as an opportunistic search for non-obvious means and possibilities.

Strategy is not about fitting an organization to its environment, nor about allocating the resources at its disposal in the most effective way. It is more concerned with creating new environments and getting hold of whatever resources are needed to achieve strategic ambitions.

Many of the topics covered in this part have been the subject of complete books rather than parts of short chapters. The current treatment is therefore necessarily brief. The object is to build up an understanding of the essential components of the strategy dimension.

Associated with each chapter is a set of questions that indicate how an individual organization measures up in terms of strategy. The questions are intended to raise issues that management might consider in relation to its own organization's strategy. They will, it is hoped, prompt some productive management action within your own organization. However, their main purpose is to profile an organization's performance in terms of the five characteristics that make up the strategic dimension of the competitive matrix, and so locate that organization on the matrix. For convenience the questions are listed in full together with a suitable answering scheme at the end of Chapter 12. Further explanatory notes on using the questionnaire are included in Appendix II.

7
Setting strategic direction

7.1 Introduction

The competitive model was briefly outlined in the opening chapter together with a thumb-nail sketch of the main strategic models that have so far been widely adopted. Clearly, each of these models is quite distinctive and appears to answer quite different questions. They share the same basic components shown in Figure 7.1, but there the similarities seem to end. What is meant by terms such as 'direction' appears to be fundamentally different in each of the models.

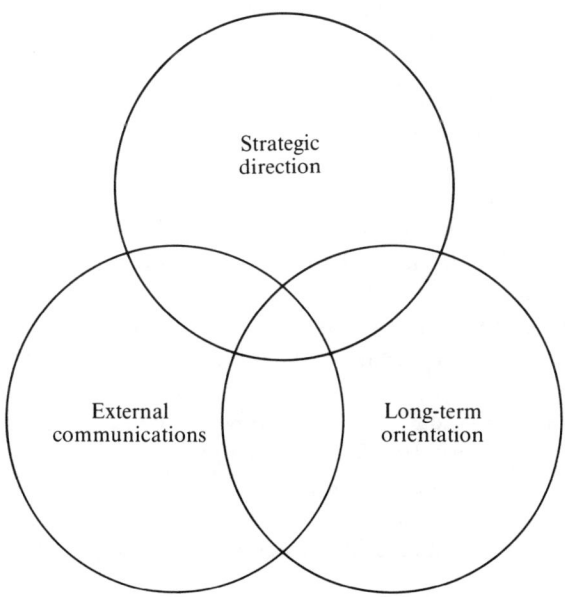

Figure 7.1 Components of strategy

The Boston model uses external communications in the form of information about market growth and market shares in order to formulate long-term decisions about direction, simply as to whether to maintain, increase or cut investment in a particular business. The generic strategy approach forces a choice between two strategies – cost leadership or differentiation – and commends an exhaustive (and exhausting) collection of information, both internal and external, in order to monitor the achievement of strategic aims primarily in relation to competitors.

Clearly, both the inputs and the outcomes of these two models are entirely different and they appear to serve different purposes. Moreover, even though the competitive matrix has not yet been described in depth, it appears to make use of inputs that are different again, to produce different outputs and also to serve yet a different purpose. However, even though there are fundamental differences in the various approaches to strategy, there is an underlying rationale that applies to them all. Every strategic model is intended to achieve the same general outcomes. This chapter outlines that underlying rationale.

7.2 Strategic responsibility

In some businesses strategy appears to emerge as the result of a more or less haphazard process of trial and error. New products, services and ways of doing things are tried out and those that appear to work become embedded in the business and its culture. In due time these successful recipes accumulate into 'the way we do things around here' – a distinctive and effective guide for future development. In other businesses, strategy is simply what the chief executive says it is. For a new business, or a small business, this may be the natural and often most effective way of establishing responsibility for strategy. However, for a larger, multi-product or multi-business company, the situation is too complex and changes too fast for the individual approach to be realistic. Under these circumstances, an individual-led strategy is likely to reduce to a financial, control-oriented mechanism of limited strategic significance.

Neither of these situations is satisfactory. An emergent strategy may not emerge quickly enough, or even at all, and reliance on the personal decisions of an individual, no matter how eminent, even if successful in the short term, is clearly fragile in the medium and long term.

It is important to recognize that being 'entrepreneurial' does not imply that strategy is the responsibility of a single entrepreneur. A quick glance at the list below will indicate how fragile such strategies often turn out to be.

The idea of a single individual having responsibility for the strategic development of a business is at first sight attractive. A benign dictatorship is surely the most efficient and effective way of running an organization. But consider the businesses run by these one-man strategists:

- Alan Bond
- Freddie Laker
- Robert Maxwell
- Clive Sinclair
- Jim Slater
- Donald Trump
- George Walker

The list could be extended almost without end. All their businesses have been successful, but in the long run may have been better off run by a team. Even Sir James Goldsmith has pointed out that conglomerates tend not to outlive their creators for very long. A winning strategy is not the result of the thought processes of some inscrutable leader with the 'vision' to see how things are and what should be done about it.

In most businesses strategy needs to take inputs from all members of management and to be developed by them operating as a team. In this way it is likely that they will all be committed to achieving the same strategic ends and also able to engage the commitment of their own people in its implementation. Making groups of people work together as effective teams is not easy. There is a natural tendency for any group to adopt a leader even if one is not formally appointed. The leader may then take on the role of decision maker with the rest of the team merely working as rubber stamps.

In strategic matters the team most often involved is the board of directors operating formally under the leadership of a chairman and a chief executive, the two roles often being combined by a singular individual. Such boards of directors rarely operate effectively as teams (Patton and Baker 1987). The executive director who acts independently or proposes the unorthodox, risky or innovative solution can be extremely vulnerable. Having spent half a lifetime building his career and achieving a good income, a satisfactory quality of life and comfortable pension arrangements, the typical executive director will be unlikely to put all this at risk by rocking the boat. Thus, most boards of directors, while accepting formal responsibility for strategy as a group, in practice do not work as a team. Decisions are taken by the chairman/chief executive and compliant co-directors merely acquiesce.

Patton and Baker suggested the following steps to make directors less compliant:

1. Separate the functions of chairman and chief executive.
2. Limit directorships for board members so that their attention is concentrated more on their own business.

3. Prune directors who don't peform.
4. Restrict board size to no more than 9–11 directors.

The board of directors should be the most important team in any business and making it operate effectively as a team is essential if it is to become an effective vehicle for setting the strategic direction of the business. Making a team operation work properly at board level is not easy in practice. Kotter referred to the process as the role of true leadership as opposed to mere management (Kotter 1990) – leadership controls change by setting the strategic direction of a business whereas management simply controls complexity. The distinction between leadership and management re-emphasizes that leadership is a team role, not the job of an individual, much less an essentially charismatic individual. Leadership of all but the most simple organizations, in this sense, is essentially a role best carried out by a team of individuals stimulating and complementing each other.

7.3 Purpose of strategy

The theoretical ideas underlying strategy are simple, but converting them into practical action is often extremely difficult. The basic idea behind most strategic planning models is extremely simple and is often expressed, as a continuous cycle, in the following terms:

– Where are we now?
– Where do we want to get to?
– How do we get there?
– ACTION
– How are we doing? i.e. Where are we now?

It could not be easier to comprehend at the theoretical level and can be illustrated by simplistic examples, such as making a journey:

> If you're in London and you want to get to Manchester, first of all you plan a suitable route and then start travelling. Every so often you check progress and, so long as everything is going according to the original itinerary, you carry on travelling. If, however, you find yourself heading towards Brighton, you need to amend your route to get back on the road to Manchester. Similarly, if you are making slower progress than intended you may need to consider corrective action. Also, if you receive information that Manchester is suffering a plague or about to be bombed, or for any other reason it appears more desirable to go to Glasgow, then you may wish to change destinations and so revise the entire journey.

However, the journey metaphor doesn't get very far in the real world; business isn't that simple. The first difficulty is in defining a suitable destination in terms that everyone can understand.

The purpose of strategy, as identified by Mintzberg (1987:11–32), is theoretically simple enough:

– set direction
– concentrate efforts
– maintain consistency

Yet most strategic models have really only contributed marginally to direction, concentration and consistency. Boston's portfolio suggests going for high market shares of high growth markets as its only contribution to the direction debate. Porter suggests either differentiation or cost leadership but is silent on the means for making the decision on what form the differentiation should take. If there is a known direction, then it may be possible to be consistent in trying to reach it. With no direction, strategy is likely to be made by a series of random leaps. In the short term they may be exciting, or disastrous, but they are unlikely to achieve any long-term success.

The definition of direction is the foundation of an effective strategy model. Yet, in practice, detailed strategic plans amount to little more than projections of the *status quo*, rather than directional strategies. These problems are often increased by the use of analytical approaches such as SWOT (the analysis of Strengths and Weaknesses and Opportunities and Threats). An exhaustive list, of strengths to be exploited, weaknesses to be eliminated, opportunities to be grasped and threats to be avoided, almost inevitably produces an allocation of limited resources that is too thin and too broad for anything substantial to be achieved. Similar objections can be raised against the detailed industry analysis commended by Porter. The analysis is so detailed, yet at the same time so undiscriminating, that the result will almost inevitably be a form of paralysis.

President Kennedy's famous target – to 'put a man on the moon by the end of the decade' – was a simple and to-the-point expression of strategic intent. This statement of direction became the crucial foundation of America's strategy in the space race. It fully achieved the purpose of strategy in a way that could never be done by the more detailed plans arising from exhaustive analyses of orthodox planning methods.

7.4 Outcomes from strategy

The outcomes from strategy are shown in Figure 7.2. First, and perhaps most important, are the many relatively minor decisions taken daily by every member of the organization. If these are taken randomly with regard to strategy the result will be a Pareto-style misallocation of time, efforts

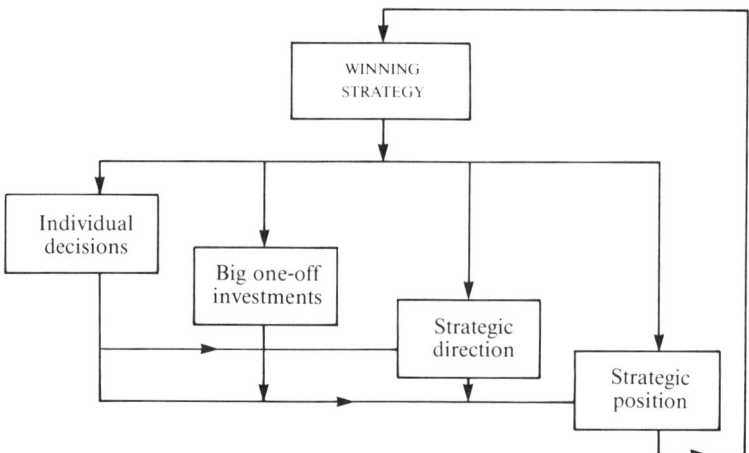

Figure 7.2 The outcomes of strategy

and the enthusiasm of people. Thus 80 per cent of time would be devoted to items contributing only 20 per cent to the organization's strategic aims.

The cumulative effect of small decisions can be decisive. The introduction of a new product, for example, may take a dominant share of a salesman's time despite the fact that it will never become a major profit earner. Meanwhile, the product that represents the core of the business gets ignored. A similar dilution of time and effort will occur in marketing, production and even administrative functional areas. Over a period of time when a number of new products are introduced the resultant reallocation of resources may well result in the unnecessary or premature decline of the core business. If the introduction of new products is carefully planned as part of the organization's directional thrust this reallocation of resources and efforts may be valid, if the new products merely represent minor diversification in order to 'spread the risk' or 'broaden the market' the result is likely to be a loss of direction, stagnation and, eventually, overall decline with the core products. On the other hand, if individual decisions are taken to support the chosen strategy then the reverse will be true and a virtuous self-reinforcing cycle can be achieved.

The second outcome of strategy relates to the taking of major one-off decisions. These are usually capital investments but, equally, may be policy-type decisions that may change the direction of the business. With no clear strategy these decisions will have a discontinuous effect, resulting in the business lurching from one direction to another, losing momentum and coherence at every change. In many cases these decisions are unavoidable: plant is worn out and has to be replaced, a lease expires or consumer tastes change. Management is therefore presented with an opportunity to make major strategic progress, or to take the decision almost by default and so pass up the opportunity. The replacement of plant opens up the possibility of reducing costs, increasing flexibility, improving service, or carrying on as before. The decision may be taken to buy new plant that merely replaces the existing equipment, or that embodies an increment in technology or even a step change to something quite new. With no clear direction it will not be possible to determine which option would be the most appropriate and the decision taken will run a high risk of being wrong. With a known direction, on the other hand, such decisions may be taken so that they further direction and reinforce concentration and consistency.

Many businesses lack any sense of direction and many others are heading up blind alleys. In such cases, it won't matter how skilled and well motivated the people are. Business success is not achieved by simply 'rowing harder if the boat is headed in the wrong direction' (Ohmae 1989a).

Both these sets of decisions – small individual decisions and the big one-off investments – impact, either positively or negatively, on the other two outcomes of strategy, direction and position, which are discussed in the following sections.

7.5 Strategic direction

Direction is the key strategic issue. Some firms deliberately adopt a clear and simply stated direction, some establish direction through repeated trial and error. Those that lack direction will underperform and in the long run probably not survive. Even when other factors are favourable lack of direction leads to underachievement through the dissipation of effort and investment and also to the frustration and ultimately alienation of people, as in the case of the company reported in Figure 7.3. Long-term objectives can encapsulate strategic direction in simple, tangible terms that are capable of initiating and galvanizing action, like Kennedy's already quoted 'man on the moon' commitment.

- 'Provide the best service in the industry.'
- 'Be the technological leader.'
- 'Offer the lowest cost product with XYZ technology.'
- 'Beat ABC Co. to the introduction of XYZ technology.'

These are all forms of long-term objectives that contain within them easy to understand and remember expressions of direction. They effectively drive the strategy process.

Traditional strategic planning models do not work like this. They operate on the assumption that the purpose of strategy is to fit the organization to its various environments through the judicious allocation

Company X, a private company established in 1973 by the present chairman, produced a comprehensive range of local area network components, boxes of electronic kit sold alongside specialist cabling that was bought in. The boxes comprised terminal servers, adaptors, coaxial repeaters, fibre optic repeaters, bridges and transceivers, i.e. all but the computer equipment needed to make a local area network operational. Most of the boxes were run by microprocessors, the software for which was developed and coded by Company X itself.

Company X gave a general impression of freedom and informality. For example, all offices were open-plan, dress was informal – no ties, no suits except the MD (the software development manager, for example, wore floral jeans and served coffee to all her staff) – two VDUs displayed the Mandelbrot set and one young programmer was doodling with it – 'it helps improve efficiency of coding'. This environment was deliberately contrived in order to be more conducive to creative, innovative activity than a tightly controlled and disciplined unit would have been.

The MD described himself as a 'self-confessed LAN fanatic'. He had joined Company X three years previously and had made many changes in personnel. He had joined the company with the aim of 'inducing more creativity and innovation'. Traditionally, he explained, Company X had been 'me too' followers (behind the leading UK networking company and four American firms). Company X was not an innovator. They had custom designed both hardware and software to customer requirements, but with very few exceptions had not initiated innovations themselves. He had brought in a lot of new people, mainly from Company X customers, 'creative, bright young people', and they were becoming more innovative – 'quite a few exciting ideas are now coming through'.

'The job is producing products to sell against the big boys. We can't compete on price, so we must do it by being creative. We must get new products out early enough to compete while the price is still high.'

The MD's suggestion that the firm was not innovative and needed to be more so was echoed by the other staff members, but it was almost the only common ground between them. Innovativeness in terms of new products was not seen as particularly relevant by the other managers, whose view was that they were no more likely to compete in terms of innovative new products than they were on price. They saw their main strength as having to lie in offering superior customer service, e.g. they needed to be most innovative in offering customized products of high reliability, with great speed.

Whereas the MD saw the open, informal, unstructured organization as the key to providing the opportunities for being creative, the managers all agreed that there was a need for 'more structure' and 'clearer direction from the top'. The organization was described by one manager as a 'butterfly' in that it flitted from development to development without any consistent underlying thread of strategy. As a consequence many such investments of cash and, more particularly, effort, were not followed through to fruition. This was the cause of considerable frustration among the Company X managers.

Figure 7.3 Company X: directionless 'butterfly' (Pearson 1989)

of resources. This process constrains strategic intentions to those that seem natural, if not almost inevitable, and eliminates a bold intent as unrealistic. The possibility of any business rising from obscurity is denied by such an approach, especially in a corporate culture dominated by macho-accounting norms where risk avoidance sometimes appears to be the main business objective.

Yet there are many examples of small obscure businesses that have refused the shelter of small market niches and had the temerity to confront and beat their industry giants (Cooper, Willard and Wood 1986). Some of the most successful of today's businesses have risen like this on the back of unrealistically bold strategic intentions. Japanese successes in consumer electronics, semi-conductors and factory automation all started off from such highly unfavourable positions.

Strategic direction goes far beyond the allocation of resources. A clearly stated direction that is known and understood by all the firm's stakeholders – employees, suppliers, customers, shareholders, technology suppliers and competitors – is the most powerful strategic tool.

7.6 Strategic position

Some statements of strategic direction are so strong they become embedded in the culture of the firm so that all stakeholders know implicitly what the business is all about. Such 'successful recipes' guide all future developments. For example, MacDonald's clearly established recipe – the way they do things around there – suggests that the Egg McMuffin fits well, but a sophisticated French menu (as Mintzberg (1987) put it, 'the McDuckling à l'Orange') would be inconsistent. MacDonald's employees, customers, suppliers, shareholders and, indeed, the population at large have a very clear understanding of what would be consistent and what would not. Concentration is therefore easy to achieve and maintain.

Many businesses have achieved a strong strategic position that would clearly determine the nature of any future development. The known positions of Porsche, Bic, Yves St Laurent, Marks and Spencer, Rolls-Royce, Dunhill and many others is so strong that it clearly determines the sort of projects that would be likely to succeed. Such businesses have a clear self-perception that guides their future actions in a way that permits the concentration of resources and the efforts and commitment of people on the same ends and in a way that is consistent over time.

The down-side of such strong strategic positions is that they become restrictive and inflexible. It would be difficult for such businesses to change their recipe in response to changes in their environment. The financial and psychological investment sunk in the existing position is so great that changing position would prove a very difficult decision to reach. Moreover, implementing such a decision would prove even more difficult; every conceivable barrier to change would be raised against such a fundamental change. Most firms do not have such strong strategic positions, and are not necessarily 'stuck in the middle' because of it. A firm with no strong position may nevertheless have a clear direction that guides strategy to achieve both concentration and consistency.

7.7 Summary

- The purpose of strategy is to:
    set direction
    achieve concentration
    maintain consistency
- Previous approaches such as Boston's portfolio and Porter's generic strategies do not help much in achieving this strategic purpose.
- The planning approach to strategy does not help much either and is very often absolutely counterproductive to achieving the strategic objective.
- The desired outcomes from successful strategy are:
    that the many individual and small decisions that affect the allocation of time, effort and enthusiasm should all be taken to reinforce the organization's strategic direction;
    that the major investment decisions are taken similarly;
    that the direction is therefore continually reinforced and progressed;
    that a strategic position may be progressively built up.
- A clear direction is the crucial ingredient of strategy: without it there will be no concentration or consistency.
- A strong position can also be a very powerful outcome that clearly guides future development, but strong positions tend to restrict flexibility and responsiveness to change.

References

Cooper, A. C., G. E. Willard and C. Y. Wood, 'Strategies of new and small firms: a re-examination of the niche concept', *Journal of Business Venturing*, Vol. 1, No. 3, 1986:247–60.

Kotter, J. P., *A Force for Change: How Leadership Differs from Management*, Macmillan, New York, 1990.

Mintzberg, H., 'The strategy concept', *California Management Review*, Fall 1987:11–32.

Ohmae, K., 'Companyism and do more better', *Harvard Business Review*, Jan–Feb 1989a.

Patton, A. and J. C. Baker, 'Why don't directors rock the boat?' *Harvard Business Review*, Nov–Dec 1987.

Pearson, G. J., 'Factors which facilitate and inhibit innovation in a mature industry', unpublished doctoral thesis, Manchester Business School, University of Manchester, 1989.

8
Developing external communications

8.1 Introduction

External communications comprise the organization's immediate transactions with suppliers and customers, its interdependent connections with technology suppliers and competitors, and its less immediate interactions with the political, economic, social and technological environments. They provide the knowledge base for setting and achieving strategic intentions.

From the Carter and Williams study onwards researchers have identified external communications as one of the key components in competitive success. Kanter's study of major American corporations (Kanter 1983) suggested that open communications were a prime characteristic of the innovative organization. Openness of communications, both externally and internally, is a key enabling characteristic, but is not necessarily sufficient. The purposive characteristic is difficult to research effectively and consequently is missing from a lot of theoretical literature. Nevertheless, it clearly underlies the new models of corporate strategy being defined by Hamel, Pralahad and others as described in Chapter 10 and is also an essential component of an effective network (see Section 8.4).

At one level external communications are concerned with a holistic view of an organization's situation and its likely future development. This provides insights that are not apparent when looking at the separate issues individually. It is not simply an analysis of the organization's strengths and weaknesses, and the threats and opportunities presented by its context, but includes also a discriminating view of what matters and what can be left on the back burner. It provides some understanding of how the important issues will develop over time and, most important of all, it offers guidance as to how to position the organization most advantageously.

Establishing external communications is not simply a process of exhaustive analysis. Each of the issues referred to above may be analysed in

82 THE COMPETITIVE ORGANIZATION

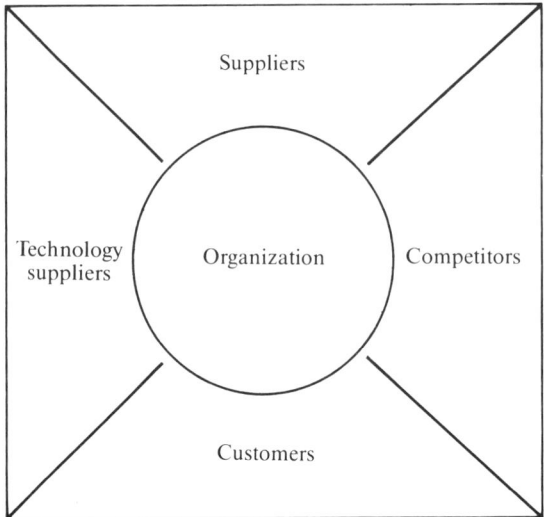

Figure 8.1 Direct relationships

detail and any sense of vision obscured in the process. Selectivity and discrimination are essential elements.

8.2 Direct relationships

The most important external communications that an organization has are with its customers and suppliers. Every transaction is a form of communication. Every order placed, product or service delivered, telephone answered, invoice received and paid, or complaint dealt with forms part of the external communication up and down the value chain. Similarly, though usually with much less freqency, every organization also has routine communications with the suppliers of its technology, whether they be the international producers of capital plant or the local PC retailer. Finally, most organizations have sporadic communications with their main competitors (Figure 8.1).

The most immediate contacts that any business has are with its customers and suppliers. Each business operation is a link in the chain stretching from raw material 'extraction' to finished good 'consumption'. Each transaction along this chain generates some economic surplus or contributes to the final economic surplus that justifies the existence of the chain of transactions. Transactions can be viewed separately or as a continuous process of transacting over time. The separatist view suggests that each participant in a transaction should attempt to maximize their share of the surplus from the transaction. Thus, every buyer will attempt to extract the best supply for the lowest cost and every supplier will try to provide the lowest cost supply at the highest price obtainable. In such a scenario the only thing that will mitigate these basically adversarial supplier–buyer transactions is the knowledge that they recur and form a continuing relationship that has to work to the continuing economic benefit of both parties.

Viewing the transaction as a continuous process suggests that the adversarial approach may not be the most economically beneficial for either party. A cooperative approach that recognizes the mutual interdependence of both parties, and the vital interests of each, leads to a completely different way of conducting such transactions.

Less frequent, but equally vital, transactions arise between the business and its technology suppliers and the business and its competitors. In some situations, the relationship with technology suppliers is less easy to recognize as a continuous relationship. In the past capital equipment may have been purchased only once every ten years or so and each such acquisition may have been treated as a highly competitive arms-length transaction, dealt with in some cases on a formal competitive tendering basis. However, as the speed of technological innovation has increased, continuous development of process and product has become a competitive necessity right across the economy and the relationship between technology suppliers and customers has become increasingly continuous.

The transaction between a business and its competitors may be less explicit and direct, but are nevertheless just as crucial to the business's viability. Every purchase a customer makes from a competitor represents a negative transaction with the business, a lost opportunity and a broken link in the continuous supplier–customer relationship. This is not a semantic point. The loss of a customer can present a competitive supplier with a unique learning opportunity – identifying the cause of the loss may result in the organization repositioning itself in its market, rebuilding its image, refocusing its resources and communicating both inside and outside the organization (Green 1989). A single broken link may not be important, but the continuous process of such negative transactions may be the most important element of external communications.

Thus, direct relationships must increasingly be regarded as continuous and non-adversarial, i.e. cooperative with open and frequent communications. Customers and suppliers have always been a prime source of awareness and now that collaborative arrangements are becoming more widely adopted instead of the old, adversarial, arms-length transactional relationships, there is a new openness in communications between many suppliers and customers. Similarly, collaborative technological arrangements are increasingly becoming the norm between the developers and users of technology. In the case of competitive relationships, the picture is

84 THE COMPETITIVE ORGANIZATION

less clear-cut. In the past there have been many industries that were characterized by mutual back-scratching arrangements, from simple price fixing to formal agreements about which firms would compete in which areas of business. These cartels, having long been illegal though not always easy to identify, even by the participants, are now much less common in most industries. However, the consequent increase in real competition does not necessarily imply that firms will cut each other's throats. There remains ample opportunity for substantial exchange of information that will operate in the interests both of the competitors and their customers.

These are obvious sources of increased awareness, but they are rarely fully developed. Most firms' relationships with their customers are still based around the buying–selling transaction itself and the opportunities for even an informal, much less a systematic, exchange of information are not exploited. This applies even more frequently to the relationship with technology suppliers and competitors.

The way these direct communications are most effectively conducted with competitors and customers are outlined in Chapters 10 and 11 respectively.

8.3 The broader context

These four different relationships take place within the broader context of the political, economic, social and technological environments, any of which may become paramount for a particular industry at a particular point in time. The strategic view of the business context is summarized in Figure 8.2.

A major consideration in the political environment has in the past been primarily related to the assessment of risk – risk of political instability, of non-payment for export sales, of inability to repatriate funds in the case of overseas operations. In the last few years political considerations have been extended in many industries where deregulation and privatization have presented opportunities for profitable new business and in other situations removed protective barriers to competition that had previously propped up unsustainable rates of return. In the 1990s one of the major political issues that will pose both threat and opportunity is the elimination of the communist threat and the opening up of Eastern Europe. Half the British government's expenditure on R&D has in the past gone on defence with negligible commercial spin-off, and total defence expenditure has been close to 4 per cent of GDP. The 'peace dividend' will have a substantial structural impact, not restricted solely to those firms directly involved in defence supply.

Factors within the broad economic environment are concerned with rates of economic growth and decline as they affect different world markets

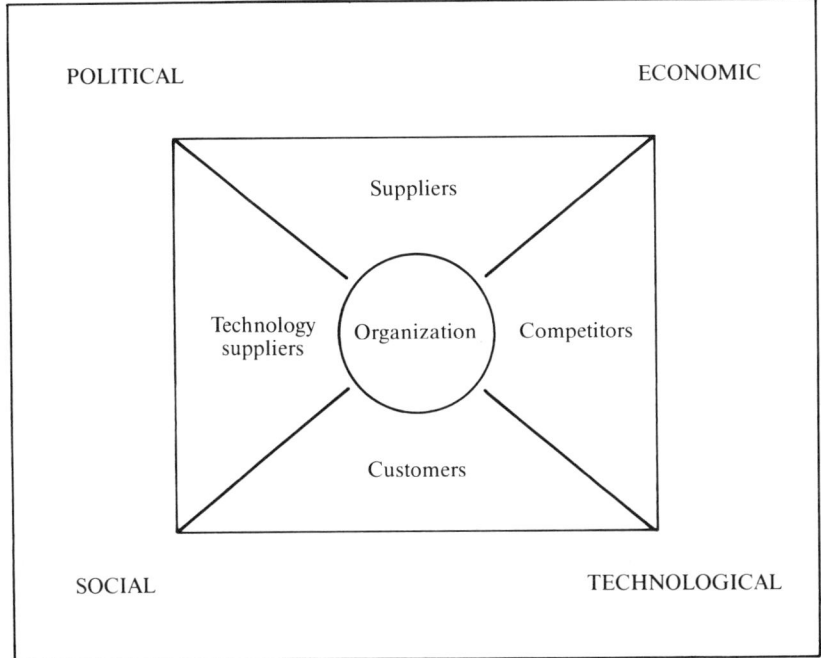

Figure 8.2 The strategic environment

and condominions and the understanding of why these differentials occur and how they are expected to occur in the future. The role of the European Community within the GATT initiative and the degree to which the EC opens up world trade or puts barriers up against it, will affect different industries differently. Similarly, Britain's relationship within the EC, especially with the single market in 1993 and the extent to which British rates of inflation and interest differ from other member countries, either within or not quite within a common European currency, will also have a structural effect within the British economy. It may also be vital to take a view on how Britain will rebuild its economic infrastructure (particularly in transport, education and health) when the public funds generated by privatization and North Sea Oil have declined.

Social factors that are currently critical to many industries relate to demographic and environmental issues. The continually ageing population and the prospective shortfall in graduate entries to the work-force will both have differential effects on industry, forcing structural changes that present both opportunities and threats. Similarly, the growing awareness of the side effects of manufacturing industry in terms of global warming and depletion of the ozone layer, as well as more localized impacts of industrial pollution, and the increasing demand for 'quality of life', will also create changes in industry structure and viability.

Technological factors, as already outlined in Chapter 2, also have differential effects on the structure of industry. Every industry has been affected by the electronic revolution and the potential benefits of information technology, but they are all at different stages of exploitation of these potentials. Some industries are more acutely affected than others by the possibilities of molecular engineering, biotechnology and the other special areas of new technology that are still sprouting.

All or any of these factors and relationships may be critical to the strategic vision of a particular business. There can be no general rules as to what is important and what is merely interesting in any individual situation. The only general rule is that every business must be aware of the important factors so that the structural changes can be anticipated and appropriate action taken. The business that has a clear strategic direction is at a considerable advantage in achieving effective external communications since it will be readily aware of what factors are potentially important to its strategy and what less so. This underlying purposiveness is the basis of an effective communications network.

8.4 Communications networks

A network is not simply a group of communicators. Such a group may be connected at random to exchange information of an undefined nature. They may well lack the essential purposive element. 'Have a nice day' is a communication – or at least it meets most of the requirements of an orthodox definition of a communication. Its purpose is, however, limited. Communications can be open, but not necessarily serve the prime purposes of the organization. They may be open entirely for social purposes that have nothing directly to do with the organization's strategic development. Such communications are not networks.

> The term *network* is the communications analogue of the sociological concept of 'group', but 'network' is distinct from 'group' in that it refers to a number of individuals (or other units) who persistently interact with one another in accordance with established patterns. (Mueller 1986)

Corporate networks take many different forms. The informal grapevine is a communications network, in most organizations fulfilling the very clear purpose of communicating corporate information that has not (yet) been communicated by official channels. Mueller describes a semi-formal network that he used to great effect: what he called his 'GWRK File' – a listing of contacts ('Guys Who Really Know'). This was really a networking system comprising various sub-networks that might serve particular purposes. For example, within the GWRK file there would be specialists on the market, on technology, on government, etc. The GWRK network system was set up carefully and very deliberately by Mueller to help him fulfil his managerial purposes more effectively.

Networks may be internal, connecting individuals and departments that have no other formal organizational links. They may have a physical form, as with electronic networks, operating as important aids to communication. Or they may be external, connecting the organization with its existing and potential customers, competitors and technology suppliers, or other external systems, such as financial markets. The science park concept derives its strength from networking. Silicon Valley is not just a geographical area, but a network. Networks are systems of communications links that overlay the formal organization. In the main they are informal and may be activated only irregularly, but they are persistent and, most important of all, they are clearly purposive.

External communications, i.e. networks involving customers and technology suppliers, both existing and potential, as well as other networks concerned with competitors (though not necessarily involving them directly), are crucial to the achievement of an effective strategy. Without such networks, the firm's strategy will be based on an inadequate understanding of customer needs, a lack of knowledge about technological developments and an ill-formed view about competitive strengths and weaknesses. Under such circumstances strategic direction is likely to be both dispersed and short-lived.

Networks are set up directly with the sources of primary information such as customers, suppliers and technology suppliers, or less directly related experts who may be useful in providing strategically relevant information in one field or another. This is a most invaluable source of information on which to base the development of strategy. However, there is an increasing amount of information that is available in already published form, and this is described in the following section.

8.5 Secondary sources of information

Very few firms exploit fully the myriad other sources of information now readily available to them largely as a result of the revolution in information technology, which has exploded both the amount of information available and its ease of access. For example, in the Science Reference and Information Service (formerly the Science Reference Library) of the British Library, holdings include:

- 229 000 monographs (including research reports, pamphlets, etc.)
- 30 500 current trade and business journals
- 31 million patent specifications
- More than 2000 directories

Also held are the following sources of specific company information:

- company catalogues and product literature (hard copy and on microfiche)
- current annual reports of British, European and international companies
- current house journals for British and European companies
- Extel cards (all series)
- McCarthy news cuttings (20 years on microfiche)
- Moody's series
- Jordan's series
- Who Owns Whom series
- Inter Company Comparisons series
- 1300 On-line databases including many general series such as the F & S Index, PROMPT, US Forecasts, Worldcasts, Economic Abstracts International, plus many industry-specific series such as Chemistry Industry Notes, Pharmaceutical News Index, RAPRA abstracts, World Textiles, Foods adlibra, etc.

All these items are held for the benefit of the general public and are supported by a free enquiry service. In addition, longer and more complex enquiries can be undertaken (on a fee-paying basis) in the areas of business, the environment, science and technology, biotechnology and Japanese Information Services, as well as patent scanning and search services. Similar, though less comprehensive information is available in the public commercial libraries of major provincial cities.

The sheer quantity of information is staggering, but more important is the ease of its access. Electronic data can be accessed selectively and efficiently by any interested party with no necessity for information technology expertise. The variety of data listed above implies a variety of means of access. In some areas this remains difficult and time-consuming, but in most instances access is quick and simple. Typically, secondary sources of information are undervalued and accessing it is often delegated to junior members of the organization, or it is even ignored altogether. As with networks of primary sources, access to published data needs to be carefully organized to fulfil the specific purposes of the organization. Potentially relevant databases, indices, abstracts, cuttings services, industry and company reports need to be reviewed, and their acquisition or access planned and reporting responsibilities allocated, so that the team with strategic responsibility is assured of routine awareness from the main relevant sources.

Setting up such a secondary information system is likely to be time-consuming, but its maintenance will be cheap and the potential returns are extremely high.

8.6 Summary

- External communications provide the knowledge base for setting and achieving strategic intentions.
- External communications include: those that occur frequently and regularly (e.g. receipt of orders, despatch of invoices, etc.) and those that occur infrequently and sporadically (e.g. items related to specific events such as major capital investments). Such transactions occur, whether or not they are explicitly planned, as means of effective communications.
- Communications need to be open and purposive. They are concerned with a holistic view of an organization's situation and its likely future development.
- Establishing external communications is not simply a process of exhaustive analysis, but of developing an active understanding.
- A firm's direct communications are with its customers, suppliers, competitors and technology suppliers. These occur by default, but need to be planned if they are to be exploited for the development of a winning strategy.
- These direct communications take place in a broader context of the political, economic, social and technological environments, any of which may become paramount for a particular industry at a particular time. Information on the broader context also needs to be planned.
- Acquiring required information can be done through networks of primary sources and systems of secondary information collection.
- A network is a number of individuals (or other units) who persistently interact in accordance with established patterns for a specified purpose. The purpose needs to be specified and the network deliberately set up.
- Access to published data also needs to be carefully organized to fulfil the specific purposes of the organization.

References

Green D., 'Learning from losing a customer', *Harvard Business Review*, May–June 1989:54–8.

Kanter, R. M., *The Change Masters: Corporate Entrepreneurs at Work*, Unwin Hyman, London, 1983.

Mueller, R. K., *Corporate Networking – Building Channels for Information and Influence*, Free Press, New York, 1986.

9
Maintaining a long-term orientation

9.1 Introduction

External communications are not simply related to a snapshot at a point in time, but rather to the dynamic position of the organization, its immediate relationships and its broader context and how these are developing over the longer term. In some of what has been said this is quite explicit. For example, the relationship between suppliers and customers is seen as continuous rather than just a series of discrete transactions. This is currently being highlighted by an increasing number of single sourcing arrangements that have to be based on positions of considerable mutual trust and reliance. Similarly, technology is recognized as developing rapidly and any awareness study must focus not simply on the current situation but on how technology is likely to develop in the long term and what the effects are likely to be.

A long-term orientation is the essential bed-rock of a winning strategy. However, some of the implications of long-term orientation are not obvious and some of the symptoms of a short-term orientation are often so disguised in 'long-term' clothing that even the managers concerned are unaware they are running a business on essentially short-term criteria. Long-term orientation therefore needs overt examination and its implications made explicit.

There are three problem areas in achieving a long-term orientation. First, there is the question of corporate objectives. These are often set in terms of financial performance, the only common language that can apply equally across all the disparate parts of a large corporation. Unfortunately, this almost always leads to a denial of strategy and a focus on short-term performance, the exceptions being those organizations that are themselves essentially financial rather than business-oriented, where the commitment is primarily to creating shareholder wealth without regard to any particular technology or market. Second, there is the fact that most strategic investments require a long time to generate any significant return. Long-term investments are more difficult to sustain in some environments than others and it is a particular problem in the UK where the financial market tail appears to wag the business/industrial dog. Third, there is a further set of short-term pressures that act directly on the individual manager. These may result directly from the need to achieve quick returns in response to the needs of the financial market, or they may arise more subtly as a result of the business and management culture that has been built up in the UK which emphasizes the 'bottom line' and 'macho-management' ways of improving it.

In the face of these pressures it remains true, almost without exception, that the most successful companies are those that have been able to take a long-term view and guide the development of individual businesses in accordance with a clear strategic direction that takes full advantage of long-term developments and change.

9.2 Strategic objectives

One way many businesses overtly espouse a long-term strategy is through a system of objectives that are intended to remain operational over the long term. For example:

- 20 per cent return on capital employed
- 10 per cent per annum compound growth in net assets, or even
- provide x per cent dividend yield to shareholders

Although these objectives are not expressed in time-dependant terms, they are intended to act as long-term guides to the level of acceptable performance. This they may do perfectly adequately, without carrying any strategic implications whatsoever. They contribute nothing to the definition of direction. Nor do they assist in the concentration of efforts, nor the maintenance of consistency in strategic thrust. In all these things such financially expressed objectives are completely silent. Their contribution to strategy is entirely illusory.

Objectives that are truly strategic are those that define direction, as outlined in Section 7.5. They are expressed in action terms and describe an aimed-for end state, such as 'provide the best service in the industry', or 'be the technological leader'. A business that is driven by strategic objectives such as these will only subordinate them to short-term considerations when short-term failure itself threatens to hazard strategic achievement. If a business aims to be the technological leader but has a short-term cash flow problem, it must first focus its attention on the short-term problem. However, generating a quantified cash surplus will not drive the business forward to any strategic achievement.

The Japanese electronics giant, NEC, identified three main strands of long-term technological and market development:

- computing would evolve from large mainframes to distributed processing;
- components would evolve from simple integrated circuits to very large-scale integration; and
- communications would evolve from cross-bar exchange to complex digital systems.

These three developing strands, computing, components and communications, 'would so overlap that it would be very hard to distinguish among them, and there would be enormous opportunities for any company that had built the competences needed to serve all three markets' (Pralahad and Hamel 1990:80).

Having established these three intertwining developments, it appears almost inevitable that NEC should set strategic objectives related to the development of technological competence in all three fields. This defines the company's direction and prescribes the types of new product (i.e. generic products) that NEC will generate in the future, as well as the broad markets in which they will plan to be active. None of these benefits would have been enjoyed had NEC proposed a level of return on capital employed as its strategic objective. NEC, like any other business, might well make use of financial targets, but the company is driven by focusing on its strategic objectives, and its financial achievements are the result.

Too many firms operate the other way round: focusing on financial achievement, which is essentially short-term, with the result that its long-term development is *ad hoc* and directionless.

But this essentially short-term requirement on British firms does not relieve them of the necessity to compete in global markets with global technologies. The example of Pilkington, whose long-term investment in glass technology made them vulnerable to a takeover bid by BTR (see Figure 9.1) showed how the long-term perspective can be difficult to maintain. Another, potentially even more damaging, example would be the takeover and break-up of ICI by Hanson. ICI and Pilkington may not be paragons of efficiency in the essentially short-term measures used by the City and espoused by BTR and Hanson, but it would be extremely surprising if their core businesses were not still generating returns for their shareholders long after BTR and Hanson have ceased to exist. It is vital that firms like Pilkington are able to retain their focus on the long-term development of technology in their industry. This is precisely the focus of most of the successful Japanese firms that are so widely quoted as examples of managerial rectitude.

The failure to support long-term technology development results in a

> BTR's one-time bid for Pilkington Glass was a watershed event in the UK battle between long-term technology development and short-term financial opportunism.
>
> Pilkington's share performance reflected the fact that short-term returns to shareholders were held down in order to invest further in R&D on glass technology. Pilkington had an enviable reputation as global leaders in glass technology, having developed float glass, and various other significant innovations.
>
> In so doing they required the cooperation and patient support of shareholders. This provided BTR with their opportunity. Had they succeeded, BTR may have continued to operate Pilkington as previously, or they could have cut all unnecessary expenses and boosted their own earnings per share by selling off 'surplus' assets and living off previous investments in R&D (e.g. float glass licence income).
>
> Since most shares are now controlled by the institutions (investment trusts, pension funds, etc.), all of whom are charged with the responsibility of making the greatest profit for their clients, the possibility of making a windfall profit as a result of such a takeover cannot be ignored.
>
> In this particular case, the issues were so stark and public feelings ran so high, that a financially irrational decision was taken by the shareholders and the takeover was frustrated. In most similar cases, the issues are less clearcut and public sentiment is not aroused. As a consequence, such takeovers may normally be expected to succeed almost without comment.

Figure 9.1 Pilkington's long-term/short-term dilemma

firm being left behind as new innovations diffuse throughout an industry. As a result a technology gap opens up between those firms that invest long-term and those that simply seek to minimize costs. Under these circumstances a cost-oriented firm is likely to find it tempting to miss a whole generation of technology altogether with the intention of climbing back aboard at a later date. However, re-establishing a leading position in technology is extremely difficult and many firms that decide to opt out find that their role progressively degenerates so that they become assemblers or distributors, marginal to the main core of activity in their industry. Missing out on technology is likely to mean a firm is unable to re-establish any significant competitive advantage.

9.3 Long-term investment

The returns from strategic investments are notoriously slow to be generated. Several researchers have shown that major new projects are likely to take as long as 8 years to come to profitability and 11 years or more to be as profitable as the base business (e.g. Burgelman 1984). Under these circumstances, if a 10-year horizon is taken as the project life when it is first evaluated (as is typical in the UK), few major projects will appear to be financially attractive. Normally, there are easier ways to achieve a superior financial return in the short term. Even these timescales understate the time required to develop the sort of technological competences needed by NEC (see Section 9.2). It may seem surprising that any such investments are ever made in these circumstances. Clearly, a long-term orientation, which can override short-term financial considerations, is essential if such investments are to be justified. Long-term orientation is frequently adduced in connection with Japanese firms such as NEC, Sony and others. These firms take a long-term view of how technologies will develop and impact on markets and consequently how they should build technology into their strategies to make the most of the situation. This is achieved through a long-term vision that emphasizes technological capability and is tolerant of failure in the short term (Morone 1989).

Structural changes are long-term. The point about the long term is all to do with whether a business will fail, survive or prosper. The development of computer technologies produced long-term structural change of markets and industries. For example, these firms were all players in the American vacuum valve market, well placed to exploit these developments:

- RCA
- Philips
- National Video
- Rawland
- Eimac
- Lansdale Tube
- Hughes
- Transitron
- Clevite

Of these, four never made the change into transistors and three others chose the wrong technology. They failed to recognize what was happening or lacked any clear direction to guide them as to what they should do about it. Only RCA and Philips are still in semi-conductors, although they have been joined by four new players – NEC, Fujitsu, Toshiba and Hitachi. These, less well placed, firms, exploiting the appropriate external communications and taking a long-term orientation, were able to develop a clear strategic direction and take over the new markets and technologies.

In the UK, long-term investments are made more difficult to sustain because of the short-term pressures that peculiarly appear to affect countries where the financial markets are most developed and most efficient, i.e. Britain and America.

9.4 Short-term pressures

A recent survey showed that the top 115 British companies pay out at least twice, and sometimes three times, as much in dividends as their German competitors (Hutton 1990). This has a direct impact on investment decisions. The easiest way to improve performance in the short term is to cut those elements of cost that make no short-term contribution: R&D, training and management development, some elements of marketing, etc. Thus, every time there is an underachievement in the short term, long-term performance is put at risk.

Focus on short-term efficiency and cost control is widely followed by firms in Britain and America in the interests of quick profits, often with disastrous results. Skinner (1986) called this the productivity paradox:

> the efforts to improve productivity actually drive competitive success further out of reach. This is because cost leadership is a syndrome, a mindset, which stunts strategic vision and inhibits innovation. Breaking loose from . . . the mindset is not easy. It requires a change in culture, in habits, instincts and ways of thinking and reasoning.

This phenomenon had been previously identified as the reason why American industry was starting to lose ground to Japanese and European competitors (Hayes and Abernathy 1980; Hayes and Garvin 1982).

> In the past, American managers earned worldwide respect for their carefully planned yet highly aggressive action across three different time frames:
>
> – *Short term*: using existing assests as efficiently as possible;
> – *Medium term*: replacing labour and other scarce resources with capital equipment;
> – *Long term*: developing new products and processes that open new markets or restructure old ones. (Hayes and Abernathy 1980)

While American managers were credited with continuing to achieve with the short-term actions, they were no longer effective in the medium and long-term requirements. Hayes and Abernathy illustrated the point with a number of quotations from American managers:

> To undertake such (medium and long term) commitments is hardly in the interests of a manager who is concerned with his or her next quarterly earnings reports.

We understand how to market, we know the technology, and production problems are not extreme. Why risk money on new businesses when good profitable low risk opportunites are on every side?

The short-term cost focus inhibits investments in new plant and new technology, which in due course results in firms losing the ability to compete effectively. In the face of price competition such firms inevitably lose, both in terms of profit and market share. Consequently, 'morale sags, performance suffers, and employees – generally the best ones – begin to leave. Faced with these circumstances, top management often concludes that a division or product line is unsalvageable and purposely continues the process of disinvestment' (Hayes and Garvin 1982). Once started, this disinvestment spiral is extremely difficult to reverse.

The Japanese, and to a lesser extent the Germans, achieve cost efficiency only in order to implement a customer-oriented strategy aimed at achieving long-term growth and profitability. This is done using the cost advantage to satisfy some additional perceived need of the customer, such as quality or some other differentiated product attribute. By contrast, in Britain and America, cost leadership is often pursued for its own sake, the motivation coming from the adoption of purely accounting norms and objectives. In this case the pursuit of cost leadership, even if it is not directly counterproductive, actually has little relevance for strategy of any kind. Ultimately, these different orientations become embedded in the culture of organizations so that they are entrenched and self-fulfilling. Thus the typical mid-ranking manager in a British or American corporation recognizes that future prospects are highly dependant on hitting budget and keeping your nose clean. Boat rocking, whistle blowing, any other form of challenging the *status quo*, or simple non-conformist behaviour are normally punished, while simply being expert in the relevant technology is unlikely to be rewarded.

The disinvestment spiral is a productivity paradox. Cutting long-term investments leads to technological incompetence, which leads to poor financial performance followed by further cuts. Breaking out of it requires a culture change that is difficult to achieve. However, the result of the culture change is to create a virtuous cycle of long-term investment, technological competence and financial performance. There are no simple recipes for achieving this result. The first step must be to recognize the syndrome, if it exists, in your own organization. Corrective measures are more complicated and in reality they are the concern of this whole book.

9.5 Summary

- A long-term orientation is the foundation of a winning strategy.
- Financial objectives are essentially short-term and inhibit the pursuit of strategy.
- Strategic objectives set direction and define action. They result from the analysis of external communications and a long-term orientation.
- Following strategic objectives is particularly difficult in the UK because of the paramountcy of the financial world and the pressures for short-term results that it imposes.
- Investment in major new projects may take 8 years or more to reach profitability, and 11 or more to reach the level of profitability of the base business.
- Such new projects may be designed to take advantage of structural changes arising from technological developments.
- Strategic investments are designed to provide the firm with some competitive advantage in the future, e.g. by building technological expertise in new or converging markets.
- The search for efficiency and reduced costs becomes a mindset that in the end is self-defeating, leading only to a spiral of disinvestment and the opening up of a technology gap that will become progessively more difficult to close.
- A long-term orientation is made even more difficult in the UK because the cost efficiency mindset is embedded in corporate cultures; this leads to managers being rewarded and promoted on the basis of achievement against short-term goals such as achieving budget.

References

Burgelman, R. A., 'Managing the internal corporate venturing process', *Sloan Management Review*, Winter 1984:23–48.
Hayes, R. H. and W. J. Abernathy, 'Managing our way to economic decline', *Harvard Business Review*, May–June 1980.
Hayes, R. H. and D. Garvin, 'Managing as if tomorrow mattered', *Harvard Business Review*, May–June 1982:71–9.
Hutton, W., 'Short-changed by short-termism', *The Guardian*, 20 June 1990.
Morone, J., 'Strategic use of technology', *California Management Review*, Vol. 31, No. 4, 1989:91–112.
Pralahad, C. K. and G. Hamel, 'The core competence of the corporation', *Harvard Business Review*, May–June 1990.
Skinner, W., 'The productivity paradox', *Harvard Business Review*, July–Aug 1986:55–9.

10
Exploiting core competences

10.1 Introduction

More than 30 years ago Selznick used the term 'distinctive competence' to denote what a particular business is uniquely good at by comparison with its close competitors (Selznick 1957). Selznick suggested how distinctive competence and what he called 'organizational character' – what we would now call 'culture' – could be combined to fulfil an organization's basic mission. Selznick's idea of distinctive competence highlighted the competitive element that differentiates one business from another. Such differentiation is no longer enough because the current speed of technological development means that competitive advantage based on a singular competence is unlikely to be sustainable for long.

Drucker developed a parallel theme in his enunciation of business leadership – i.e. a business must be the leader in *something*. It didn't matter much what that something was so long as the customer genuinely wanted it and was prepared to pay for it (Drucker 1964). Leadership has often wrongly been taken to relate to market leadership, most often measured simply in terms of market share. This was the basic assertion of the Boston Consulting Group model and was also supported by some analyses of statistics taken from the PIMS database. However, it was never intended by Drucker:

> examples abound of companies that have the largest share of the market but are far behind in their profitability compared to competitors of much smaller apparent stature (Drucker 1964:38)

The idea of core competences promulgated by Pralahad and Hamel (1990) is different from both these antecedents. The idea resulted from studies of the way succesful firms, mainly Japanese, appeared systematically to acquire and exploit combinations of fundamental technologies in order to develop generic or core products with which to dominate global markets.

Thus many of the quoted examples of the exploitation of core competences relate to manufacturing technology and to global business. However, the concept also has validity for non-manufacturing and for non-global businesses. Core competence is not simply the possession of a particular technological or managerial capability. This would be unlikely to differentiate a firm from its competitors possessing a similar capability. Core competence is a combination of such capabilities that provide the firm with a leadership position in the development of certain generic or core products. This is what gives the business a sustainable competitive advantage.

10.2 Globalization

Globalization is a chicken and egg process. The ever-increasing scale of investment required by advancing technology means that there must be a rapid exploitation of that technology in order for it to be profitably exploited. Speed of exploitation means that a large market is required, preferably global. Thus changes in the global environment arise from global technology development (Miller 1990). The assiduous pursuit of a global market results inevitably in convergence of consumer tastes (Ohmae 1989b). Just a few decades ago, the cultural differences between, say, Japan and Britain meant that it would be difficult to envisage the same consumer product succeeding equally in both markets. Now, tastes for many technically advanced consumer durables clearly coincide and the same product can be marketed in London and Tokyo with only superficial differences.

The globalization of technology makes it essential that all businesses, large and small, take a global view. Even a localized business like Carter's (see Section 1.2), with no global pretensions themselves, must take full account of global developments in markets and technologies potentially relevant to their business. This global awareness is essential to the maintenance of technological position (Clark 1989).

10.3 Identifying core competences

A firm's existing core competences can be identified by analysing its product or service. What are the fundamental skills and knowledge on which successful products are based? They may relate to straightforward world leadership in specific technologies or they may be more related to particular organizational or managerial skills. Some examples of core competences are:

- *Benetton*: Fast cycle times through computer-aided, just-in-time manufacturing, rapid customer response, distinctive product aesthetic design
- *Toyota*: Fast cycle times
- *Honda*: Engines, power trains
- *Coca-Cola*: Brand strength, geographic spread
- *Carter's Gold Medal Soft Drinks*: Flexibility of bottling facilities; responsiveness to customer requirements

Companies that successfully build global leadership in more than one core competence are few and far between; those that have done so in several are extremely rare. Global leadership in two or more complementary fundamental competences provides the ability to create a stream of new products, some of them (e.g. personal hi-fi, electronic personal organisers) unimaginable, with no known demand.

Most of the firms exampled in this chapter are global players, but their cases are instructive for every business whether or not their intentions have a global dimension. After all, most of the global players began their quest for core competences as small and relatively obscure firms and only became global through persistence over decades of following an explicit and well understood strategic intent (e.g. 'beat Xerox'). Moreover, every business, whether in services or manufacturing, is affected by the new technologies, which are themselves global. Even for those businesses that have no global ambitions whatsoever and appear not to be vulnerable to global competition, the concept of core competences, though writ small, is equally relevant.

Every management team needs to know what competences form the foundation of its most successful products, so that they can develop those competences and nurture the people on whom they depend.

For many businesses, the acquisition and development of core competences is somewhat haphazard. As Mintzberg (1987) noted, even the clearest strategic positions may emerge from a process of repeated trial and error, or even as a result of simple good luck. The extent to which strategic positions emerge, as opposed to being deliberately planned, can never be known – many emergent strategies are post-rationalized to give the impression of careful and sophisticated planning. For example, while Honda's development is apparently based on the overt exploitation of its position in engines and transmissions, its ultimately successful entry into the American motorcycle market was a saga of learning from trial and error. Honda simply had a product, the lightweight Super-Cub bike, which they wanted to sell in an America dominated by Harley Davidson. In 1957, Soichiro Honda thought he had agreed to sell 7500 bikes a month while his American agent had thought they were talking about an *annual* sale – 'Seventy-five hundred a month!' the agent exclaimed when he realized the misunderstanding. 'That's out of the question. Preposterous!' (Gilder 1986:187) A few years later Honda were selling around 20 000 bikes a month in America.

The breakthrough idea, or product, is by definition 'preposterous'. If it were not so, it would already have happened. Such breakthroughs themselves can lead to the development of new core competences that provide the basis of sustainable leadership positions.

The idea that Canon should set out, as a leading camera manufacturer, to beat Xerox in the copier market was preposterous, but they did it. Such successes do not arise solely as a result of trial and error or good luck, but are based on a clearly articulated strategic intent which is painstakingly implemented over many years. Canon's attack on the photocopier market involved the following eight steps:

1. Establish the strategic intent to 'beat Xerox'.
2. Identify Canon's existing core competences.
3. Understand the Xerox technology and patents in order to identify the necessary core competences.
4. License the technology to gain market experience and begin to acquire the core competences not already owned.
5. Invest in R&D to improve on the existing technology to acquire and start to exploit core competences, primarily to achieve cost reductions, e.g. by standardization of components, improving ease of maintenance and replenishment, etc.
6. License out own technology to fund further R&D and thus further consolidate the core competences required to beat Xerox.
7. Open challenge, first by attacking markets where Xerox is weakest, e.g. Japan, and then Europe.
8. Finally, an innovative, rather than imitative, attack on markets where Xerox is strongest, e.g. by selling rather than leasing, distributing through office equipment retailers rather than direct, and focusing promotion on end-users rather than corporate functional heads (Hamel and Pralahad 1989).

Core competences are the basis of competitive advantage in achieving strategic intent. Acquiring and nurturing competences that are not core is simply a waste of resources and effort and serves only to dissipate concentration. It is much better to buy in non-core competences (Quinn *et al*. 1990) and focus all internal efforts on the acquisition and development of what really matters.

10.4 Acquiring core competences

A firm's capacity for competitive innovation is based on its ability to acquire relevant core competences and to apply them effectively in the development of core products. Capability is infinite. It is not constrained by the competences you already have, or even the resources at your disposal, but can be extended by careful definition of the competences required and the means of their acquisition and development.

Missing competences can be painstakingly developed internally through focused investment in R&D or acquired externally through various forms of collaborative arrangements. Success by internal development may provide a sustainable leadership position where the acquisition of new technology is a continuous process with each advance laying the foundation for the next. However, internal development is extremely expensive and beyond the means of all but the largest organizations. Moreover, in an era when the diffusion of technology is rapid, the resultant competitive advantage may be short-lived. Also a lot of new technology is not protectable and there is little commercial benefit in being the holder of patents the essence of which is immediately copied by competitors. As Ouchi and Bolton (1988) suggest, internal development is not the best way to progress in areas where the intellectual property may be 'leaky'.

So, for a variety of reasons, the acquisition of core competences through collaboration has become an attractive proposition. It is a way of reducing costs and eliminating wasteful competition, especially in R&D (Telser 1987). It is also likely to be quicker to buy in technology than to develop it in-house. And it also opens up the potential of a business to the establishment of core competences far beyond what it could develop with its own resources, as the example of Canon shows. Canon used primarily a combination of external licensing and internal R&D in order to build the competences to compete with Xerox.

It is a way forward that accords very well with the business environment of the 1990s. Communications with suppliers, customers, competitors, shareholders, technological suppliers and independent sources of knowledge and expertise, such as research associations, universities and commercial technology consultants, have never been more important to the success of a business. Diffusion of innovations has never been more rapid, so that the need to know what is happening in new technology throughout Europe, America, Japan and elsewhere has never been greater. Consequently, we are operating in an era of increasingly open communications.

Buyer–seller relationships have moved from the adversarial to the collaborative (Spekman 1990) so that transactions are not seen as one-off profit-maximizing deals, but as part of longer-term mutual dependencies where close collaboration can work to the mutual benefit of both parties. It used to be thought that to compete globally you had to be big (Chandler 1990), but it is no longer true. The logic behind the trend to alliances and collaborations is based on the need to globalize when clearly it is beyond the scope of the businesses concerned if they operated alone.

Collaboration, even between competitors, has thus become one of the key business issues and examples of successful and disastrous collaborations abound. Businesses are having to adjust to this more open world of technology exchange, alliance and research (Ramo 1989). The tremendous cost of maintaining a leading position in a globalized market or technology is beyond the capacity of all but the very largest corporations. Collaboration rather than cut-throat competition is becoming an imperative for smaller businesses if they are not to be left hopelessly behind.

Nowhere is industry technological cooperation growing more rapidly than in Europe. In the early 1980s, European companies were being outgunned by superior technology in the US and Japan. Now, recognizing that in a unified market it will be imperative to leverage technology continent-wide, they are jumping into technology partnerships that anticipate the abolition of economic frontiers in 1993. In addition there is an increasing public investment in technological collaboration – Europe has become 'the world's hot spot for industrial cooperation and the growth of coalitions' (Madia 1990):

- European Community's *Framework* programme financing co-operative R&D projects between EC member states;
- EC's multi-billion *Esprit* programme to improve microelectronics technology in areas such as Computer Aided Manufacturing and integrated circuit design;
- Industry-led *Eureka* programme spending £1 billion p.a. on advanced technology projects such as the submicron silicon project to leapfrog current Japanese/American chip technology, high-definition TV and external vehicle guidance systems;
- European Space Agency's *Hermes* space shuttle and satellite projects;
- The 14-nation *Joint European Torus (JET)* project in energy research, especially nuclear fusion;
- Many other multi-state, multi-company manufacturing collaborations such as *Airbus Industrie*.

Many of these collaborative ventures involve large firms that are already multinational, but this is by no means the whole truth. There are many opportunities for smaller businesses to be involved in publicly sponsored collaborative projects or directly with other firms. The potential benefits from collaboration are tremendous, but the risks are also considerable. Many firms seem to enter such arrangements for reasons which are not very apparent, possibly even because they are fashionable, and as a result they lose out to their collaborative partner, sometimes disastrously. The overriding principle in engaging in any collaboration is to *make sure you know exactly what you are trying to achieve* when you enter a collaborative arrangement and then to make sure you achieve it. Some firms have adopted forms of alliance and mutual collaboration in order to close the competence gap, while others have simply opted out and bought in technology from elsewhere as a cost-saving device. More often than not this form of cost reduction is the first step down the disinvestment spiral. Alliances must be strategy-driven (Devlin and Blackley 1988).

An interesting analogy is provided by Hamel (1987) that highlights two different attitudes to collaboration. Typically, the Japanese adopt the role of students or learners in their approach to collaboration. They seek to learn and understand as much as they can from the arrangement. Western countries on the other hand typically adopt the role of teacher. The result is that the Japanese firms learn and the Western company's give up their special expertise. The Japanese may learn a technology, but more often nowadays it is market understanding they gain from collaborations. The Western participants may gain today's technology (or even yesterday's) relatively cheaply, but in so doing stand out of the technology race and miss the long-term development, making it very difficult for them to climb aboard at some later stage.

So, 'collaborate with your competitors, but be careful' (Hamel, Doz and Pralahad 1989). Know exactly what you are trying to achieve through collaboration.

10.5 Using core competences

The strength of a business is not seen in terms of a particular product, sector of the market or distribution channel, but in the underlying capability to generate a range of rapidly evolving products or markets. The traditional rationale for structuring an organization as a collection of business units, each with maximum autonomy, becomes questionable. Instead, the overriding requirement is for the development and acquisition of common strands of expertise that cut across products, markets and business units. This may lead to some apparently strange combinations of business activities. For example, 3M's products include 'Post It' notes, magnetic tape, photographic film, pressure-sensitive tapes and coated abrasives. These all have quite different production technologies, end consumers and channels of distribution. The rationale is based on the core competences in substrates, coatings and adhesives. Or again, what would be the justification for a product range including lawn mowers, generators, motor cycles and cars? These are all quite different markets with their own unconnected distribution channels. Honda's success with this diverse range – 200 per cent growth between 1980 and 1988 – is based on the deliberate exploitation of their core competences in engines and power trains.

Pralahad and Hamel (1990) quote several such examples of the use of core competences. The success of NEC (discussed in Chapter 9) resulted directy from this approach. NEC adopted the core competences approach by systematically exploiting the convergence of core competences in computing and communications (C&C). A 'C&C' committee oversaw the development of these core competences and resulting core products. This was supported by other coordination groups and teams which cut across the traditional organization structure and ensured that each member of the organization knew and understood the strategic intent. They developed competences internally and also through more than 100 purposive collaborations and alliances with other organizations. Between 1980 and 1988 NEC's sales grew from $3.8 billion to $21.9 billion and the company became the world number one in semiconductors and a leading player in telecommunications and computers. Over the same period, its American competitor, GTE, enjoyed sales growth from $10 billion to $16.5 billion and had to withdraw from several of its major business areas (Pralahad and Hamel 1990:79–91).

In similar vein, between 1980 and 1988, Canon grew by 264 per cent to beat Xerox with a range of core products including image scanners, laser printers, copiers and cameras, based on core competences in precision mechanics, fine optics and microelectronics. Honda's application of its core competences resulted in the introduction of four-wheel steering and multi-valve engines, among others. These developments can be introduced to give the competence owner enhanced competitive advantage. For example, Canon manufacture about 80 per cent of desk-top laser printer engines even though sales under their own name are relatively small. The Hewlett Packard IIP laser printer, which led the personal laser market using a Canon engine, was quickly faced by a Canon product with the same engine but with the added feature, at no additional cost, of infinitely scalable fonts. Hewlett Packard were forced to respond with a similar feature built into the IIIP model.

Core competences are not the sole preserve of manufacturing industry. The same concepts apply equally in services, though the competences may be related to technology imported from manufacturing. For example, fast cycle times are a critical factor in providing customer service in many industries. Sportswear producer and retailer, Benneton, owes its success and explosive growth almost entirely to fast cycle times made possible by the use of information technology (Bower and Hout 1988). It starts in new product development with a CAD system that automatically explodes a new design into a full range of sizes, and transmits the patterns to computerized cutting machines to await customer orders. Undyed fabric is stored at demand-scheduled just-in-time factories and cut and dyed strictly to order. Retail outlets are also run on a minimum stock JIT basis. Cycle time, from placing the order at the retail store to receiving the specially made product, takes 15 days, which both satisfies customers and avoids over- and underproduction.

Most firms, whether in manufacturing or service sectors, are not competing on a global front and do not seek to be global leaders. Nevertheless, every firm is operating in a global context: the technologies used are available globally and every customer is conditioned by standards of quality and service that apply globally. Thus, every firm must ensure it is aware of all the available technological capabilities and must also decide which are the core competences that are needed to implement its particular strategic intent.

10.6 Competitive challenges and competence gaps

Strategic direction is about which way a business is headed in the long term and if identified simply and succinctly can have a profound effect on the firm's stakeholders, both internal and external. Employees know what they are trying to achieve and therefore how they should make their greatest efforts; customers know what the firm's products and services embody; suppliers understand what the key elements are when dealing with the firm. Direction needs to be defined with precision and it also needs to be supported by indications of how fast the firm proposes to travel and how far. Thus milestones along the route need to be spelled out, progress at each stage monitored and the people involved rewarded according to progress.

'Become the leading world producer of photocopiers' is a statement of strategic direction that could be a powerful organizing and motivating concept. The strategic intent of 'beat Xerox' is nevertheless still more powerful, focusing as it does on the major competitor and thus identifying standards to be beaten, or mechanisms to be avoided, right across every aspect of the business. The way Canon achieved their strategic intent was indicated earlier in this chapter. In essence the process is one of spelling out the strategic intent in terms of a competitive challenge, identifying the existing and required competences and then setting about acquiring those competences that need to be added in order to achieve the challenge set.

Here are some examples of strategic intent expressed in simple unambiguous terms:

- *Komatsu*: Encircle Caterpillar.
- *Canon*: Beat Xerox
- *Coca-Cola*: Put a Coke within 'arm's reach' of every consumer in the world.
- *NEC*: Exploit competence in computing and communications.
- *US space programme*: Put a man on the moon by the end of the decade.

These are statements of mission or long-term objectives capable of initiating and galvanizing action and able to be converted into competitive challenges, which are staging posts along the way. The expression of strategic intent in terms of a competitive challenge identifies a gap between the actual competences possessed and those required in order to achieve the strategic intent.

10.7 Summary

- Core competence is the possession of particular technological or managerial capabilities which in combination provide the firm with a leadership position in the development of certain generic or core products.
- Core competence is the foundation of a winning strategy.
- All firms are affected by the trend to globalization of markets and technologies. Even quite small and localized firms have to take full account of global developments, which present both threats and opportunities.
- The acquisition of core competences enables a business to respond flexibly as technologies and markets evolve, and facilitates the process of new product development.
- Core competences are not the sole preserve of manufacturing industry – the same concepts apply equally in services.
- The breakthrough idea, or product, is by definition 'preposterous' but can lead to the development of new core competences that provide the basis of sustainable leadership positions.
- A firm's existing core competences can be identified by analysing its product or service in terms of the fundamental skills and knowledge on which it is based.
- Core competences are the basis of competitive advantage in achieving strategic intent. Acquiring and nurturing competences which are not core is simply a waste of effort.
- Strategic intent needs to be defined with precision and supported by indications of how fast the firm proposes to travel and how far.
- Milestones along the route, i.e. competitive challenges, need to be spelled out and progress at each stage monitored.
- Required competences can be painstakingly developed internally or acquired externally through various forms of collaborative arrangements. Collaboration is generally quicker and cheaper than internal development.
- Collaborative ventures may involve large or small firms. There are many opportunities for smaller businesses to be involved in publicly sponsored collaborative projects, or directly with other firms.
- The potential benefits from collaboration are tremendous, but the risks

are also considerable. In any collaboration, make sure you know exactly what you are trying to achieve, and then work at achieving it. Collaborate, but be careful.

References

Bower, J. L. and M. Hout, 'Fast cycle capability for competitive power', *Harvard Business Review*, Nov–Dec 1988:110–18.
Chandler, A. D., 'The enduring logic of industrial success', *Harvard Business Review*, March–April 1990:130–40.
Clark, K. B., 'What strategy can do for technology', *Harvard Business Review*, Nov–Dec 1989.
Devlin, G. and M. Blackley, 'Strategic alliances – guidelines for success', *Long Range Planning*, Vol. 21/5, No. 111, October 1988:18–23.
Drucker, P. F., *Managing for Results*, Harper & Row, New York, 1964. (Currently available from Heinemann Professional Publishing, Oxford, 1989.)
Gilder, G., *The Spirit of Enterprise*, Penguin Books, Harmondsworth, 1986.
Hamel, G., 'Corporate Strategies and Technological Cooperation', paper presented to a UACES Conference on European Technological Collaboration, Brunel University, 14 May 1987.
Hamel, G., Y. L. Doz and C. K. Pralahad, 'Collaborate with your competitors – and win', *Harvard Business Review*, Jan–Feb 1989.
Hamel, G. and C. K. Pralahad, 'Strategic intent', *Harvard Business Review*, May–June 1989.
Madia, W. J., 'EC technology partnerships', *Strategic Direction*, February 1990.
Miller, W. F., 'Technology and global strategy', *Strategic Direction*, January 1990.
Mintzberg, H., 'The strategy concept', *California Management Review*, Fall 1987:11–32.
Ohmae, K., 'Managing in a borderless world', *Harvard Business Review*, May–June 1989b.
Ouchi, W. G. and M. Kremen Bolton, 'The logic of joint research and development', *California Management Review*, Vol. xxx, No. 3, Spring 1988.
Pralahad, C. K. and G. Hamel, 'The core competence of the corporation', *Harvard Business Review*, May–June 1990.
Quinn, J. B., T. L. Doorley and P. C. Paquette, 'Beyond products: services-based strategy', *Harvard Business Review*, March–April 1990:58–68.
Ramo, S., 'National security and our technology edge', *Harvard Business Review*, Nov–Dec 1989.
Selznick, P., *Leadership and Administration*, Harper & Row, New York, 1957.
Spekman, R. E., 'Buyer–seller relations' *Strategic Direction*, February 1990.
Telser, L. G., *A Theory of Efficient Cooperation and Competition*, Cambridge University Press, Cambridge, 1987.

11
Focusing on the customer

11.1 Introduction

Focusing on the customer is the foundation of strategic direction. It guides the development of external communications and long-term orientation. Core competences are developed with the sole object of delivering value to existing customers and creating new ones. Thus, customer focus underpins much of the content of the previous four chapters; it is the glue that holds a winning strategy together. Peters and Waterman found that being 'close to the customer' was one of the key factors in the 'excellent' companies (Peters and Waterman 1982) and since then management texts have advocated developing 'a passion for customers', becoming 'a service fanatic' and various other forms of customer focus. Serving customer needs has become a watchword to which every business at least pays lip service – competitive strategy is driven by the identification and satisfaction of customers' real needs (Ohmae 1988).

It seems that many traditional British and American businesses had drifted so far away from their customers that these simple blandishments may often have been wholly appropriate. But it is difficult to imagine that many businesses which have survived into the 1990s are unaware of the need for customer orientation. However, they may not all be fully aware of what is meant: customer focus is an analytical approach to the customer, designed to achieve a long-term relationship that is of mutual profit.

Each viable sale results in the generation of a certain economic surplus, and the customer – the other half of the selling transaction – will share the surplus generated. The relationship therefore has to be calculated and not passionate. The success of Japanese manufacturing is not based on passion for the customer, but on an analysis of needs and a calculation as to how those needs can be met, profitably and without waste. Failure to deliver what the customer wants will undoubtedly lead to disaster, but delivery of more value than the customer requires just as certainly leads to ultimate failure.

11.2 Defining value

The traditional concept of value for money is a function of both the price and quality of a product or service. Too high a price, or quality that is too low, results in less than value for money. Too low a price, or an unrequired level of quality, results in wasted value. Management's aim must, in this simple two-dimensional model, be to achieve the right balance of price and quality, i.e. the balance required by the customer. However, this two-dimensional model is not very revealing. The concept of quality is not simply unidimensional, but complex. Moreover, its definition clearly depends on the type of product or service being delivered. For example, in the case of food products, distribution is clearly critical:

> Japanese firms have increased their penetration of the US food market by achieving much superior delivery service. Two food distribution studies were carried out by management consultants A. T. Kearney. In Japan a study of 79 manufacturers and 30 wholesalers found that 76 per cent of manufacturers target their products for delivery in less than 1 day, and 15 per cent in less than 12 hours. A total of 94 per cent of wholesalers aim for 24-hour delivery. A similar study of 64 US grocery manufacturers found that their order cycle time averaged 7.7 days. 'Customer service will become a key differentiating factor for the major players,' commented W. J. Best, MD of A. T. Kearney's Tokyo office.
> Source: (Best 1990:14-15)

In the case of RAM chips, however, failure rates and reliability are more important to the customer:

> Hewlett Packard's Data Systems Division tested 300 000 16K RAM chips from three US and three Japanese manufacturers. At goods received inspection the Japanese chips had a failure rate of zero, the American chips had 11-19 failures per 1000. After 1000 hours of use the Japanese failure rate was 1-2 per 1000, compared with an American failure rate of up to 27 per 1000. There were three responses by American manufacturers to these data:
> - some suggested the Japanese were only importing their best product;
> - others disputed the basic data;
> - a few noted the connection between enhanced quality and increased market penetration by Japanese manufacturers. (Garvin, 1987:101-9)

Garvin suggested eight characteristics of quality, any of which might be crucial in particular circumstances (Garvin 1987):

1. primary performance
2. secondary features
3. reliability
4. conformance
5. durability

6. serviceability
7. aesthetics
8. perceived quality

Performance refers to the product or service's primary operating characteristics, and Garvin noted that these were usually capable of objective measurement. In the case of cars, for example, performance would include such measures as speed, acceleration, noise levels, etc. In the case of fast food, or airlines, performance may be mainly a matter of prompt service.

Secondary features are also usually amenable to objective measurement. They are the extras which may differentiate an otherwise standard product. The following are examples of secondary features:

- customer selection of detailed product specification, e.g. General Motors dealers provide computer terminals which allow customers to select the features they want and the specified car is delivered within seven days;
- free drinks on an airplane;
- 'clever' remote controls for a hi-fi set;
- flexibility and a wide variety of options in personal investment plans.

Flexibility and responsiveness in satisfying customer needs is an increasingly powerful feature in the current environment. New technology is making flexibility as economical as standardization for the leading producers and service providers and they are consequently establishing new standards that consumers increasingly come to expect as the norm.

Reliability refers to the probability of a product breaking down in use. Clearly, this is the key characteristic of many industrial and, increasingly, consumer durable products. Improved standards of reliability achieved in one sector, notably in electronics, appears to have a knock-on effect in other sectors. Customers are now generally less tolerant of poor product reliability than previously.

Conformance refers to the achievement of product specifications, for example dimensions within agreed tolerances. Again this is most usually critical in industrial products, particularly where they are to be assembled with other products of similarly defined specifications.

Durability is the expected product life and may be determined either by technical or economic factors. For example, the expected life of cars has increased significantly over the past decade because the rising cost of petrol and general economic stringency have reduced average annual mileages. Durability is a characteristic that differed widely between brands – Garvin examples washing machines with expected lives of 5.8 to 18 years, and tumble dryers from 6 to 17 years, for makes of differing quality.

Serviceability refers to the ease, speed, competence and courtesy with

> A product or service is comprised of some combination of the following attributes:
>
> | Physical | Implied | Psychological |
> |---|---|---|
> | price | distribution | corporate image |
> | quality | delivery | brand image |
> | performance | reliability | product image |
> | design | warranty | |
> | packaging | after sales support | |
> | | advertising | |
> | | service | |
>
> 'What matters about this complex product is the customer's perceptions of its attributes.'

Figure 11.1 Product attributes (Pearson 1990:116)

which service is provided (i.e. products delivered, queries answered, repairs achieved, etc.). Clearly, this characterisitic is in some respects less amenable to objective measurement. Actual machine down-times resulting from breakdown may be open to accurate measurement, but the competence and courtesy of the service engineer are clearly subjective measures, likely to be influenced by individual circumstances. Subjectivity highlights the importance of customer complaint handling and, in particular, obtaining the maximum amount of information about customer perceptions as a result of these transactions.

Aesthetics, the look, feel, sound, taste or smell of a product, is clearly a subjective measure, which again means deliberate and calculated steps being taken to achieve any measure of consumer perceptions.

Perceived quality refers to consumer perceptions of quality, which may or may not be the same as reality. A firm may have established a reputation for quality that naturally attaches to any product the company offers. The corporate or brand image affects the way potential customers will perceive the product even before its introduction. Clearly, this is a powerful factor, which may make the difference between success and failure with the introduction of a new product.

These eight dimensions of quality accord to a great extent with the orthodox product characteristics attributed by marketeers (see Figure 11.1). The main omission is the price attribute. However, Garvin's dimensions of quality strike much deeper into the organization than the marketeer's product attributes, affecting the way each individual in the organization does their job. The marketeer's product attributes may, in organizational terms, be quite superficial even though they may be important aspects of the product or service itself. For example, packaging may contribute substantially to the customer's perception of the product, but the impact of packaging on individuals in the organization may be minimal.

Below is a profile of a ten-attribute product, based on Garvin's dimensions of quality but including also the essential attribute of price, plus a tenth attribute labelled 'ingredient X'. This is not simply a selling proposition (unique or otherwise), or a marketing gimmick of some kind, but an extra attribute which arises directly from the core competences of the producer.

The ten-attribute product
primary performance
price
perceived quality
aesthetics
reliability
serviceability
conformance
durability
secondary features
ingredient X

Canon's infinitely scalable fonts on its low-cost laser printer was an added ingredient which gave it an extra competitive advantage over its main rivals. Similarly, Honda's four-wheel steering is another 'ingredient X' example. In the case of service sector business, ingredient X may well relate to special elements of superior service which differentiate the business from its competitors. Ingredient X is not simply a marginal additional factor in differentiation – it is a remarkable added attribute that takes the customer by surprise. It is a fundamental attribute, stemming directly from the firm's core competences, and is therefore not easy for competitors to replicate. Clearly it will not be possible for every business to develop a product or service with a real ingredient X but, for those that do, it may be the most important attribute of all.

These ten attributes are the components of value which the firm delivers to its customer. No firm can successfully pursue all ten attributes; being leader simultaneously in all ten is simply not possible. Being the price leader may well preclude leadership on any other attribute, and several of the others may well conflict. Management's aim must be to provide a balance of attributes that accords with the requirements of customers. This is the business of delivering value and is clearly a far more demanding task than simply aiming to be either cost leader or differentiator.

The first step in this process is finding out what the customers need, that is what they regard as value. This obvious step is one that is still often avoided both in America and the UK. For a company where product failure rate is high or product durability or reliability is dubious, or a company that falls down on delivery promises or offers unsatisfactory serviceability, contact with customers is likely to be a painful experience. For a company that delivers value, on the other hand, contact with customers is regular, constructive and fruitful. Both situations are self-reinforcing but too many British firms still experience the vicious cycle of too little customer contact, too late, and customer contact that is too often oriented to negative damage-limitation exercises.

11.3 Identifying customer needs

There are various sorts of customer contact that most businesses make. First, there are those routine aspects of the sale transaction involving possibly the following elements:

- advertisement
- personal selling contacts
- technical advice
- order placement
- progess enquiry/response
- delivery
- invoicing
- credit control
- after-sales service
- customer complaints

Each of these points of contact represents an opportunity to increase understanding of the customer's needs and desires, but it is rare for a British business to regard these routine transactions as the learning opportunity they really are. As in the case of developing core competences, adopting the learning role seems more typical of the Japanese approach than the Anglo-Saxon. Learning about customers' requirements from these routine contacts is far from automatic and therefore needs to be planned and managed if real gains are to be achieved.

Losing a customer is another learning opportunity that many businesses fail to exploit fully. Failure to achieve a major contract, or the loss of a regular customer, may cause a business to review its shortcomings, but apparently less important losses may go unnoticed. A learning organization will, on the other hand, treat all such occasions as opportunities to increase understanding of customer needs and how they may be better satisfied. But, again, the learning exercise must be planned and managed if the maximum benefit is to be achieved (Green 1989). Customers who defect to the competition can tell you exactly what parts of the business you must improve. In 1982, the credit card company, MBNA, faced a crisis with high rates of customer defections. The president called all 300 employees together and announced his determination to satisfy and keep every customer. They began a systematic programme of collecting feedback from defecting customers and acting on the information, regularly changing products and processes as required. By 1990, MBNA's defection rate was half the average for the industry. Over the eight years it had grown from 38th to 4th position without acquisitions, and profits had increased sixteenfold (Reichheld and Sasser 1990:105–11).

Customer contacts are too often restricted to sales personnel, with little opportunity given for customers to talk directly to the people involved in manufacturing their product, or designing their service. Great benefits can accrue from opening up these communications links. For example, Tektronix, maker of oscilloscopes, inserts a postcard with each finished product listing the names of workers involved in its production and giving a Freefone number for customers to ring any queries direct to the shop floor (Chase and Garvin 1989).

All these customer contacts should be managed so as to find out what customers really want, but it is not easy. Deschampes (1990) points out four difficulties:

1. Customers all want different things.
2. Customers do not know what they want.
3. Customers do not always buy what they think they want.
4. Customers keep upgrading their expectations.

Clearly all these problems do not always apply to all customers, but they offer sufficient difficulty for managers to be sceptical about the meaning and face value of feedback obtained directly from customers. Such directly obtained information from routine contacts appears to require validation by less suspect sources. This is where formal marketing research methods play an important role. Deschampes reviewed six broad categories of marketing research particularly relevant to the problems listed above:

– lifestyle analysis
– customer watching
– concept testing
– needs vs. buying motives analysis
– perceived value analysis
– competitor dissection

These analytical approaches are used widely in fast-moving consumer goods and to a slightly lesser extent in automotive products, but in most other sectors they are infrequently used, though Japanese firms tend to make more use of them than others (Deschampes 1990). The purpose of marketing research is to ensure that we fully understand customers' perception of their own needs and of our product (which is an amalgam of perceptions of the various product attributes).

The customer's perception of products is not necessarily based on any objective fact. Too great a divide between perception and reality is likely to be only short-lived, but there will nevertheless be differences, and some of them may be important. Even an attribute as apparently unambiguous as price may be affected by this dichotomy between customer perception and reality. A product that is actually cheap relative to its competitors may, in fact, be perceived as being relatively expensive. If customers regard price as the critical attribute, then it is their perception of the product's price that will dictate the buying decision. If they perceive Brand A as cheaper than Brand B, they will buy it, even if the reality is that Brand B has the lower price. Customers may have perceptions about every product attribute, though many of them may not be sufficiently strong to affect the buying decision. An attribute as potentially woolly as perceived quality can be a powerful determinant of customer behaviour.

The process of identifying what need customers satisfy when they buy the product can be approached through systematic marketing research methods. First, it is necessary to know which product attributes the customer perceives as important. Second, it is important to know what the customer perceives as being ideal performance on these important attributes. Third, it is important to establish how the customer perceives the firm's product as performing on the same attributes. Finally, it is important to know how the customer perceives competing products in the same way.

Such precise information is unlikely to be achieved simply by being 'close to the customer'. Obsessions with service and quality, effective nichemanship and listening to the customer are what Peters and Waterman identify as 'close to the customer', but understanding customers' real needs and perceptions implies a more systematic form of customer orientation, which has to include a technically reliable form of enquiry. Such methods are available and are fairly straightforward. Preference mapping is one approach which enables the customer's perceptions about the product and its competitors to be identified. The technique has been described in operational detail in many other texts (e.g. Green and Tull 1970), so a simplified explanation is sufficient for the present purpose. A common consumer product such as instant coffee is ideal for illustrating the process.

First, orthodox qualitative methods such as unstructured and semi-structured interviews and consumer panel tests are used to establish a list of potentially significant attributes of instant coffee. As far as possible these attributes are generated without prompting or leading in any way by the researcher. Possible attributes of instant coffee might include price, strength, flavour, aroma, country of origin and brand image.

Second, the list of potentially significant product attributes is then tested with selected samples of consumers to establish which attributes appear to be regarded as important. The apparently unimportant attributes can then be disregarded. In our instant coffee example let us assume just two attributes are found to be perceived as important – price and strength. Thus a simple two-dimensional 'map' could be constructed. In practice the number of important attributes is unlikely to be restricted to only two and computer methods are used to 'draw' multidimensional maps. Third, selected consumers are tested or questioned as to the nature of their 'ideal' instant coffee in terms of the important attributes of strength and price. This is done using methods which result in some sort of scaled response, such as placing responses along a seven-point scale from 'very strong' to 'very mild'. In this way the response can be scored and the respondent's position plotted on the map. Then the aggregate 'ideal' instant coffee can be positioned on the map, being simply the aggregate of all responses.

Similarly, other 'ideal' instant coffees can be positioned relating to various subsets of the sample of respondents. The ideal coffee of people living in Greater London may differ substantially from that of people in, say, Scotland or Wales. The samples used for testing may be selected on any basis (geographic, demographic, psychographic, etc.) so long as the market segments they represent are actually measurable, accessible (i.e. capable of being focused on) and of sufficient volume to be economically worthwhile. Having established 'ideal' positions, research is then conducted to establish the position of actual brands of instant coffee. Again this can be done either by testing or by direct questioning or a combination of the two. Thus the map is completed, showing consumers' ideal product positions and the positions of actual brands.

This example is highly simplified, but the principles can be widely applied. For any product, a picture of customer preferences can be built up which shows what key leadership position, if any, the product enjoys, as perceived by its actual and potential customers. It is then possible to identify how this strength could be improved, i.e. moved closer to the customer's perceived ideal, in order to position, or reposition, the product on the customer's preference map.

Marketing research can help validate customer feedback obtained by more direct methods. The aim is to identify customers' real needs and assess how adequately they are currently being satisfied. If used on a regular basis these methods make it possible to detect changes in customer perceptions and needs, and in the position of competing products, before they make themselves apparent in reduced product sales.

11.4 Delivering value

Identifying customer needs is the easy part; satisfying those needs by delivering value is more problematic. At the start of this chapter value was defined in terms of product or service attributes. Delivering value means providing the customer with a product or service that embodies the mix of attributes the customer regards as most desirable. The way attributes have been defined means that delivering value is not simply a matter of presentation, packaging or image building, though these may all play a part. It goes bone deep, involving all the activities in a business and the way every member of the business performs.

External linkages are crucial between key functions within the firm and its customers, so that existing products or services can be modified and developed to satisfy customer requirements more exactly and so that new product concepts can be extensively tested, involving users in product definition at each stage of development. Similarly, internal linkages are also vital: between marketing and development functions, between R&D and production, and between all these functions and the financial systems within which they operate.

Ensuring the product or service satisfies the customer is an ongoing process involving all the people in the organization. Their involvement in and commitment to these ends must be achieved, and this is the subject matter of Part Three.

11.5 Analysing the competitor

The delivery of value needs to be seen in relative terms, that is in relation to the particular industry and the position relative to competitors. Some markers relating to industry assessment were laid down in the opening chapters, but only the briefest comments have been made about analysing competitors in terms of setting up external networks and making full use of secondary research.

There are a number of approaches to competitor analysis. Most firms take account of competitors' general position and activity in the market, focusing on relative market shares, pricing policies, the introduction of new products, etc. Porter's generic strategy approach (Porter 1980) suggests an infinitely detailed analysis of every conceivable aspect of a competitor's operation, which is far beyond practicality. Others advocate detailed comparative financial analysis. However, there is a more focused approach, using the components of strategy now being described, based on the research support indicated in Part One. These factors are just as important to competitors as they are to one's own business. Therefore, competitor analysis should concentrate on an assessment of

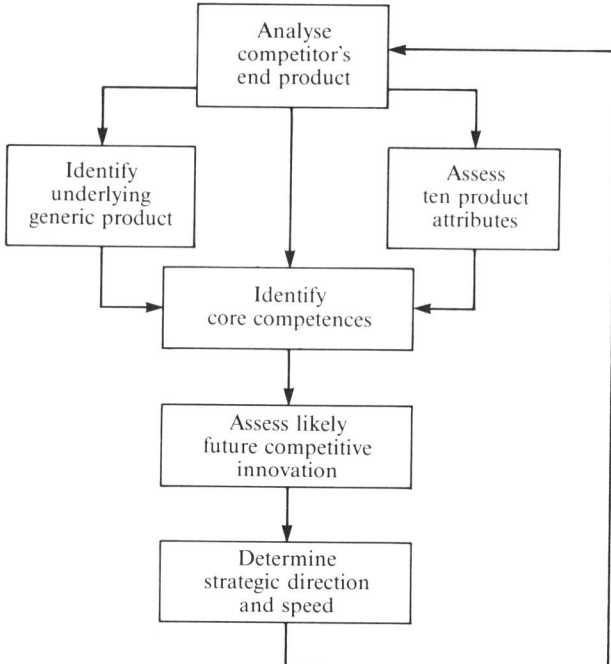

Figure 11.2 Competitive analysis

the competitor's relative positioning in terms of these strategic characteristics.

The key to this analysis is the competitive product or service. There is no substitute for buying, using and taking apart a competitor's product or experiencing their service at first hand, or testing their after-sales service, the way they handle complaints, and how they exploit the learning opportunities in all these transactions. The five characteristics of strategy, being outlined in this part of the book, provide a structure for competitive analysis (see Figure 11.2). Analysing the competitor's end products can reveal the strength of the ten attributes embodied in them, as well as the underlying generic product that springs directly from the particular mix of core competences on which the competitor's business is based. The core competences suggest the likely forms of future competitive innovation and thus can be deduced the direction in which competitors are headed and how fast they are going.

11.6 Summary

- Customer focus is the glue that holds a winning strategy together. It is an analytical approach to the customer, intended to achieve a long-term relationship of mutual profit.
- Too high a price, or too-low quality, results in less than value for money. Too low a price, or an unrequired level of quality, results in wasted value.
- The eight characteristics of quality are *primary performance, secondary features, reliability, conformance, durability, serviceability, aesthetics* and *perceived quality*.
- A useful product categorization includes these eight attributes plus price and 'ingredient X'. 'Ingredient X' is not simply a selling proposition or marketing gimmick, but an extra attribute arising directly from the producer's core competences.
- These ten attributes are the components of value, which the firm delivers to its customer.
- The first step in delivering value is finding out what the customer needs, only achieved through direct customer contact.
- Losing a customer is a learning opportunity.
- Because of the uncertainty of customer needs, it is necessary to validate direct feedback from customers with formal marketing research. Preference mapping is one approach that identifies customer perceptions about the product and its competitors.
- Delivering value is an ongoing and problematic process that involves everyone in the organization.
- The key to competitive analysis is the competitive product or service. There is no substitute for buying, using and taking apart a competitor's product.

References

Best, W. J., 'Japanese logistics', *Strategic Direction*, June 1990:14–15.
Chase, R. B. and D. A. Garvin, 'The service factory', *Harvard Business Review*, July–Aug 1989:61–9.
Deschampes, J. P., 'Market driven product development', *Strategic Direction*, June 1990:8–11.
Garvin, D. A., 'Competing on the eight dimensions of quality', *Harvard Business Review*, Nov–Dec 1987.
Green, D., 'Learning from losing a customer', *Harvard Business Review*, May–June 1989:54–8.
Green, P. and D. S. Tull, '*Research for Marketing Decisions*,' Prentice-Hall, Englewood Cliffs, 1970.
Ohmae K., 'Getting back to strategy', *Harvard Business Review*, Nov–Dec 1988.

Pearson, G. J., *Strategic Thinking*, Prentice-Hall, Hemel Hempstead, 1990.
Peters, T. and R. H. Waterman, '*In Search of Excellence*', Harper & Row, New York, 1982.
Porter, M. E., '*Competitive Strategy: Techniques for Analyzing Industries and Competitors*', Free Press, New York, 1980.
Reichheld, F. F. and W. E. Sasser Jr., 'Zero defects: quality comes to services', *Harvard Business Review*, Sept–Oct 1990.

12
Plotting the strategy profile

12.1 Introduction

This chapter draws together the various strands of strategy that have been outlined in Part Two. The purpose is to serve as a reminder of these separate elements and at the same time to set up the strategy dimension of the competitive model that is developed in full in Part Four.

The different components of strategy have been discussed separately, but it should be apparent that they in fact intertwine and overlap. Active external communications are fundamental for a competitive business, and in discussing this aspect it is impossible not to refer also to customer focus. The product attributes that are of value to the customer, described in terms of quality dimensions, are closely tied into the concept of core competences, which may be developed through a process of external communications, collaboration and alliances. All these elements in strategy overlap and complement each other so that they form a self-reinforcing orientation for the business to achieve. A weakness in one factor is likely to lead to weaknesses in others; a strength in one will support complementary efforts in others. It is useful to discuss the items separately, but their interrelatedness should be recognized.

A set of questions designed to enable a business to identify its relative strength on each component of strategy is presented at the end of this chapter. This questionnaire serves two purposes – it helps a business to identify possible problems that should be addressed if it is to achieve an effective strategy, and it permits the business to locate itself in one dimension on the competitive matrix. Both these purposes are explained below.

12.2 The components of strategy

The five main components of strategy have been identified as:

1. strategic direction
2. external communications
3. long-term orientation
4. core competence
5. customer focus

Each component is itself comprised of various subsidiary elements.

The business with a robust and lasting strategic direction will be most effectively managed by a group who work as a team, not by a single individual, no matter how benign an autocrat the individual may be. The direction will be clear enough and well enough understood to achieve a concentration of resources, efforts and enthusiasm to progress in that direction. The strategy will be maintained consistently over time, and should eventually define a known strategic position that will itself work to sustain the strategic direction. Thus within this one factor there is a virtuous cycle which will tend to reinforce itself once established.

The importance of external communications is often overlooked by firms who may merely give lip service to the concept without making any real attempt to exploit the opportunities available to them. Some of these opportunities arise from routine transactions of the business. The firm's direct relations with suppliers, customers and technology suppliers proceed whether or not the firm makes any deliberate efforts to maximize its learning from the process. In many cases, relations with competitors are also an essential part of normal business operations, whether in the form of fairly routine collaboration, or through the auspices of a trade association or industry research body. Again, few businesses manage these relations with the intention of maximizing corporate learning. Every firm also has interactions in a broader context – the political, social, economic and, most important, the technological environments which may critically determine the future of the business. A firm may adopt a variety of approaches to external communications ranging from straightforward avoidance to a proactive programme of networking and systematic analysis of secondary sources.

Long-term orientation is simple to describe but, in the UK at least, difficult to achieve. It is not easy, in the face of short-term external pressures, notably from institutional shareholders, to espouse and focus all attention on long-term objectives which by their nature are not expressed in financial terms such as earnings per share or returns on investment. The average quoted British business pays out around twice as much dividend as its German counterpart and three times as much as its Japanese competitor. Long-term orientation is therefore not easy to achieve consistently, but consistency is exactly what is required if firms are to maintain their position in the technology race.

The achievement and nurturing of valuable core competences can be achieved through long-term investment in technology, either directly through R&D or indirectly through collaboration. The first stage in achieving core competences is awareness of global technological and market developments. The second stage may be through direct investment in technology development or through the spreading of these costs by way of collaborative arrangements or some form of strategic alliance. However they are achieved, it is clear that the establishment of core competences is the driving force of strategic development, rather than the pursuit of some quantified financial target.

The last key component of strategy is customer focus, which drives all the other elements. Development of core competences that are not related to delivering value to the customer is futile. Long-term orientation that is independent of the long-term development of customers and their needs is unlikely to provide any benefit. External communications that are unrelated to providing the customer's needs are unlikely to be particularly useful. And strategic direction that is not aimed at serving the customer will not provide an adequate focus for concentration and consistency. If all these elements are present then the organization is likely to have a focused strategy, that is members know what the organization is trying to achieve and how they can contribute to its achievement.

12.3 The strategy profile

Completion of the questionnaire at the end of the chapter will generate average scores for each component of between -3 and $+3$ which can then be plotted on the strategy profile chart (see Figure 12.1). In addition, an overall average strategy score can be calculated, which is used to locate the business on the competitive matrix. Interpretation of the absolute scores in these profiles is industry-dependant, and some pointers to interpretation were given in the industry assessment questionnaire in Chapter 6. These issues will be discussed further in Chapter 18. For the present purpose attention is focused on the shape of the profile and the action pointers arising from it.

A competitive organization should achieve a strategy profile that is fairly even across all five component parts. An uneven profile, i.e. with one or more scores substantially out of line with the others, suggests areas that warrant management attention. For example, a firm with a profile as indicated in Figure 12.2 clearly has undeveloped external communications and an ill-defined strategic direction. Management should investigate the reasons why scores were low in these areas. Investigation starts from a

126 THE COMPETITIVE ORGANIZATION

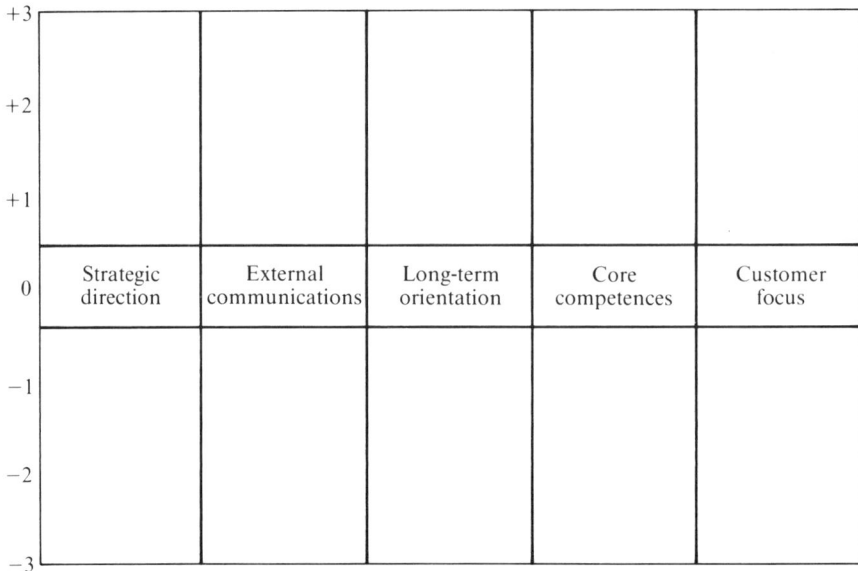

Figure 12.1 The strategy profile

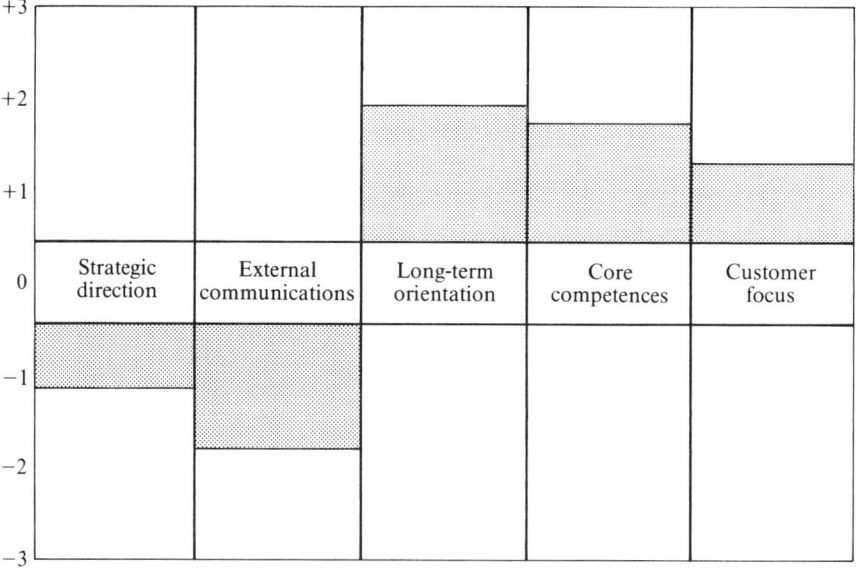

Figure 12.2 Sample strategy profile

detailed examination of answers to the assessments to highlight which aspects have produced the low score. These then serve as pointers to areas that warrant management action.

In most industries, a competitive organization should expect to score around +1.5 or more on the strategy profile. This would be particularly important in new high-growth high-technology industries and also in decline situations where an old industry has not yet made use of new technology. Industries which are less affected by the rapid rate of technological development and which appear to be operating in a quiet backwater may well be extremely vulnerable to the technological revolution. In such a situation, for example, a low score on external communications and long-term orientation is likely to signify only that, when change comes, the firm will be taken by surprise and will probably only survive with extreme difficulty.

The impact of the technological revolution has been just as profound in its effects on distribution and service industries as it has been in manufacturing, and competitive analysis of services is just as vital. The rates of change in high street retailing, for example, have been as rapid as in factory production, but the trends have so far taken a different direction. In the 1950s and 1960s the emphasis of manufacturing was on standardization, both to reduce costs through long production runs and to achieve standard quality of product. New technology has permitted flexible production and product variety to be achieved without loss of quality and at no extra cost.

In contrast the move in high street retailing over the past few decades has been to increased standardization. The dominance of national chain stores has led to the centralization of all significant management decisions and standardization of products, prices, shop layouts and displays, and promotions. Standardization is now so complete that entire city shopping centres have become virtually indistinguishable and local store managements are prevented from exercising any managerial discretion. New technology (e.g. in electronic funds transfer at point of sale and other integrated computer control systems) has eliminated problems of stock control and reordering as well as financial reporting. Thus branch managers now work as little more than personnel supervisors and high-calibre managers are therefore hard to recruit into the retail sector.

The opportunity is, however, clearly available to give store managers substantial local autonomy and so take advantage of the new flexibility available from their suppliers. So far this has only been done to a limited extent (e.g. in perishable foods within the supermarket sector), and the opportunities for flexibility and satisfying customer desire for variety have not yet been grasped in the UK. Child indicates that the acquisition of new technology in retailing has been more entrepreneurial in Germany, and ultimately the full exploitation of innovations in this field is inevitable (Child et al. 1987).

The strategy profile is equally valid whether your business is in manufacturing or services.

12.4 Assessing the strategy profile of your business

To assess how effective your organization is in terms of its strategy, organization members should be asked to consider the truth of statements 7.1 to 11.10 (listed in the strategy profile questionnaire in Section 12.5) as they apply to your organization. The statements are numbered according to the chapters containing the subject matter to which they refer, i.e. statements 7.1 to 7.10 are concerned with strategic direction; statements 8.1 to 8.10 refer to external communications, and so on.

The truth of the statements is scored in the range from −3 to +3 as indicated below each statement. This quantitative scaling of responses enables scores to be aggregated and averaged.

Responding organization members can be grouped hierarchically and functionally and their answers analysed accordingly, so that differences in the perceptions of different groups can be identified. It is not uncommon, for example, for the perceptions of chief executives to differ from those of other board members, and for the directors as a group to differ substantially from other organization members. Such variances may be of crucial importance and have frequently been the first indication to top management that the aims and purposes of the organization are widely misunderstood by most employees.

If the overall average score for any of the strategy components is negative, then the organization management clearly needs to consider a programme of remedial action. The starting point for this would be an analysis of scores for the individual statements. These should be examined and those with the most negative scores considered in detail. For example, an overall negative score on strategic direction may arise even though there is a valid and clearly stated strategic intent. Organization members other than the directors, say, may simply be unaware of it. This suggests immediate and obvious action for management to open communications on strategy throughout the organization to make sure that everyone knows and understands the chosen strategic direction.

Alternatively, a negative overall score may arise because organization members' perceptions that there is no clear strategy are correct. Again, a management action plan is suggested, this time for the formulation of a valid strategy and its subsequent communication.

In considering responses to statements 8.1 to 8.10, related to external communications, it may be that there is a general awareness of external factors but that the organization has not explicitly set up any means of ensuring that this awareness is maintained. This is likely to result in the organization becoming aware of major changes in technology, competition, consumer tastes, etc. when they have already occurred and become established. In many instances this lateness in external communications may not matter but, for some changes, being early may be vital to success or even survival. Thus, even for an organization that espouses a devout 'me too' follower stance, a lack of explicit external communications systems demands immediate remedial action – establishing contacts with technology leaders, setting up a formal system for the routine collection of carefully specified secondary data, or the establishing of relevant networks by all members of the management team.

Any statement that attracts an average score that is negative warrants further investigation as to the causes and possible remedies.

In addition, variations in perceptions of different groups of organization members may suggest other remedial management actions. These possible action plans may be suggested only tentatively. Nevertheless they may support or confirm suspicions that already exist, or they may prompt further investigation that would confirm or deny the need for additional management action. As other questions are raised, related to the subject matter of other chapters, responses may progressively crystallize into a strategy profile with clear weaknesses that must be addressed.

The simple dichotomy of negative–positive average scores is only part of the story. First, a marginal positive score is clearly not as beneficial as a score of 2 or more. A solidly competitive organization will be likely to score around 1.5 or more on the strategy dimension overall and any scores below this may be significant flags for action. In some industries (i.e. those for which industry assessments of under 25 per cent or over 75 per cent were achieved in the questionnaire in Chapter 6), a minimum score of $+1$ may be requisite and consequently a score of 2 or more may be regarded as desirable for an effective competitor.

The interpretation of scores clearly has implications at various different levels. First, there are the direct implications relating to the subject matter of the individual question. Then there are implications for the component to which it contributes (strategic direction, external communications, etc.). There are implications for the overall dimensional profile (in this case the strategy dimension). Finally, there are implications for the ultimate positioning of the organization on the competitive matrix. The organization's position is determined at all these levels and the action prescriptions emanating from the duly administered questionnaire start at the highest level, the position on the matrix, proceed to the detail of the dimensional profile, down to the individual characteristic and the particular question. At each stage the data extracted from the questionnaire can be used to define the management action required to address the particular shortcoming identified by the question, thereby improving the characteristic that contributes to the dimensional profile, and so reposition the organization on the matrix.

12.5 Strategy profile questionnaire

Read the following statements and score each one according to how true you feel it is of your organization. Use the following 7-stage rating scale:

1. completely true
2. mainly true
3. slightly true
4. 50% true: 50% untrue
5. slightly untrue
6. mainly untrue
7. completely untrue

Score by ringing your answer, totalling the scores for all questions and calculating your average score. Further guidance on the use of this questionnaire is included in Appendix II.

Strategic direction

7.1. Strategic aims are stated clearly and simply and communicated to all employees.
Completely true +3 +2 +1 0 −1 −2 −3 Completely untrue

7.2. Few people make any contribution to formulating strategy – the chief executive takes all the key decisions.
Completely true −3 −2 −1 0 +1 +2 +3 Completely untrue

7.3. The strategic planning system operates to a set timetable.
Completely true +3 +2 +1 0 −1 −2 −3 Completely untrue

7.4. Most members of the organization know how their jobs contribute to strategy.
Completely true +3 +2 +1 0 −1 −2 −3 Completely untrue

7.5. We have tended to move in several directions at the same time in order to exploit opportunities as they arise.
Completely true −3 −2 −1 0 +1 +2 +3 Completely untrue

7.6. The company's products (or services) are clearly different from the main competitor's.
Completely true +3 +2 +1 0 −1 −2 −3 Completely untrue

7.7. We have an established position in the market which is recognized by everyone, both inside and outside the organization.
Completely true +3 +2 +1 0 −1 −2 −3 Completely untrue

7.8. We tend to get involved in fire-fighting and this deflects us from pursuing the stated strategy of the business.
Completely true   −3   −2   −3   0   +1   +2   +3   Completely untrue
7.9. We have a system for monitoring the progress we make in achieving our strategic aims.
Completely true   +3   +2   +1   0   −1   −2   −3   Completely untrue
7.10. Most decisions, big and small, are made with the intention of helping achieve the stated strategic aims.
Completely true   +3   +2   +1   0   −1   −2   −3   Completely untrue

Total score: _____   *Average score*: _____

External communications

8.1. The organization makes special efforts to keep in close touch with customers in addition to normal routine sales contacts.
Completely true   +3   +2   +1   0   −1   −2   −3   Completely untrue
8.2. Most managers have good working contacts in the industry.
Completely true   +3   +2   +1   0   −1   −2   −3   Completely untrue
8.3. We regularly meet our competitors and exchange real information.
Completely true   +3   +2   +1   0   −1   −2   −3   Completely untrue
8.4. Most members of the organization know who our three main competitors are.
Completely true   +3   +2   +1   0   −1   −2   −3   Completely untrue
8.5. We work closely with the suppliers of our technology (plant and equipment) and run (or would be keen to run) trials of prototype equipment for them.
Completely true   +3   +2   +1   0   −1   −2   −3   Completely untrue
8.6. We know what the next developments in our technology are going to be.
Completely true   +3   +2   +1   0   −1   −2   −3   Completely untrue
8.7. We know why people may wish to buy products from our competitors.
Completely true   +3   +2   +1   0   −1   −2   −3   Completely untrue
8.8. The organization maintains regular contacts with technology leaders (e.g. machine manufacturers, research associations, consultants, universities, etc.).
Completely true   +3   +2   +1   0   −1   −2   −3   Completely untrue
8.9. We have a routine system of regularly updating our information on customers, technology, products and market trends.
Completely true   +3   +2   +1   0   −1   −2   −3   Completely untrue

8.10. We know what the government's next moves are likely to be in relation to our industry.
Completely true +3 +2 +1 0 −1 −2 −3 Completely untrue

Total score: _____ *Average score*: _____

Long-term orientation

9.1. Top management puts more emphasis on keeping costs within budget than on long-term issues.
Completely true −3 −2 −1 0 +1 +2 +3 Completely untrue
9.2. We try to make sure we know which way the market is likely to go over the next 5 years.
Completely true +3 +2 +1 0 −1 −2 −3 Completely untrue
9.3. The company invests heavily in its future – e.g. in new technology, R&D, market research, etc.
Completely true +3 +2 +1 0 −1 −2 −3 Completely untrue
9.4. Our long-term objectives are mainly financial ones, such as return on capital employed.
Completely true −3 −2 −3 0 +1 +2 +3 Completely untrue
9.5. The organization is invariably working on at least one large-scale investment in a major new development.
Completely true +3 +2 +1 0 −3 −2 −1 Completely untrue
9.6. New technology is seen as an opportunity to improve rather than a threat.
Completely true +3 +2 +1 0 −1 −2 −3 Completely untrue
9.7. We are continually improving the quality/performance of our product.
Completely true +3 +2 +1 0 −1 −2 −3 Completely untrue
9.8. The company actively seeks to attract shareholders who invest for the long term, rather than a quick return.
Completely true +3 +2 +1 0 −1 −2 −3 Completely untrue
9.9. Cutting costs is really the driving force of this business.
Completely true −3 −2 −1 0 +1 +2 +3 Completely untrue
9.10. A lot of effort is put into protecting ourselves against takeover.
Completely true +3 +2 +1 0 −1 −2 −3 Completely untrue

Total score: _____ *Average score*: _____

Core competence

10.1. We know which major competitor we need to beat if we are to succeed.
Completely true +3 +2 +1 0 −1 −2 −3 Completely untrue

10.2. We have a well understood plan that sets out how we will beat the main competitor.
Completely true   +3 +2 +1 0 −1 −2 −3   Completely untrue
10.3. Top management is expert in the company's core technology.
Completely true   +3 +2 +1 0 −1 −2 −3   Completely untrue
10.4. We are well aware of the latest global trends in our industry.
Completely true   +3 +2 +1 0 −1 −2 −3   Completely untrue
10.5. We are actively pursuing international collaborations so that we can keep up with technology in a way we couldn't achieve on our own.
Completely true   +3 +2 +1 0 −1 −2 −3   Completely untrue
10.6. We (would) license technology in order to develop the business, not simply to cut costs.
Completely true   +3 +2 +1 0 −1 −2 −3   Completely untrue
10.7. We have analysed our competitor's product and know what competences they have that we do not build into our product.
Completely true   +3 +2 +1 0 −1 −2 −3   Completely untrue
10.8. We make little use of publicly funded research programmes.
Completely true   −3 −2 −1 0 +1 +2 +3   Completely untrue
10.9. We know what new technological competences we are trying to develop and how we will make use of them.
Completely true   +3 +2 +1 0 −1 −2 −3   Completely untrue
10.10. We have no global ambitions so we do not need to know the latest Japanese technology.
Completely true   −3 −2 −1 0 +1 +2 +3   Completely untrue

Total score: _____   *Average score*: _____

Customer focus

11.1. The company invests a lot of time and money in finding out what customers really want.
Completely true   +3 +2 +1 0 −1 −2 −3   Completely untrue
11.2. We know exactly what the customer means by value and that's what we try to deliver.
Completely true   +3 +2 +1 0 −1 −2 −3   Completely untrue
11.3. The company tries to be efficient in order to make more profit rather than to give the customer better value.
Completely true   −3 −2 −1 0 +1 +2 +3   Completely untrue
11.4. Management's most important responsibility is to ensure we give the customer real value.
Completely true   +3 +2 +1 0 −1 −2 −3   Completely untrue
11.5. Sales and marketing is more important in this company than production or accounting.
Completely true   +3 +2 +1 0 −1 −2 −3   Completely untrue

11.6. Keeping costs down is more important than increasing market share.
Completely true −3 −2 −1 0 +1 +2 +3 Completely untrue
11.7. The company's main competitive strength is the quality of its product.
Completely true +3 +2 +1 0 −1 −2 −3 Completely untrue
11.8. The company meets all its major customers at least once a year to consider how its relationship with them can be improved.
Completely true +3 +2 +1 0 −1 −2 −3 Completely untrue
11.9. Our product has no special attribute that might give the customer a pleasant surprise.
Completely true −3 −2 −1 0 +1 +2 +3 Completely untrue
11.10. We know how the customer rates our product in relation to our main competitors in terms of all the important attributes.
Completely true +3 +2 +1 0 −1 −2 −3 Completely untrue

Total score: _____   *Average score*: _____

Overall average strategy score: _____

Reference

Child, J., H.-D. Ganter and A. Lieser, 'Technological Innovation and Organizational Conservatism' in J. M. Pennings and D. Buitendam (eds) *New Technology as Organizational Innovation*, Ballinger, Cambridge, Mass., 1987.

PART THREE
THE CULTURE DIMENSION

These following few chapters are about engaging the intelligence, expertise and commitment of people in achieving the organization's strategic aims. This is not simply a matter of giving people the freedom to take initiatives, though this is important. It is more about involving them in the leadership of the organization and motivating them to a personal commitment to the organization's success.

The opening chapter is about the management philosophy that underlies an achievement culture. McGregor defined two extremes of self-fulfilling management attitude and advocated the adoption of the people-empowering Theory Y as the more productive approach. Belief in empowerment is an important part of the achieving management philosophy, but it is not the whole story. If people are to use their freedom and power effectively they must also have the core skills and knowledge. Thus, empowerment is not simply a question of giving people freedom but also of developing their intelligence and aptitudes through training and education.

Progressive management creates what has been called a 'learning organization', which is an organization that facilitates the learning of all its members and in so doing continuously transforms itself. Members are encouraged to develop to their full potential and the learning process is encouraged beyond the boundaries of the organization itself to include customers, suppliers and other relevant stakeholders. In an era of rapid change this is of crucial importance. This open, flexible, responsive organization is at the opposite extreme to the rigid, control-oriented bureaucracy where Theory X might flourish. Yet the ideas about organizational culture that are currently fashionable are being used widely to reimpose control rather than to empower people. This is likely only to recreate the same sorts of rigidities that afflicted old-style bureaucracy.

The problem of how to give people freedom while not losing control is one of the fundamental management dilemmas. The problem has been approached theoretically through the application of generalized rules to such issues as delegation, leadership, motivation and so on. In practice, however, people are not managed on the basis of universal laws. Their differences are recognized, and they are treated accordingly. One convenient way of categorizing the differences is through the idea of psychological contracts. Some people may seek to work only from 9 till 5 to earn their money with no out-of-hours interest in or commitment to the organization; they may nevertheless be highly intelligent, experienced and skilled, with a lot to contribute. Others may be totally dedicated to their work, offering a completely open-ended commitment.

Management's task is to achieve the best contribution from both groups of people whether their psychological contract is calculative or cooperative. A first step to achieving this is through the maintenance of high corporate integrity. This is fundamental to the relationship of the organization with all its stakeholders, both internal and external. This seems to be one of the few universal truths in management theory. Beyond this, management must adopt a pluralist view of its people, recognizing that some of them may well have dominant life interests that lie outside the work arena. They can nevertheless become involved in the expert leadership of aspects of the organization and also motivated to a commitment to the achievement of organizational aims.

These are the components of a progressive culture. It is people-oriented, but at the same time is focused on achieving strategic aims.

13
Empowering people

13.1 Introduction

The organizational requirements of innovation and efficiency are usually thought to be directly opposite. To be innovative people need to have freedom, while to be efficient they need to be tightly controlled. Much of the research over the past thirty years, from Burns and Stalker on, appeared to support this general contention. It was clearly an oversimplification, but seemed to have a lot of truth in it. However, since the current technological revolution has got under way, this general contention has been increasingly questioned. The old orthodoxies seem to hold no longer. The maturest of mature businesses can be innovative and outperform young and aggressive high-tech operators! Perhaps the old orthodoxies never were wholly valid.

Freedom is not a sufficient condition to ensure creativity and effective innovation and, equally clearly, tight control is not enough to ensure that a business is efficient. Nor, in an era of rapid change, is it clear that efficiency will result in an acceptable financial performance. Freedom needs to have a focus and to be well informed by strategic awareness, as outlined in the chapters on strategy. Otherwise, innovation and creativity will be directionless, inconsistent and incapable of concentrating people's efforts. Focused freedom is what empowers people in an organization to achieve the organization's strategic aims. Empowerment is the basis of a progressive culture as described in these next few chapters. Empowerment is the end result of management action, and the underlying conditions that result in empowerment need to be fully understood so that they can be effectively managed, according to particular circumstances, to achieve the desired results.

Underlying consideration of these issues is something which goes right to the core of every manager's personal philosophy. Are particular conditions created in order to achieve results by exploiting the available talents to the full, i.e. is culture managed in order to manipulate people? Or are conditions created as desired by people so that their enthusiasm may be naturally stimulated to the achievement of results which are also in the organization's best interests?

In practice is there any substantive difference between these two propositions? At first sight, the differences may seem slight. It is a difference in management philosophy, of attitude to people. An early expression of management philosophy was McGregor's Theory X and Theory Y dichotomy. This was a rather crude expression of basic attitudes which were fundamental to a manager's every interaction with people.

Theory X and Theory Y
Assumptions about people at work

Theory X
- People are lazy and do as little as they can get away with.
- They dislike responsibility and prefer to be told what to do.
- They are completely self-interested and not concerned with the organization's aims.
- They always resist change.
- They are not very clever and will believe anything.

Theory Y
- People are inherently the opposite of what is assumed in Theory X.
- If people behave in a way that is consistent with Theory X it is because of their experience at work.
- It is management's responsibility to organize work so that people can achieve their own personal goals by directing their efforts towards organizational aims.

(Based on McGregor 1960)

McGregor made it clear that Theory Y was not a soft option, but his advocacy of Theory Y management was often naively followed by human relations devotees whose simplistic view was that management was just a question of being nice to people and they would respond in kind. Not surprisingly, the result of such a simple-minded approach, often resulting in management losing the legitimacy to manage, were frequently disastrous. Over the years Theory Y has fallen into some disrepute.

A model with possibly greater relevance to the current managerial situation was outlined by Carl Rogers (1969) in the field of education. His dichotomy of traditional–progressive was used to describe approaches to the process of learning. Not only is this particularly relevant to the role of management in this period of rapid change, but it also describes a way of achieving the 'freedom to learn' which can achieve results not obtainable from traditional control-oriented methods. The progressive approach is outlined in this chapter together with guidelines to its limitations and applicability.

13.2 Progressive and traditional management

Rogers' ideas were consistently based on what he called a 'personal philosophy' which confronted traditional or conventional attitudes to teaching. He was not commending a singular new technique, or a limited change in the curriculum. What Rogers hoped to achieve was a fundamental change in the attitude of teachers, from the directive and traditional to the student-centred, facilitative and progressive. Rogers said that he had 'found a way of being with students that . . . did not involve teaching so much as . . . the facilitation of learning'. The student discovered knowledge and experienced the process of learning with careful guidance or facilitation. The methodology for achieving such learning was quite different from the traditional approach. Instead of simply disgorging knowledge through formal lectures, the facilitator set up experiences and activities for the students, in which they acquired both knowledge and competence. Instead of learning material prescribed in a formal syllabus, students would negotiate their own learning contracts. Instead of testing memory by sitting traditional examinations, students would continually assess their own progress. Such a change implied many and various changes in teaching methods and approaches and, as Rogers emphasized, the changed attitude would inevitably inform everything that the teacher did.

The two approaches to teaching, that Rogers identified as traditional and progressive, are generally expressed in rather extreme terms as being diametrically opposed. As such they are perhaps best regarded as 'ideal types'. The traditional approach is characterized as authoritarian and directive, with large elements of compulsion or coercion; the method of teaching centres round 'chalk and talk', discipline is maintained by fear and threat and the curriculum is restricted entirely to the essential business of passing exams. The progressive approach, on the other hand, is characterized by a negotiated curriculum more loosely related to exams; teaching methods are democratic, student-centred, experiential and discursive, with discipline held to be largely a matter of self-discipline. the parallels between this approach and McGregor's Theory Y are clear. However, Rogers appears to have been more concerned than McGregor with achieving outcomes and the processes of achievement.

Most teachers and most teaching situations exhibit characteristics from both sides of the divide. There appears to be not so much a dichotomy as a continuum with the extreme ends as described above. The same clearly applies in managerial situations, which most often exhibit elements of both Theory X and Theory Y. Both Rogers and McGregor reflect a dichotomy between the traditional and progressive approaches; McGregor's Theory Y and Rogers' facilitative learning share a basic philosophical view of the employee/student which is one of trust and respect. They both believed that the two opposing views in their separate fields were actually self-fulfilling – if you treated people as though they were lazy, untrustworthy and basically irresponsible, then that is how they might be expected to behave. If on the other hand you give them responsibility and trust then, it is asserted, they will respond positively.

The approaches of McGregor and Rogers seemed deceptively simple to understand, but not so simple to implement effectively. Being nice to people, using democratic methods, even being *laissez-faire*, does not produce good results. Neither McGregor nor Rogers were advocating this simple approach – effective student-centred facilitating is undoubtedly more difficult to achieve than traditional directive teaching. Effective employee-centred management requires more skill and commitment than traditional carrot and stick methods. In some circumstances the progressive approach has seemed to be less effective than more traditional methods. The same has appeared to hold true in management situations where autocratic methods may seem to be most appropriate for certain conditions, at least for short periods of time (e.g. crisis and turn-around situations). However, where these conditions no longer exist, there would seem to be no valid role for traditional methods.

Rogers' view was that the 'personal philosophy' was all-pervasive. A teacher could not genuinely hold one set of values in one situation and adopt a quite different, even opposing set, in other situations. Values go deeper than that. Rogers was above all else concerned with values; he built on the democratic ideal and emphasized the dignity of the individual, the importance of personal choice, the significance of responsibility and the joy of creativity. The same applies in management. Superficially held values are an unsatisfactory foundation for an effective organizational culture. Lorsch (1986) defined culture as

> the shared beliefs top managers in a company have about how they should manage themselves and other employees and how they should conduct their business(es). These beliefs are often invisible to the top managers but have a major impact on their thoughts and actions.

A manager's personal philosophy will pervade and influence the whole of his or her work, if the values are firmly held. Lorsch strongly advocated making these beliefs explicit in the form of a published statement of company credo in order to reinforce them and ensure their consistency so that they became the foundation of a coherent organizational culture. Attempting to create an organizational culture that is falsely based, on aspirations not genuinely held by management, or on beliefs that are only superficially held, is unlikely to succeed. The inconsistencies will inevitably become apparent and result in a cultural dissonance that can only produce disaffection and alienation among members of the culture. Subsequent attempts at culture management will then prove counterproductive.

Purcell (1987) surveyed firms about their management philosophy and found that, although 80 per cent said they had an underlying management philosophy, which was in most cases written down, this was in fact largely ineffective. Philosophy stated by corporate headquarters was actually the least likely style to be practised at the sharp end, and in many cases was couched in terms of 'generalised banality'. Moreover, as the processes of diversification, decentralization and conglomeration proceed, this dissonance is likely to become even more pronounced.

The illustration here of Rogers' approach to learning is more than just an analogy. The facilitation of learning, in this period of rapid change, is becoming a more important and more explicit responsibility of all managers. Empowerment embodies not only the creation of freedom to act but the development of skills and knowledge on which appropriate action can be based. It is important for the management philosophy to be genuinely held so that managers can fulfil not only the broad managerial functions but also those specifically related to the development of their own staff, that is to make their contribution to what has become known as the 'learning organization'.

13.3 The learning organization

A learning organization has been defined as 'an organization which facilitates the learning of all its members and *continuously* transforms itself' (Pedler, Boydell and Burgoyne 1988).

The learning organization places an emphasis on the development of the individual and the organization together. In a learning organization human resource development is an important part of corporate strategy, not merely an output from it, and it is linked closely to concepts such as participation, openness, trust and responsibility. These ideas have become more important in the past few years in response to increasing rates of technological development and competitive global markets demanding higher levels of quality and service, greater flexibility and sensitivity to customer needs. This has led to the need for companies to create and manage organizational cultures that foster commitment, responsibility and the development of individual potential for the corporate good.

The FME/Ashridge project (Barham, Fraser and Heath 1988) proposed what it called a 'focused approach' to personnel development. This involved continuous learning by individuals as a competitive weapon linked to organizational strategy. Individuals, in full knowledge of organizational strategy, staked out their own training requirements. Training was generally non-directive unless knowledge-based and new forms of training were utilized, e.g. open learning and self-development programmes. There was also more concern to measure the effectiveness of training and development. This stands in stark contrast to the fragmented approach where, typically, individuals are told which courses to attend and their performance on the course is ignored. The main responsibility for training in the focused approach lies with line management, while trainers adopt a wider role. There is a new emphasis on learning as a process ('learning to learn') and tolerance of some failure as part of the learning process. The approach has been called focused because training and development activities are driven by both the strategic goals of the organization and the needs of the individuals. The process follows Rogers' progressive prescription and is learner-centred and problem-oriented. This is what characterizes the 'learning organization'.

The findings of the FME/Ashridge project are confirmed by Burgoyne (1988) who describes a six-stage management stepladder as follows:

1. *Laissez-faire* with no systematic management developments;
2. *Ad hoc* with isolated tactical management development;
3. Integrated and coordinated structural and development tactics;
4. Management development strategy to implement corporate policy;
5. Management development strategy input to corporate policy formation;
6. Strategic development of the management of corporate policy.

Thus the management stepladder climbs from the *laissez-faire* approach at the bottom to total integration with corporate policy at the top in a way similar to the development from fragmented to focused approaches already discussed. Both these models see a hierarchy of approaches to training and development with the strategically integrated approach, characterized as the learning organization, at the top of the hierarchy.

Pedler *et al.* (1988) used the matrix shown in Figure 13.1 to depict the idea of the learning organization. This suggests that a learning company

- has a climate in which individual members are encouraged to learn and develop their full potential;
- extends this learning culture to include customers, suppliers and other significant stakeholders;
- makes human resource development strategy central to business policy;
- undergoes a continuous process of organizational transformation, i.e. the organization develops itself rather than being changed by outside intervention.

The learning organization seems the almost inevitable result of a progressive philosophy of management, as exemplified in Rogers' approach to learning. It is essentially a deeply held view that seeks to provide opportunities for people to exploit their potential in contributing to organizational aims, rather than seeking to manipulate individuals to achieve those aims.

EMPOWERING PEOPLE   143

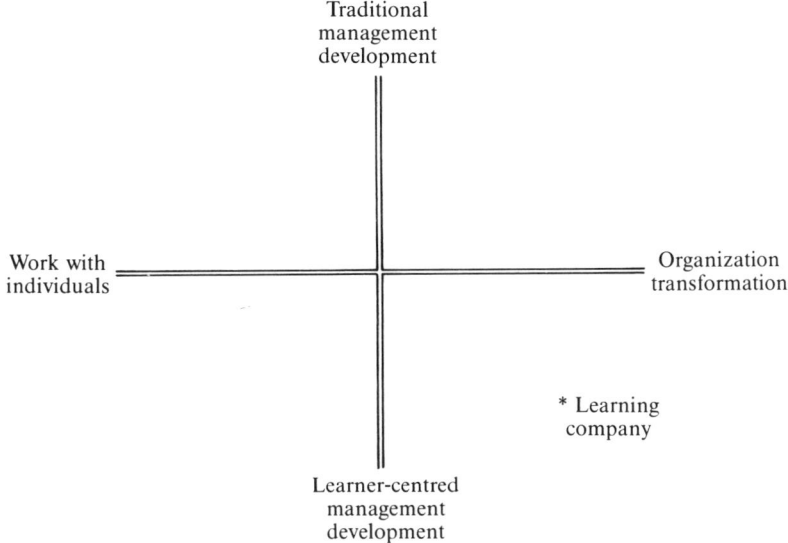

Figure 13.1 The learning company (based on Pedler, M., T. Boydell and J. Burgoyne 1989, Crown copyright)

13.4 Control through structure and culture

A learning organization may seem on the face of it to be a rather delicate organism. When the going gets tough, management's attention is automatically focused on 'the bottom line' and they seek naturally to exercise tight control in order to achieve efficiency. To achieve an efficient operation, they feel they need to know who does what and who reports to whom for what. Thus the argument is made for a classical hierarchical structure with simple but effective controls.

Yet, the learning organization is not so delicate. It is flexible. It is responsive to changes in technology, customer requirements and other extraneous developments. In times of rapid change it is a more robust organizational form than the rigid mechanistic form. Few managers would disagree, and yet many still feel the need for control.

It is easy to draw many false analogies to support the rationale for this much-felt need. For example, 'If you're driving down a steep, windy hill, control is vital and it's best if there is just one person in the driver's seat'. The analogy seems intuitively valid, but like many oversimplifications its relevance is limited. The occupants of the car comprise simply the driver and passengers, but the drivers of a business include its designers, manufacturers, assemblers, distributors, salespeople and maintainers as well as drivers and passengers. The analogy is false. Nevertheless, the perceived need for apparent control is strong.

Bureaucratic controls have failed and management naturally seek an alternative which seems appropriate to the current situation. The management of organizational culture may be one such possibility. Certainly, culture management has many advocates. Japanese firms have used various tools of culture control to create the desire and confidence in employees continually to evolve their contributions to the organizational effort:

- security of tenure – Japanese workers are taken on for life, new product/market requirements mean new jobs not new organizations;
- greater emphasis on security;
- a slower, more measured and participative approach to strategy formulation;
- the use of cultural 'propaganda' (e.g. organizational stories, company songs, down-to-earth anecdotes, etc.);
- training and education (average Japanese workers spend two of their first ten years of employment in the classroom and are employed in a variety of jobs during their career);
- participation of all in the drive for *continually* increased efficiency and quality (Based on Jaeger and Baliga 1985).

The term 'culture' has already been used quite frequently in this volume without any agreed definition being offered. Lorsch's view that it is no more than the 'the shared beliefs top managers in a company have about how they should manage' the business seems somewhat limited. The widely quoted 'the way we do things around here' probably comes closer to the generally understood concept. The most obvious characteristic of culture is that it is not quite 'up front'. Many new employees are shown an organization chart and told, rightly or wrongly, that it shows the structure of the company. Few will receive such a simple summary of the organization's culture. You can't see it, touch it, smell it, hear it or count it, but you know it's there.

In some companies it is more apparent than in others. These 'strong culture' companies appear to use culture as a control mechanism. Pascale (1985) showed how a systematic process of socialization is used initially to exert control over new employees. The process consists of these steps:

1. Only bright, young, suggestible, conformist people are recruited.
2. New recruits are exposed to 'humility-inducing' experiences during the first few months.
3. On-the-job training in a core discipline is provided.
4. There is meticulous assessment of results and employees are rewarded accordingly.

5. Careful adherence to the organization's 'transcendent values' is required.
6. Culture-reinforcing stories, etc. are heavily promoted to employees.
7. Consistent role-model high flyers are created and promoted to employees.

At first this may seem to be a rather subtle use of new knowledge to achieve perfectly sensible management aims. The fact that it may be regarded as manipulative, or may be manipulative in the wrong hands, seems hardly relevant; if management's underlying philosophy is progressive the management of culture will surely help to achieve both the aims of the organization and those of the individual.

However, the creation of a strong culture in this way has problems. While it serves to replace the control mechanisms once effectively wielded by powerful bureaucracies with something that appears more congenial, it also replicates the problems created by those control mechanisms. Culture is by definition long-lasting, and strong culture may be particularly so. Thus all the old rigidities and loss of responsiveness that caused mechanistic firms so much trouble when confronted with change are equally present in the strong culture businesses. Control is control, whether or not it comes in the guise of a nineteenth-century bureaucratic structure, or a 1990s strong culture. Either way tight control implies lack of flexibility and ability to innovate.

13.5 Psychological contracts

An implicit assumption made so far is that people at work are all essentially similar – whether they accord with Theory X or Theory Y they all share similar needs and desires. But this is patently not the case. We are all different and we go to work for a wide variety of reasons. And the way we respond to experiencing freedom or control at work will also differ.

Handy suggested that one way of looking at this difference was through the idea of a psychological contract:

> Just as in most work situations there is a legal contract between the organization and the individual which states who gives who what in consideration for what, so there is an implied, usually unstated psychological contract between the individual and the organization. . . . This psychological contract is essentially a set of expectations. The individual has a set of results that he expects from the organization, results that will satisfy certain of his needs and in return for which he will expend some of his energies and talents. Similarly the organization has its set of expectations of the individual and its list of payments or outcomes that it will give to him.
> (Handy 1981:39)

Handy distinguished just three forms of psychological contract: coercive, calculative and cooperative. The coercive contract is where individuals are held as organization members against their will (e.g. in prison) and is not applicable to a normal work situation. The calculative contract is where the two parties discuss specific terms and all aspects of the contract are agreed and probably written down. A cooperative contract is more open-ended and less clear-cut, the parties to it operating on the basis of mutual trust and interdependence and sharing the same broad goals and intentions.

Traditionally, most companies have employed most of their people on the basis of a calculative contract, and only a relatively small minority of senior managers and professional specialists have worked on the basis of a truly cooperative contract. However, this is not entirely the case. There are echoes in this analysis of Burns and Stalker's mechanistic and organismic organizations: employees in the mechanistic organizations, even senior management, would be retained on the basis of a calculative contract. Employees in an organismic organization, even quite junior people, would probably be retained on the basis of a cooperative contract.

The move from mechanistic to organismic forms in response, say, to the revolution in technology seems to imply that an increasing number of people are likely to be employed on the basis of rather open-ended, flexible, cooperative contracts, This may seem to be an essential prerequisite to the prosperity or even survival of an increasing number of businesses. Nevertheless, it must be remembered that both calculative and cooperative contracts are essentially voluntary arrangements. There may well be people with whom an organization would like to enter a cooperative contract, who, on the other hand, are only prepared to enter a calculative contract. This does not mean that they must necessarily be written off as 'not one of us'; they may be highly talented and skilled individuals whose contributions to the organization are potentially immense. The common practice of entering calculative contracts with the majority and cooperative contracts with the chosen few risks the widespread rejection of invaluable contributions from the many.

Management's task is clearly to make the maximum use of the talents at its disposal, and this means offering as many cooperative contracts as will be taken up. For those who seek only a calculative contract, management must devise new ways of gaining their enthusiastic cooperation and commitment to organizational goals within the limitations of their psychological contract, whatever they may be.

The psychological contract idea provides a way of looking at the management and motivation of different sorts of people, all of whom can contribute crucially to organizational success.

13.6 Summary

- Freedom is not sufficient to ensure that an organization is creative and innovative. Freedom needs to have a strategic focus for it to be used effectively.
- Control is not sufficient to ensure that an organization is effective. In an era of rapid change, simple efficiency is not enough.
- Empowerment is achieved through focused freedom, which depends on the manager's underlying philosophy towards people in the organization.
- Management philosophy has been described by McGregor in terms of Theory X and Theory Y, an approach widely interpreted as suggesting that trusting prople and being nice to them will create an effective organization. It doesn't often work.
- Another approach to management philosophy is that of Carl Rogers who distinguished two approaches to the teaching-learning process: the traditional approach is directive and prescriptive and bears some comparison to Theory X; the progressive approach is employee-centred and empowering and is particularly pertinent in today's environment because developing people is one of the crucial tasks of management.
- The importance of people development is recognized in the learning organization.
- Progressive management and the development of a learning organization is a process that works through the culture of the company. Culture management is sometimes seen as the way to achieve control now that former mechanistic controls are no longer available or are seen as inappropriate.
- A strong culture can be as inflexible and unresponsive as the mechanistic bureaucracy it seeks to replace.
- Empowerment of people involves sensitivity to individuals and their differing psychological contracts: a calculative contract is one where the terms are explicit and limited; a cooperative contract is one where the terms may not be explicit, but are agreed on the basis of trust and acknowledged interdependence – they are likely to be open-ended and unlimited.
- Management's task is to organize work so that the fullest use can be made of everybody's intelligence, knowledge and skills for the mutual benefit of both parties.

References

Barham, K., J. Fraser and L. Heath, 'Management for the Future' – a research project sponsored by the Foundation for Management Education and Ashridge Management College, 1988.

Burgoyne, J., 'Management development for the individual and the organisation', *Personnel Management*, June 1988.

Handy, C. B., *Understanding Organizations*, Penguin, Harmondsworth, 1981.

Jaeger, A. M. and B. Baliga, 'Control systems and strategic adaption: lessons from the Japanese experience', *Strategic Management Journal*, Vol. 6, 1985:115–134.

Lorsch, J. W., 'Managing culture: the invisible barrier to strategic change', *California Management Review*, Vol. xxviii, No. 2, Winter 1986.

McGregor, D. M., '*The Human Side of Enterprise*', McGraw-Hill, New York, 1960.

Pascale, R., 'The paradox of "corporate culture": reconciling ourselves to socialization', *California Management Review*, Vol. xxvii, No. 2, 1985:26–41.

Pedler, M., T. Boydell and J. Burgoyne, 'Learning Company Project Report', Training Agency, 1988.

Purcell, J., 'Mapping management styles in employee relations', *Journal of Management Studies*, September 1987.

Rogers, C. R., *Freedom to Learn*, Charles Merrill, Columbus, Ohio, 1969.

14
Building corporate integrity

14.1 Introduction

> One of the surprises in our interviews at chief executive level and below was the passion with which our successful companies embraced integrity as an essential part of their culture. This clearly was not window-dressing. Each company was convinced that without absolute integrity the business simply could not operate.

So starts Chapter 9 of *The Winning Streak* (Goldsmith and Clutterbuck 1985). At first sight it seems a curious statement. Clearly, it all depends on what is meant by integrity, and particularly 'absolute integrity'. It seems unlikely that most businesses 'could not even operate' without absolute integrity, whatever it means. The concept of integrity seems to invite cynicism – chief executives *would* say their businesses embraced total integrity, wouldn't they! Financial institutions, which used to operate on the basis of 'my word is my bond', now frequently hit the headlines for unethical, dishonest and even criminal behaviour. In such an environment integrity might seem to be synonymous with naivety.

The cynic might suggest the social responsibility of business is an academic concern. The purpose of business is to satisfy the customer and make a profit, not to fulfil some greater social purpose – the two are incompatible. The phrase 'business ethics' is a contradiction in terms. Business is about maximizing profit by whatever legal means are available and the only way of ensuring that businesses operate in a socially acceptable way is to impose statutory constraints on their profit-maximizing behaviour.

This cynical view has made considerable impact and restrictive legislation is now far more comprehensive than ever before. The law governing the workings of financial institutions around the stock market is a good example. Until the 1960s the stock exchange operated largely under a system of self-regulation. In those days the major institutions were controlled by members of a relatively small number of families whose interdependence was recognized and understood. If a member of a family were to break a verbal commitment, he would have been drummed out of the club and his life would have become, by their lights, intolerable. This system of self-regulation could be extremely harsh and on occasions led to the suicide of individuals who broke the rules. At the same time, it was common practice in those days for a merchant bank to buy blocks of shares and only decide subsequently, and in the light of their performance, whether the purchase had been made for the bank or on behalf of one of its clients. Today, when the grip of the old families has weakened and some elements of meritocracy are starting to gain ascendancy, self-regulation by any form of social sanction is inadequate, even laughable, and a more comprehensive statutory framework is being created. This not only replaces the old system of voluntary control, but broadens it to eliminate many of the abuses that used to be accepted and taken for granted.

However, there are limits to what legislation can achieve. The chief executives in the *Winning Streak* enquiry are not simply saying that firms must act within the law, but that there is much to gain from maintaining standards of integrity which are set much higher than this. Maintaining high integrity is, as Goldsmith and Clutterbuck indicated, a basic component of an achievement culture. It helps a firm to develop fruitful long-term relationships with suppliers and customers, and is vital in enlisting the intelligence, expertise and commitment of people in achieving a winning strategy.

14.2 The scope of integrity

Figures 14.1 to 14.4 show examples of ethical issues affecting various personal or corporate transactions.

Integrity, or its lack, is manifested whenever a firm or an individual takes part in some interaction with another interdependent entity. These interactions may be simple and direct, as between a firm and its customer when a product is sold. Or they may be extremely indirect, even circumstantial, as between a firm and the whole human race when a potentially pollutant by-product is disposed of into the atmosphere. This rather extreme case serves to emphasize how interdependent we all are, such interdependence being the foundation of the concept of integrity. Were there no such interdependence, integrity simply would not be an issue. For a business, these various interdependencies exist in the following forms:

1. the firm and its macro-environments: global ecology, society at large, the political, economic and technological environments, etc.

BUILDING CORPORATE INTEGRITY   151

The Purchase of Freehold

Some years ago the National Coal Board purchased the freehold of some land under which they held mineral extraction rights. The land was in four parcels, then owned by three farmers and the widow of a fourth. Each parcel was approximately the same size and of approximately equal value.

Coal Board officials started purchase negotiations with the four landowners. The three farmers drove a fairly hard bargain and a price was finally agreed of about £100 000 in each case. The fourth landowner, the farmer's widow, unaware of the value of land, would have been prepared to accept a figure of about £25 000.

After due consideration the NCB purchased the fourth parcel for £100 000. Their view was that being seen to act ethically was paramount. Moreover, though they could have made a short-term gain of £75 000 they could have lost far more in the long run. For example, future planning consents from the local authority could well be affected by the NCB's local reputation for ethical behaviour.

Figure 14.1   Local community transactions

2. the firm and its more immediate micro-environments: local community, competitors, employee markets, etc.
3. the firm and its direct external stakeholders: customers, suppliers, shareholders, lenders, etc.
4. the firm and its direct internal stakeholders: employees.
5. internal relationships between employees, especially between top management and others.

Ethical dilemmas may arise in any or all of these interdependencies. For example, the personal integrity of top managers is likely to affect the commitment of people working for them. The integrity of a company's relationships with suppliers, for example in regard to cooperation in future work scheduling, is likely to affect the priority the supplier gives to that company. The integrity of a company's dealings with its customers will clearly be crucial to the development of future business. Examples can be readily recognized for each category of transaction.

Repeated individual transactions gradually accumulate into relationships which themselves embody the level of integrity invested in individual transactions. The integrity of a customer–supplier relationship is defined by the adherence to agreed behaviours such as paying on time, or adherence to the delivery of a product with known and consistently achieved attributes.

> ### Board salaries soar as economy dives
> 'Pay rises for top executives in Britain's largest companies have consistently outstripped inflation, average earnings and corporate financial performance during the past five years.
>
> '. . . the average rise for highest paid directors in the country's 100 biggest corporations totalled 120% between 1985 and 1989. . . . That compares with growth in average earnings of 50% . . .
>
> 'At Barclays Bank, for example, remuneration for the highest paid director has risen by more than 215% to £9000 per week even though earnings per share have fallen by 30% while at Midland Bank, earnings ended in the red whereas the highest paid director's salary was 500% higher . . .'
> (*The Guardian*, 3 May 1990)
>
> ### Concern grows over boardroom bonanza
> 'Britain's biggest institutional shareholders yesterday weighed into the debate on top executive pay following a series of boardroom rises which have vastly outstripped profits growth.
>
> 'The Association of British Insurers which, with £200 billion invested in UK industry, owns around one in three of all shares, has issued a discussion paper on the role of directors, including their emoluments.
>
> '. . . In the past opposition to specific examples of corporate greed have been handled on an individual basis, with large shareholders often working behind the scenes.
>
> 'The ABI is aware that its members have attracted criticism for appearing to be inactive in the face of what has been perceived as an unrestrained free for all in Britain's boardrooms . . .'
> (*The Guardian*, 20 June 1990)

Figure 14.2 Personal integrity of top management

Above all, integrity is manifest in the firm's strategic intent. A strategic intent which would depend on unethical behaviour for its achievement would be unlikely to engage the intelligence and commitment of many people. Only when you have integrity can most people have fun at work.

A number of questions arise:

– Does it matter whether a firm actually behaves ethically, or is merely seen to do so?
– Is being ethical a fundamental characteristic that an individual or

> The president of Falcon Computer, erstwhile rising star of Silicon Valley, expressed the intended corporate culture in a document called *Falcon Values*. It covered such things as attitudes to customers and colleagues, styles of communications and decision making and the cultural aspects of the working environment.
>
> For example, under *customer orientation* it said: 'Attention to detail is our trade mark; our goal is to do it right first time. We intend to deliver defect-free products and services to our customers on time'. But at the same time defective computers were being delivered, on top management instructions, to squash industry rumours that Falcon would miss its announced release date.
>
> The disparity between Falcon's official culture and the way it actually did things was extreme. 'Almost everyone knew that the operative values at Falcon Computer were hierarchy, secrecy, and expediency – regardless of what the official culture said.'
>
> The result – a cynical alienated workforce, loss of more than $32 million invested capital, and debts of millions more. Just two and a half years after its founding, it closed its doors for good.

Figure 14.3 Theory and practice of values (Reynolds 1986)

organization either has or does not have, or can an individual (or organization) be, or be seen to be, ethical in some respects and unethical in others?
– Is there a universally accepted way of assessing whether or not behaviour is ethical?

A possible answer to the first question may lie in the marketing literature on *image*. Perceptions of a product, or an organization, may well differ significantly from the reality and there are well researched ways of influencing these perceptions. However, attempts to influence perceptions to create a false product or corporate image (i.e. one that differs substantially from the reality) generally fail – in the long term the truth will out. The same probably applies in the case of ethical behaviour. Even though it may be appearances which are perceived by the various stakeholders and so impact on long-term profitability, it is unlikely that the appearance of being ethical will be long maintained unless it is based on the reality of consistently ethical behaviour.

Regarding the second question, even though an individual or organization may make explicit choices as to whether to behave ethically or otherwise, stakeholders are likely to perceive an organization as being to a greater or

> **Africa – ashtray of the world**
>
> 'Cigarette sales are declining in the health-conscious West, so tobacco giants are turning to the Third World, where poverty and ignorance provide a population that is easy prey to modern marketing. The British company BAT is heading this drive and believes it is doing nothing wrong . . .
>
> 'An investigation by Insight into BAT's marketing strategy has revealed that it is operating a double standard – one for the West and another for the Third World.
>
> 'It is taking advantage of loosely enforced or non-existent government health restrictions to target millions of poor and ignorant people in what is becoming tobacco's final frontier. Its strategy entails:
>
> – Marketing brands of cheap, highly addictive cigarettes;
> – Making misleading claims to governments in developing countries that smoking is not harmful and that health warnings are counterproductive;
> – Using political and economic leverage to support its market dominance;
> – Designing advertising to play on the desire in developing countries to mirror Western sophistication.'

Figure 14.4 Double standards (*Sunday Times*, 13 May 1990)

lesser extent ethical, i.e. as possessing, in some degree or other, the fundamental characteristic of integrity. Some managements are only constrained by the law in their single-minded pursuit of the 'bottom line'. Others regard integrity as a fundamental aspect of organization that influences the perceptions of all stakeholders. In both cases the ethical stance is not a matter for individual management decisions explicitly made as situations arise. The ethical position is a more or less permanent organizational/culture characteristic that prescribes decisions on a continuing basis.

For example, the British retail chain, Body Shop, has a unique marketing thrust based on a particular ethical stance. These high principles are fundamental to Body Shop's success. If it became known that Body Shop had acted unethically in other areas (an entirely hypothetical proposition!), would this adversely influence customer perceptions of the Body Shop concept?

Is the Japanese reputation for quality of manufacture affected at all by Japanese bribery scandals or stories of Japanese patent piracy?

There are no final answers, but evidence of the all-pervasive nature of integrity is mounting. If a company is seen to be acting unethically in one respect, it may be widely expected to behave unethically in other respects also. So, if it is important for an organization to be seen to be ethical, it will be important for it to behave in a consistently ethical way.

The third question then becomes important. Most situations, like those illustrated in Figures 14.1 to 14.4 are not all simple, black and white situations, but pose genuine dilemmas that may require more than simple common sense to resolve. We need to know, if we possibly can, what is generally held by all stakeholders to constitute ethical behaviour and we need to be able to apply these rules, or this form of analysis, to ethical dilemmas when they arise.

The next section describes some of the main perspectives that are available for analysing ethical dilemmas.

14.3 Business ethics

If it is important for business to be ethical, then it will be necessary to agree what *is* ethical behaviour in a way that can command general support. The distinction between ethical and unethical behaviour needs to be capable of achieving a broad consensus of support among stakeholders. This is not necessarily straightforward because value systems are situation-dependant – what is considered unethical in Britain in the 1990s may well be perfectly okay in Borneo, or may have been so in medieval England. Nevertheless, some generalizations can be made.

Since the ancient Greeks, people have tried to define a set of ethical principles that would apply to all situations at all times. Not surprisingly, the result has not been one single principle or truth, but a variety of approaches and theories. Among this great variety there are certain broad streams which are distinguished by common fundamental assumptions. One such broad stream, the consequentialist approach or utilitarianism, is concerned with the consequences of an action, while another broad approach, sometimes known as universalism, is concerned more with acting on principle, that is the motivation underlying an action, rather than its consequences.

Utilitarianism was originally based on the idea that actions are right in proportion as they tend to promote happiness and wrong as they produce the reverse of happiness. Happiness was defined by Bentham in 1789 as intended pleasure and absence of pain:

> Nature has placed mankind under the governance of two sovereign masters, pain and pleasure . . . The principle of utility recognizes this subjection and . . . approves or disapproves of every action whatsoever according to the tendency

which it appears to have to augment or diminish the happiness of the party whose interest is in question.
(Jeremy Bentham, *Introduction to the Principles of Morals and Legislation*, 1789)

Utilitarianism focuses on the consequences of each individual act, but simplifying general rules have been developed (e.g. always tell the truth). 'Rule utilitarianism' focuses on the application of these general rules and is concerned with the consequences *if everyone did it*.

Universalism is based on the idea that the moral worth of an action depends on the intentions of the person taking the action. Thus, duty is the foundation of morality and some acts are morally obligatory regardless of their consequences. This approach can sometimes lead to behaviour which under utilitarian analysis would seem to be very clearly unethical. For example, involvement in the production of contraceptives – traditional Catholics who follow the teachings of the church as currently promulgated might believe that the production and open sale of contraceptives is unethical, whereas, in terms of the consequences, population control might be regarded as highly ethical.

The two approaches are in many circumstances incompatible with each other and so do not together produce a coherent system of ethical rules. In an atheistic (or agnostic) society it might seem inappropriate to admit a notion of duty based on some religious (or otherwise metaphysical) motivation. But even then the two approaches may often be in conflict. The simple universal rule, always to tell the truth, may in some circumstances cause great harm, while telling an untruth may have no adverse consequences at all.

Philosophical sources of ethical rules do not therefore appear to offer a complete answer to the problem of integrity. Donaldson (1989) proposes 'three ground rules': pluralism, the golden rule and autonomy.

By pluralism he means simply to acknowledge that there is no single ethical perspective or criterion which will be appropriate in all circumstances, and therefore it may be advantageous to assess ethical dilemmas from two or more perspectives.

The 'golden rule', the nearest thing to such a criterion, is simply the maxim (or categorical imperative); 'do unto others as you would have them do unto you'. This has found expression in most religions and creeds over the ages and may well be the most universally applicable ethical criterion. Confucius, for example, asked whether the true way could be summed up in a single word responded, ' "Reciprocity" is such a word'.

Autonomy is the principle that we all have the power to make our own ethical judgements. Blaming the system within which we operate, for example, is simply not good enough.

The application of these three ground rules may be as effective a set of guiding principles as can be obtained from philosophy. The study of business ethics, which is now gathering momentum in America and Europe, has probably not developed anything of more general practical application than this.

It would be possible to develop guidelines to ethical business behaviour without regard for moral principles but simply on the basis of long-term self-interest. Such an amoral guide might commend behaviour that, if it were apparent, would increase rather than decrease the level of trust felt by the stakeholder or other party to the transaction or relationship in question. For example, paying on time would increase the level of trust felt by the supplier while paying late, or irregularly, would reduce the level of trust. Remunerating all members of an organization on an open and equitable basis would increase trust in management, whereas behaviour such as that referred to in Figure 14.2 would reduce it. Similar examples could be provided for all transactions across the whole scope of integrity. The injunction to behave ethically applies whether or not the behaviour in question is apparent or not since, as already noted, unethical behaviour will in the long term not remain hidden. And it applies equally to all stakeholders and all transactions because in the long term, as also noted previously, integrity is a fundamental characteristic rather than a chosen form of behaviour applicable to individual transactions only.

14.4 Openness

Even though, in the long term, the truth will out, it remains true that unethical individuals frequently delude themselves that their behaviour is not seen and recognized.

This is especially the case with top management who are often placed in a position of extreme personal power within their organizations. In many cases they create the rules of behaviour by which their organizations are managed.

When a chief executive instructs his finance chief to pay an invoice for, say, an item of furniture that has been purchased for his own home, he may believe he is justified since he entertains many business contacts at his own home. He may believe that it will be known only to himself and his finance chief who will also understand the moral justification. When the transaction is repeated with other similar deals, an ongoing relationship is progressively set up and the parties to that relationship are likely to include most of the other members of the organization, who understand exactly what is going on but lack a full comprehension of the moral justification involved.

The extreme personal power is evident in the way such transactions and relationships remain covert. It is extremely rare that any employee will blow the whistle on such dealings. Whistle blowing is notoriously damaging to a management career. So the finance chief, aware of responsibilities to wife and family, both now and after retirement, is extremely unlikely to reveal what he knows. More distantly involved employees are also unlikely to take any action, again because of personal fear, plus the feelings of diminished responsibility that distance provides.

This crude and obvious example stands proxy for all the other transactions which have been referred to above, but emphasizes the all-important contribution of top management in establishing and nurturing corporate integrity. Their personal influence cannot be overemphasized.

The only way round a culture of secretiveness and lack of whistle blowing is to bring ethics into the open. Set up an ethics committee specifically charged to review corporate integrity in *all* its scope. This explicit openness will not only inhibit dishonesty at all levels, but will also serve to ensure consistency of integrity so that trust can be built up with all stakeholders. Without taking such deliberate steps, an organization or even an individual will tend to behave ethically on some occasions and unethically on others, or even drift into the sort of situation at Falcon Computer described in Figure 14.3.

14.5 Summary

- In the *Winning Streak* enquiry it was found that successful companies embraced integrity as an essential part of their culture.
- Maintaining high integrity is a basic component of an achievement culture.
- Integrity, or its lack, is manifested whenever a firm or an individual takes part in some interaction with another interdependent entity. These interactions may be simple and direct or extremely indirect.
- Repeated individual transactions gradually accumulate into relationships which themselves embody the level of integrity.
- Above all, integrity is manifest in the firm's strategic intent.
- A firm must actually behave ethically, not merely be seen to do so.
- Being ethical is a fundamental characteristic which an individual or organization either has or does not have. It is not simply a matter of behavioural choice.
- Philosophical sources of ethical rules do not offer a complete answer to the problem of corporate integrity.
- Donaldson proposes 'three ground rules' – pluralism, the golden rule and autonomy – which offer some practical principles.
- Alternatively, a guide to ethical business behaviour might commend behaviour which, if it were apparent, would increase rather than

decrease the level of trust felt by the stakeholder, or other party to the transaction or relationship in question.
- Top management are in a position to establish and nurture corporate integrity, by bringing the full scope of ethical issues into the open. For example they may set up an ethics committee specifically charged to review corporate integrity in *all* its scope.
- This explicit openness will inhibit dishonesty at all levels and also serve to ensure consistency of integrity so that trust can be built up with all stakeholders.

References

Bentham, J., *Introduction to the Principles of Morals and Legislation*, 1789.
Donaldson J., *Key Issues in Business Ethics*, Academic Press, London, 1989.
Goldsmith, W. and D. Clutterbuck, *The Winning Streak*, Penguin, Harmondsworth, 1985:123:
Reynolds, P. C., 'Corporate culture on the rocks', *Across the Board*, October 1986.

15
Involving people in leadership

15.1 Introduction

The previous two chapters have both emphasized the importance of value systems to an achievement culture. Empowerment and integrity are vital if the organization is going to be able to gain people's involvement and commitment at work. But values alone are not enough.

This – how to engage people's involvement and commitment – is what Bailey (1983) described as the 'basic organizational management problem'. The costs of failure are high and include restriction of output, absenteeism, labour turnover, strikes and disputes, even sabotage, poor quality, inflexibility of work practices, overmanning, late deliveries and resistance to change. Moreover, beyond all this is the cost of failing to engage and develop the talents, skills, efforts and enthusiasm of all the people working in the organization – resources which could be deployed in the continous improvement and development of the business operation.

Individuals have first to be involved in the organization, and then they have to be motivated to a commitment to achieving the strategic aims. This chapter is about involving individuals in the organization, and Chapter 16 about motivating their commitment.

15.2 A pluralist view

The traditional management perspective on industrial organization assumes that there is one source of authority and one focus of loyalty. According to this view, employees in a successful enterprise might be expected

> to strive jointly towards a common objective each pulling his weight to the best of his ability. Each accepts his place and his function gladly, following the leadership of the one so appointed.

Also:

> If the members have an obligation of loyalty towards the leader, the obligation is certainly reciprocated, for it is the duty of the leader to act in such ways as to inspire the loyalty he demands. Morale and success are closely connected and rest heavily upon personal relations. (Fox 1966)

This indicates a picture of industry that employers and managers might feel *ought* to be realistic, but is widely acknowledged to be just wishful thinking. This idealistic approach was exemplified by the proceedings of the Industrial Co-partnership Association which ran its annual conferences under such title themes as 'Team Spirit in Industry: the vital factor in Britain's recovery' and published pamphlets under such titles as 'All on the Same Side' and 'Partnership in Industry'. Such expressions as 'team spirit', 'team work' and 'working together' are emphasized in what Fox labelled the *unitary* approach and which he summarized as 'an orgy of avuncular pontification' (Fox 1966).

Most of management literature, including this present volume, is aimed at bringing this idealized situation into being. However, Fox suggests we might be better to acknowledge that other views exist and then try to understand these other perspectives 'so that industrial relations can be seen more realistically and laid more open to solution'. This *pluralist* view holds that a business or industrial organization is essentially a plural society which contains many related, but separate interests and objectives that must be held in some kind of equilibrium. A firm is made up of sectional groups with divergent interests, possibly their only shared interest being the survival of the business they work for, though this is only a remote long-term consideration and provides no common ground on which to base the day-to-day running of the organization.

Within the unitary frame there may be two quite different subsets, one deliberately exploitive of labour, the other emphasizing mutual loyalty and commitment. Similarly, within the pluralist frame there may also be two subsets, one highly structured, formal, often with antagonistic relations with employees through their trade unions, the other emphasizing dialogue, understanding and cooperation between management and labour.

The pluralist frame of reference may have been more realistic than the unitary view in the 1960s, before the 'new realism' of trade unions, but even in the 1990s, with union power so reduced, the pluralist view still provides insights. For example, it is likely that some members of any organization will remain impervious to the unitary view. Their psychological contract may be calculative, e.g. closed and restricted to a highly prescribed arrangement covering the hours between, say, 8.30 a.m. and 4.30 p.m. This does not mean that these individuals are necessarily in any way inferior to those with more open-ended cooperative psychological contracts, but that they have so arranged their personal priorities that they satisfy whatever intrinsic needs they may have, away from work. Nevertheless, they may be highly intelligent, skilled and experienced and capable of making valuable contributions to the achievement of a winning strategy. Where both the organization and the individual want a cooperative contract there is no problem. Similarly, where both the organization and the individual want a calculative contract, there is also no problem. However, where the organization seeks a calculative contract and the individual wants a cooperative contract, problems inevitably arise. These problems, relating to the nature and extent of individual participation, are further exacerbated where the organization wants a cooperative contract and the individual seeks simply to have a limited calculative involvement.

Treating all people alike would clearly be ineffective. Some may be best managed as groups through formal cooperative systems covering communications (team briefing, joint communication and consultation committees, formal worker participation arrangements such as representative directors, etc.). Others may be best managed through more individual processes of development. The expectation that all members will be motivated by recognition and increased responsibility is unlikely to be realized. The management of individual managers through standard collective structures will inevitably lead to frustration, disappointment and ultimately alienation.

This was shown in an interesting survey carried out by Purcell (1987) which identified two ways of categorizing approaches to management: individualism and collectivism.

Individualism refers to the extent to which the firm gives credence to the feelings and sentiments of individual employees and seeks to develop and encourage them (see Figure 15.1). There are various degrees of individualism and Purcell provides some revealing quotations from his survey:

'People are our most important resource.'

'We recruit above average employees . . . invest time in their development and . . . promote from within the company.'

These two quotations come from firms emphasizing employee development, and which are thus individualist in orientation. Other comments were included from firms at the opposite end of the individualist dimension:

'a bit ruthless . . . people are just numbers'

'very tight fiscal control . . . we look at the cost of . . . manpower'

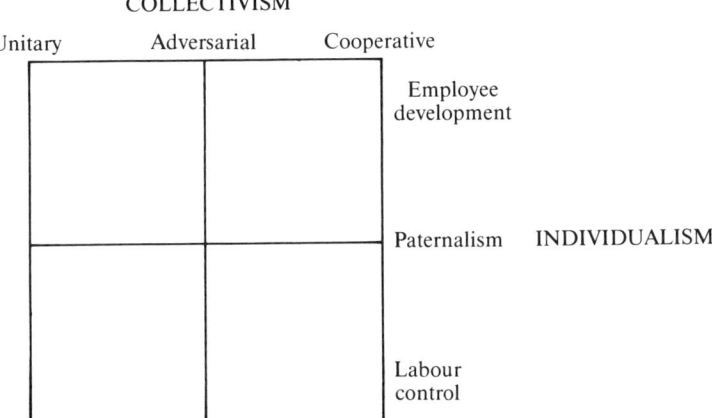

Figure 15.1   Dimensions of management style (Purcell 1987)

These remarks emphasize labour control and a group orientation. Between these two, there is a paternalistic view, 'a caring attitude, tolerant of employees within the constraints of successful business', 'limiting the freedom of the subject by well meant regulations' (Purcell 1987).

Collectivism concerns the extent to which the organization recognizes the right of employees to have a say in those aspects of management decision making which concern them. It is difficult to measure, but has two critical aspects. The first is the degree to which there are collective arrangements or structures within the firm (e.g. Do employees have the right to elect individuals to represent their views in management decisions? Do they have formal consultative and participative structures, pension scheme trustees, worker directors?). These are essentially measures of involvement. The second aspect is the degree to which management restrict or cooperate with these collective structures. For example, they may have been won through bitter fights between management and unions, and not be facilitated by management in any way, or they may have been instigated by management who encourage them to the fullest possible extent.

Thus the collectivism dimension goes from unitary at one end to cooperative at the other with an adversarial position in between (see Figure 15.1).

Purcell quotes several other researches which support this contention that management style can reasonably be defined along these two dimensions of individualism and collectivism, and the observation that style was likely to apply differently to different categories of employee. Gaining the involvement of different individuals is likely to be achieved by different means – there is no 'one best way'.

15.3 Participation in decision making

The term 'participation' is used widely and generally without it necessarily always being recognized that what is meant is 'participation in decison making'. It is a measure of the degree to which members of a social system participate in the decision-making process. Participation can be either formal or informal, according to the nature of the decision, the individual concerned, the individualist/collectivist perspective of management and the psychological contract between the two.

Most of the research on participation seems to derive directly from the unitarian school of thought and, perhaps naïvely, emphasizes the virtues of all pulling together as a team for the greater good of the organization and all those working in it. It does not yet carry the statutory overtones implied by participation in the European Community.

The power of participative systems derives from the often repeated findings that member acceptance of, and satisfaction with, decisions, particularly decisions relating to innovation and change, increase as members' participation in those decisions increases. Moreover, as participation increases, so members of the social system experience increasing cohesion with the system. Thus, participation appears to offer a possible means of making people more prepared to accept the unpleasant consequences of inevitable decisions, such as the application of new technology and the consequential job losses. As a consequence, a low-integrity management may pay lip service to participation in order to achieve acquiescence to a hidden agenda. Suspicions of this nature led many British trade unions to reject the formal participative arrangements set up by the Labour government in the mid-1970s.

However, participation is a 'hearts and minds' issue and goes far beyond formal structures. It is one of the often quoted distinctions between Japanese and Western management styles. A management that is jealous of 'the right to manage' tends to take decisions in a top-down, technique-oriented fashion, emphasizing speed and regarding the ability to take decisions as a test of managerial virility. This is more typical of Western management decision-taking style. The Japanese, on the other hand, tend to be slow but sure, consensus-building and consultative.

This contrast is best exemplified by considering a substantial, potentially risky capital investment. In Britain, this is regarded as the strict reserve of top management who may use various financial techniques (e.g. discounted cash flow) to aid, or disguise, the decision process. In accordance with accounting philosophy, a risky project such as an innovation will be required to achieve a higher than normal return by using a risk premium of between 5 per cent and 10 per cent, and not infrequently 15 per cent.

A risk premium cannot be justified either in practice or in theory. It is simply a manifestation of the accountant's natural desire to avoid risk. But the fault does not seem to lie in accounting methods as such, but rather in the clinical logic of statistical decision theory. This asserts that if a firm has two courses of action, one with a pay-off of £100 and a probability of 0.8 and the other with a pay-off of £800 and a probability of 0.1, the 'expected' outcomes are the same, despite the fact that the riskiness of the two projects is very different. The expected outcome is simply the value of the outcome multiplied by the probability of its occurring. Thus a project with a probability of less than 1 needs to earn a higher return than a risk-free project if its 'expected' outcome is to be the same. This extra return is a risk premium, and the higher the risk the greater the premium will have to be to equate the expected outcome with that of the risk-free project.

The application of this sort of thinking to investment appraisal is fallacious. A risk premium can only serve to change a firm's overall risk profile by rejecting risky projects. It can have no other effect. The application of a premium in no way increases the return from a project – it merely reduces the probability of it going ahead. If all innovative projects are risky, as they are, then it serves only to limit innovative investment.

By contrast, the Japanese rarely use this mechanical application of a risk premium (as indicated in Figure 3.2). Instead, they follow through the details of a project analysis and identify precisely what it is that makes it risky. For example, in the case of a new product innovation, is it the probability of a punitive competitive reaction? If so, what can be done to limit or avoid that reaction? What marketing or production tactics might make the short-term competitive advantage, achieved by the innovation, sustainable in the long term? What will each of the main competitors do? What will be the effect of their action? What could be done about it?

This detailed analysis of what might inhibit the achievement of the innovation's potential return involves all professional specialists and members of the management team. The project is discussed in detail at all levels of the organization, risk is investigated in every aspect and programmes devised to circumvent the possible adverse outcomes. If a credible programme for the circumvention of risk can be devised, then the project is likely to go ahead because its appraisal will not be clouded by the blind application of an arbitrary risk premium.

The participative Japanese approach not only increases understanding of the risk involved and identifies how it could best be handled, but also becomes a means of communication among members. It provides a genuine way for members to participate in organizational decisions. Japanese practice endeavours to establish a consensus among organizational members. If consensus is difficult to achieve, then the appraisal process takes longer. Achievement of consensus, after widespread communication and participation, means that all organizational members know and understand what the business is trying to achieve and which way it is headed.

Western practice still generally emphasizes decision making as an essentially managerial role and focuses considerable attention on the task of leadership. The nature of the leadership of an organization is clearly a major determinant of the nature and extent of participation and involvement of other organization members in the decision-making processes of the organization.

15.4 Leadership

The empirical work on leadership is extensive – more than 3000 separate studies by 1979. However, a basic dilemma remains: whether, or to what extent, leaders are born or made. If they are born, then theory is not going to be much use – all that can be done is to recruit the appropriate people.

Adair quotes an eminent lecturer on leadership at the University of St Andrews in 1934:

> some men possess an inbred superiority which gives them a dominating influence over their contemporaries, and marks them out unmistakably for leadership. This phenomenon is as certain as it is mysterious . . . in every association of human beings . . . there are those who, with an assured and unquestioned title, take the leading place, and shape the general conduct. (Adair 1983:7)

Many researchers, apparently taking 'leaders are born' assertions seriously, have tried to identify the God-given ingredients of 'unquestioned title'.

Stogdill carried out two surveys of such studies (Stogdill 1948 and 1974) and highlighted a number of personality traits, abilities and social skills that were identified as being most frequently associated with effective leadership. The most frequently identified traits were:

- above-average intelligence, but not too far above;
- initiative, i.e. independence and inventiveness – the ability to see the need for action and the urge to take it;
- self-assurance.

In addition, most successful leaders appear to enjoy good health, be above average height or well below it, and come from the upper socioeconomic strata of society. More recently, Kotter confirmed these earlier findings (Kotter 1990) and identified four essential prerequisites of an effective leader:

- *drive/energy level*: leaders are self-starters with the ability to persist in spite of obstacles and the stamina to endure long hours.
- *intelligence/intellectual skills*: above-average intelligence is required to go to the heart of a complex situation and set the right direction.
- *mental/emotional health*: this allows a leader to develop good interpersonal skills.
- *integrity*: large numbers of people will only follow someone for a long time if they believe he or she values their well-being.

(Ferguson 1990)

Kotter is not suggesting these basic requirements are sufficient in themselves, but that an individual possessing them could, with training and experiential development, become an effective leader.

Fiedler developed a system for categorizing leaders and identifying the sort of tasks and situations in which they would be most effective (Fiedler 1967). His approach has been repeated a number of times and, while his method of categorizing leaders (by testing their attitude to their least preferred co-workers) is sometimes regarded as idiosyncratic, the model appears to work. However, his model does not indicate ways in which leaders should adapt their behaviour to be more effective, but simply assumes the leader's personal attitudes and characteristics are fixed.

A potentially more fruitful line of enquiry has been developed through researching leadership styles. The underlying assumption to these approaches is that it is more important what leaders do than what they are. Leadership *behaviour* is what counts. Leaders are not born, but can be developed and trained and may deliberately adopt various leaderships strategies. Lewin, Lippitt and White (1939) published the first classification of leadership styles based on their research at the University of Iowa. They identified three separate decision-taking styles:

- *authoritarian*: the leader makes decisions alone and tells subordinates what they must do as a result.
- *democratic*: the leader actively involves subordinates in decisions, shares problems, solicits inputs and shares authority for arriving at decisions.
- *laissez-faire*: the leader avoids taking decisions at all costs and leaves subordinates to make decisions without guidance.

Individuals under democratic leadership were more satisfied, had higher morale, were more creative and more inclined to continue working in the absence of the leader. On the other hand, individuals under authoritarian leadership produced the highest quantity of output. *Laissez-faire* style offered no compensations. Subsequently, researchers at Ohio State University developed an alternative classification based on just two categories of leadership behaviour:

- *consideration*: e.g. friendly, consultative, offering recognition, encouraging open communications, supportive and representative of subordinate interests;
- *initiating structure*: e.g. planning, coordinating, directing, problem solving, clarifying subordinate roles, criticizing bad work and pressuring subordinates to perform more effectively.

Researchers have since found that consideration style produces a higher degree of subordinate satisfaction, but whether this is necessarily allied to higher output has never been resolved. Concurrently with the work at Ohio, researchers at Michigan developed an alternative but similar classification of leadership style:

- *employee-oriented*: concerned with welfare and development of employees, engages in two-way communications, supportive, non-punitive, delegates responsibility and authority to subordinates;
- *production-oriented*: emphasizes planning, goal-setting and meeting schedules, more likely to give explicit instructions, makes use of power, evaluates subordinates and stresses importance of production.

Over the past few decades these ideas have been picked up by Blake and Mouton who derived their widely known 'managerial grid' which seeks to identify managers as to their orientation to task completion or to people (Blake and Mouton 1964). Employee-oriented leadership generates a higher degree of satisfaction among subordinates, but the problem remains that this is not necessarily associated with higher output.

This lack of connection between job satisfaction and productivity might seem on the face of it disappointing. However, all the researches indicate that the jobs that are likely to benefit most directly from the factors that make up job satisfaction (e.g. those which permit of initiative and creativity) are not the most susceptible to having their output measured. The connection between, for example, democratic style and high morale and creativity has been made, and the connection between creativity and real productive contribution may be regarded as extremely likely, though inherently difficult to demonstrate empirically. Moreover, this connection is likely to become more pronounced as the nature of employment changes, becoming more technical and professional in the face of the technological revolution.

The path–goal theory of leadership, based on research by Evans (1970 and 1974), House and Dessler (1974) and House and Mitchell (1974), provides yet a further classification of leadership styles that may be adapted to different circumstances:

- *directive leadership*: gives instructions and guidance, schedules work and sets standards of performance, rules and regulations;

- *supportive leadership*: friendly, supportive leader concerned for well-being of subordinates;
- *participative leadership*: consultative of subordinates, solicitous of suggestions, and takes ideas seriously when reaching decision;
- *achievement-oriented leadership*: emphasizes excellence in performance and expresses confidence in subordinates, sets challenging performance goals and encourages subordinates to accept personal responsibility for performance.

Through a series of diagnostic questions this model seeks to identify the most effecitve leadership style for different management situations. For example, participative leadership is identified as the most effective approach when dealing with a high degree of instability and uncertainty which requires the input from various professional specialists.

While there is a variety of terminology in these leadership studies, there is a clear and close connection between the styles identified and the degree of employee involvement in organizational processes, including decision making. Democratic, participative, supportive, considerate, employee-centred characteristics would all appear to encourage and nurture employee involvement; authoritarian, directive, task-oriented, initiating characteristics, on the other hand, would appear likely to minimize involvement.

Research into the leadership question is still ongoing. Kotter (1990) defines the key roles of leaderhip as:

- setting direction;
- getting everyone lined up together in that direction by consistent communication of the new direction; and
- motivating a commitment to action.

This corroborates several aspects of the competitive model being developed in this book. Setting direction is a key element in winning strategy while Kotter's other two factors are key parts of an achievement culture. Kotter's leadership is thus more pervasive than the previous versions described above. His research takes account of the current revolution in technology and the consequent competitive and organizational change.

> In 1970, in a business environment that was both favourable and changing relatively slowly, sufficient leadership could be supplied by the CEO and several other people. By 1985, in a much tougher and rapidly changing environment, hundreds of individuals, both above and below the plant manager level, were also needed to provide leadership. (Ferguson 1990)

This concept of leadership crystallizes the basic thrust of this chapter. Whereas the word participation implies *participation in decision making*, the word involvement implies *involvement in leadership*. Leadership is not the sole preserve of top management, but requires the involvement of members at all levels of the organization. For a traditional, bureaucratic organization, suited to stable environments, involvement of all levels in leadership would only signal chaos. But, for an enterpreneurial organization, widespread involvement in leadership is a vital ingredient. Without a pervasive involvement in leadership there could be no effective organization through teamwork, and no possibility of making the best use of the intelligence, expertise and commitment of people in achieving the strategic intent.

15.5 Organization through teams

Traditional organizations were caricatured in the description in Chapter 5 of an employee's first day at work (see page 56). The observation of such an organization implies the characteristics advocated by Henri Fayol (1916), Urwick (1947), Brech (1957) and others:

- division of labour
- authority to issue commands
- discipline
- unity of command
- centralization
- span of control, etc.

These are, of course, wholly inappropriate for today's environment. But the problem is what to replace them with. It seems intuitively obvious that every member of the organization has to report to someone and, that being so, it seems difficult to eliminate the old-fashioned 'garden rake' form of organization with all that it implies. Various alternatives have been advocated. Matrix management, in various forms, has had its adherents, but, as Peters and Waterman noted,

> People aren't sure to whom they report for what. The most critical problem, it seems, is that in the name of 'balance' everything is somehow hooked to everything else. The organisation gets paralysed because the structure not only does not make priorities clear, *it automatically dilutes priorities*. In effect it says to people down the line: 'Everything is important; pay equal attention to everything.' The message is paralysing.   (Peters and Waterman 1982:307)

Some organizational solutions are emerging through the application of information technology which can eliminate the necessity for middle management (Drucker 1988). Drucker shares the view that future organization will be based not on a line structure, nor even a matrix, but on project teams, which will operate organically, forming to fulfil specific tasks and solve particular problems and dissolving when their task is complete, to be replaced with other teams to fulfil other roles.

There is nothing new about the creation of temporary, or even permanent, project-based teams. What is new is the extent to which they can become the dominant organizing structure in a highly volatile environment where innovation and change are the norm. Under these circumstances day-to-day maintenance of a stable business unit becomes a relatively simple task and can, to a great extent, be delegated to computers. However, the development and improvement of a business, involving innovation and the management of change, are much more demanding and it is these tasks that are more appropriately taken over by project teams rather than traditional structures.

The top team in any organization is the board of directors. As was noted in Section 7.2, boards are most often dominated by their chief executive officer surrounded by compliant co-directors. Getting the board to operate as a team is by no means straightforward and yet the board's prime responsibilities should be to ensure the development and improvement of the business, not merely to be custodians of shareholder interest reviewing past performance.

Project teams have long been used as the appropriate organizational means for managing major change projects, particularly those involving either substantial capital investments or significant changes in technology. Less frequently they have been formed, generally on a very short-term basis, to seek out the solutions to specific problems. The bringing together of individuals from different functions, with complementary skills and expertise, has been recognized as a source of multidisciplinary synergy, with the potential for creative problem solving which is lacking in traditional functional or departmental structures. However, the potential use of teams goes far beyond major change projects and problem solving. In Section 10.3 it was noted how NEC had formed a 'computing and communications committee' to oversee the development of core competences which were recognized as the key sources of future core products. They also used a network of coordinating groups and teams, which cut across the traditional organizational structure, to ensure that each member of the organization knew and understood the strategic intent.

The NEC experience is duplicated by many organizations both in Japan and elsewhere and could be extended to encompass each of the components of strategy and culture included in this competitive model. They all represent targets for organizational development and improvement and as such lend themselves to a team solution. Organization through teams is the key to involvement in leadership. The job of leadership has been summarized by Adair (1983) as comprising three key roles:

172 THE COMPETITIVE ORGANIZATION

- getting the job done
- building and maintaining the team
- developing the individual

As the competitive organization adopts teams as the dominant organizational form, members of the organization gain experience and expertise in each of the three essential team roles and the team organization provides the vehicle for the leadership training and experience which Kotter noted was such a vital requirement.

The composition of teams, their building and development and their flexible/rotating leadership by expertise is the subject matter of a sister volume by J. Rodney Turner in the Henley Management Series. For the present purpose it is sufficient to note that they are increasingly used as the solution to the competitive organization's problem of structure and that they provide an exciting means of engaging the involvement of people in achieving an organization's strategic intent.

15.6 Summary

- The 'basic organizational management problem' is how to engage people's involvement in and commitment to the organization's strategic intent.
- The traditional management perspective on industrial organization assumes there is one source of authority and one focus of loyalty. This is widely acknowledged to be just wishful thinking.
- A firm is made up of sectional groups with divergent interests.
- Some organization members will seek only a limited calculative psychological contract, having personal priorities that they satisfy away from work. The expectation that all members will be motivated by recognition and increased responsibility is therefore unlikely to be realized.
- Two ways of categorizing approaches to people management are individualism and collectivism. Individualism is the extent to which the firm gives credence to the feelings and sentiments of individual employees and seeks to develop and encourage them. Collectivism concerns the extent to which the organization recognizes the right of employees to have a say in those aspects of management decision making that concern them.
- Participation is a measure of the degree to which members of a social system participate in the decision-making process. Member acceptance of, and satisfaction with, decisions increases as member participation in those decisions increases.
- The participative Japanese approach increases understanding of issues

and identifies how best to handle them, and also becomes a means of communication among members.
- Western practice still generally emphasizes decision making as an essentially top management role and focuses considerable attention on the task of leadership.
- Kotter identified four essential prerequisites of an effective leader: drive/energy level; intelligence/intellectual skills; mental/emotional health; and integrity.
- Democratic, participative, supportive, considerate, employee-centred leadership characteristics would all appear to encourage and nurture employee involvement; authoritarian, directive, task-oriented, initiating characteristics, on the other hand, would appear likely to minimize involvement.
- Involvement implies involvement *in leadership*. Leadership is not the sole preserve of top management, but requires the involvement of members at all levels of the organization. The most effective way to achieve this is through project teams, a likely future organizational norm. Teams operate organically, forming to fulfil specific tasks and solve particular problems and dissolving when their task is complete.
- Project teams, their composition, building and development and their flexible/rotating leadership by expertise, provide an exciting vehicle for leadership training and experience.

References

Adair, J., *Effective Leadership*, Gower, London, 1983.
Bailey, J., *Job Design and Work Organization*, Prentice-Hall, Englewood Cliffs, 1983.
Blake, R. R. and J. S. Mouton, *Managing Group Conflict in Industry*, Gulf Publishing Company, 1964.
Brech, E. F. L., *Organization: The Framework of Management*, Longman, Harlow, 1957.
Drucker, P. F., 'The coming of the new organization', *Harvard Business Review*, Jan–Feb 1988.
Evans, M. G., 'The effects of supervisory behaviour on the path goal relationship', *Organisational Behaviour and Human Performance*, No. 5, 1970.
Evans, M. G., 'Extensions of a path goal theory of motivation', *Journal of Applied Psychology* 59, 1974.
Fayol, H., *General and Industrial Management*, Pitman, London, 1949. (Translated by C. Storrs from the original French *Administration Industrielle et Générale*, (1916).)
Fiedler, F. E., *A Theory of Leadership Effectiveness*, McGraw-Hill, New York, 1967.
Ferguson, A., 'The myth of leadership dismantled', *The Independent on Sunday*, 10 June 1990.

Fox, A., 'Industrial Sociology and Industrial Relations', Royal Commission on Trade Unions and Employers' Associations, Research Paper 3, HMSO, 1966.

House, R. J., and G. Dessler, 'The path goal theory of leadership: some post hoc and a priori tests' in J. G. Hunt and L. L. Larson (eds) *Contingency Approaches to Leadership*, Southern Illinois University Press, 1974.

House, R. J. and T. R. Mitchell, 'Path goal theory of leadership', *Journal of Contemporary Business*, Autumn 1974, 3:91–8.

Kotter, J. P., *A Force for Change: How Leadership Differs from Management*, Macmillan, New York, 1990.

Lewin, K., R. Lippitt and R. K. White, 'Patterns of aggressive behaviour in experimentally created "social climates"', *Journal of Social Psychology*, No. 10, 1939.

Peters, T. and R. H. Waterman, *In Search of Excellence*, Harper & Row, New York, 1982.

Purcell, J., 'Mapping management styles in employee relations', *Journal of Management Studies*, September 1987.

Stogdill, R. M., 'Personal factors associated with leadership: a survey of the literature', *Journal of Psychology*, No. 25, 1948.

Stogdill, R. M., *Handbook of Leadership: a survey of theory and research*, Free Press, New York, 1974.

Urwick, L. F., *The Elements of Administration*, Pitman, London, 1947.

16
Motivating commitment

16.1 Introduction

The pluralist view of organization suggests that Theory X and Theory Y are not necessarily mutually exclusive, but may coexist in the same organization, not necessarily as sets of managerial assumptions but as crude approximations to the way people may actually behave at work. Theory X assumes that people at work tend to be feckless, idle and wholly self-interested. Theory Y suggests they have an almost infinite potential for commitment and dedication to the achievement of corporate aims. The expression of these assumptions is loaded with unnecessary value judgements about the nature of people as employees. The reality is that some of the people, some of the time, appear to behave in accordance with Theory X, while at other times they appear to accord with Theory Y. Which tendency is dominant no doubt depends on many factors, including perhaps the history of employee relations in the organization, and also on individual psychological contracts. Some people, who may be highly intelligent and skilled, are fundamentally uninterested in organizational aims; others, who may be of limited experience and aptitude, may dedicate 100 per cent of their finite capability to the achievement of strategic aims. Management's job is to try to ensure that all the people contribute to organizational aims as fully as is feasible.

Involvement in leadership is one step in this direction, with the next being to motivate members to a commitment to the organization's strategic intent. Behavioural scientists and practitioners have spent a great deal of time and effort investigating what it is that motivates people at work, and there is sufficient knowledge to develop a simple working model. As with everything else in management it has to be admitted that there is no one best way that will serve to guide the motivation of all people in all situations. Nevertheless, there is sufficient to be able to focus on just a few key elements that may be useful in gaining the commitment of tomorrow's higher skilled, more technical and better educated employees.

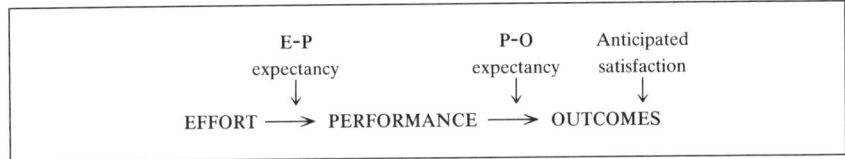

Figure 16.1 Expectancy theory

16.2 The mechanics of motivation

Motivation is the driving force that arouses and directs action towards the achievement of a desired goal. It is based on a person's expectations, first that their actions will have certain anticipated outcomes and, second, that certain anticipated levels of satisfaction or dissatisfaction will be experienced as result of these outcomes. A model of this kind of cause and effect was described by Vroom (1964) and Lawler (1973).

Figure 16.1 shows a simple expectancy model of this kind. The individual inputs a certain effort and expects as a result to achieve a certain level of performance. This performance expectancy can be expressed as the subjective probability that if one puts effort in then a certain level of performance will be achieved.

The second expectancy in this model refers to a person's beliefs that certain outcomes will result on the achievement of those levels of performance. The outcomes may be intrinsic or extrinsic. Intrinsic outcomes are those which are personal and not dependant on the organization, e.g. feelings of competence, personal accomplishment and satisfaction. Extrinsic outcomes are those which depend on the organization or other individuals within the organization, e.g. pay, promotions, verbal praise, etc.

The final component in this model is the amount of satisfaction or dissatisfaction that a person *anticipates* will be experienced when an outcome is attained. It is the anticipation that is crucial, rather than the actuality, because it is the anticipated outcome that motivates.

All three components of the model (E-P expectancy, P-O expectancy and anticipated satisfaction) must be present for motivation to be achieved. If any component is absent a link in the model will be broken and there will be no motivation. Research (e.g. Mitchell 1974; Campbell and Pritchard 1976) has tended to confirm that all three components are positively and significantly related to motivation and performance.

While the model is simple and may seem obvious, it has some pertinent practical implications suggesting that management should clarify and emphasize the connection between effort and performance. In many organizations this connection is not clearly perceived because individuals are unaware of the organization's strategic intent and where their efforts should best be concentrated. Management should also clarify and emphasize the connection between performance and desirable outcomes, so that everyone accurately perceives what these connections are. Finally, the organization needs to employ outcomes, or rewards, that are highly valued by employees.

The practical application of an expectancy model such as that outlined above can be completetly invalidated if it is done in a way that is perceived as unfair. The motivation of people in an organization is influenced by the extent to which they feel they are being treated in a fair and equitable manner. When they feel they are being treated unfairly they are likely to engage in activities, many of which may be against the organization's best interests, aimed at restoring feelings of equity (Adams 1965).

Equity is perceived as a result of two comparisons, which may well be made at a subconscious level. The first comparison is between an individual's inputs and the resultant outcomes. Inputs would include a person's education, training, experience, time and effort; outcomes would include pay, promotion, praise, recognition, friendship and feelings of personal achievement. The second comparison is between the individual's ratio of inputs to outcomes with a perceived other person's ratio. It is not specified who the other person is; it might be a colleague, a boss, or even some theoretical construct. If the individual's ratio is less than the other's then he or she will feel unfairly treated. If it is greater it may make them feel guilty or uncomfortable.

This may seem a rather mechanical way of repeating that the employer/employee relationship must be based on a high level of integrity, if employees are to be motivated to a commitment to organizational aims. More specifically, lack of perceived equity may produce various behaviours aimed at improving the equity ratio. This can be done by altering either the level of inputs or the outcomes. For example:

– altering inputs, e.g. reducing effort, or informally imposing restrictions on outputs of others, or even a whole work group;
– altering outcomes, e.g. those paid on piecework, could increase output by reducing quality;
– avoidance of the situation, e.g. by the individual seeking a job move either out of the department where the ratio applies, or out of the organization altogether.

Much of the evolving theoretical and empirical work on motivation emphasizes the importance of the relationship, first, between effort and performance and, second, between performance and reward. To be motivated, individuals must first perceive that there is a direct connection between their own efforts and a certain level of performance; they must also perceive that achievement of that level of performance will result in the rewards they desire; and they must also perceive that these relationships are fair and equitable.

The critical management roles in motivation are therefore:

- providing subordinates with just rewards;
- making the rewards contingent on achieving certain performance goals;
- helping subordinates to obtain the rewards by enabling them to understand exactly what they must do to obtain the rewards (House and Mitchell 1974).

A crucial aspect of this explanation of the mechanics of motivation is understanding what it is that constitutes a reward, i.e. what outcomes are highly prized by organization members.

16.3 Intrinsic human needs

Highly prized outcomes are those which satisfy intrinsic human needs. Understanding these needs and how different needs may be salient in different situations for different individuals may show how individuals will change their behaviour in order to satisfy salient needs.

Maslow's name has long been associated with the theory of human needs although, like Herzberg, he has attracted criticism for the unscientific method of his research. Maslow's hierarchy of needs starts with physiological needs (food, sleep, sex, etc.) at the lowest level, rises through safety needs, love needs, esteem needs and finally, at the top level, the need for self-actualization (Maslow 1943). His model suggested that needs had to be satisfied strictly in order, progressing up the hierarchy. Thus physiological needs must be satisfied first. When they are satisfied safety needs become salient. When these are in turn satisfied love needs become operative, and so forth. If at any time a lower level need ceases to be satisfied, it becomes dominant, or prepotent. As soon as it is again satisfied it ceases to motivate.

The model is simple to understand and seems plausible common sense as well as good theory. However, there is no empirical evidence of the five layers of needs, nor of how people move from one layer to another.

Other approaches may be less elegant, but may get nearer the truth. Murray's original work in the 1930s (Murray 1938), later enhanced by McClelland (McClelland *et al.* 1953) and Atkinson (1964), suggested there were more than twenty intrinsic human needs, any of which might be potent at any one time. There was no evidence of any hierarchy and no structured progression from one need to the next. They suggested that needs were primarily learned, rather than inherited, and they tended to be activated by external cues in the environment. This picture of human needs is clearly much less structured than Maslow's. It offers a diversity and flexibility of needs that looks messy, but which may be realistic.

Not all the intrinsic needs in McClelland's model are of equal importance. Most attention has been focused on just three needs: the need for affiliation, for achievement and for power. Empirical work on these three suggests they can be useful in identifying individuals who will find different types of situations differentially motivating, so the theory has found frequent application in the design of tests used in selection and recruitment.

Needs for achievement and affiliation appear to have wider application, but the power motive may have little relevance beyond this context. While there is evidence that the need for power has a strong motivational effect in certain individuals, there is no evidence to suggest that a strong need for power is any indicator of effectiveness as a leader. There are many examples of individuals who appear to derive satisfaction from the exercise of power for itself, rather than in the service of some other achievement. Such individuals are eminently unsuited to any involvement in leadership in todays's rapidly changing environments.

Alderfer produced a simplified model suggesting just three basic human needs: existence, relatedness and growth (Alderfer 1972). Existence can be taken as similar to Maslow's physiological and safety needs. Relatedness is similar to Maslow's love and esteem needs and also to McClelland's need for affiliation. Alderfer's growth need is equivalent to Maslow's self-actualization and McClelland's needs for achievement.

Thus it may be possible to draw out some consensus, in the most general terms, from these various theoreticians that there are perhaps three relevant groups of human needs which might motivate behaviour:

– *basic needs*: existence, physiological, safety, etc.
– *social needs*: love, esteem, affiliation, relatedness, etc.
– *growth needs*: achievement, self-actualization, etc.

There is no suggestion that these needs have a hierarchical arrangement of the sort proposed by Maslow. The only further assertion that can be made is the simple statement that a satisfied need is not a motivator of behaviour. Thus, if basic needs are satisfied, motivational systems will only be effective if they offer satisfaction of one or both of the other two needs. Furthermore, it seems probable that social needs are generally likely to fall into the category of what Herzberg called hygiene factors, with growth needs being the real motivators. Management's job then would be to ensure that work provides opportunities to satisfy social needs, but that, beyond this, motivation is achieved through opportunities to grow and achieve.

This conclusion, that people are posivitely motivated only by growth needs, contrasts starkly with earlier, carrot and stick approaches to motivation. As McGregor pointed out:

> the carrot and stick method of motivation works reasonably well under certain circumstances. The *means* of satisfying a man's physiological and, within limits, his safety needs can be provided or withheld by management. Employment itself is such a means, and so are wages, working conditions and benefits. By these means the individual can be controlled so long as he is struggling for subsistence. Man lives by bread alone when there is no bread. But the carrot and stick theory does not work at all once man has reached an adequate subsistence level and is motivated primarily by higher needs.
>
> (McGregor 1960:41)

If this was pertinent in 1960, it is probably much more pertinent now when living standards have improved so much further. It is sometimes argued that the higher levels of unemployment that have recently emerged are revitalizing the carrot and stick. This may be true for the unemployed, but the basic needs for the vast majority of those at work have probably long been satisfied, and will probably remain so.

Herzberg identified positively motivating factors as including achievement, recognition of achievement, work itself, responsibility and advancement. Herzberg had actually found that pay and working conditions, along with company policy and administration, technical supervision and interpersonal relations with one's supervisor, were ineffective as motivators, but could be the source of serious job dissatisfaction and therefore demotivation (Herzberg, Mausner and Snyderman 1959). Herzberg's research has received some criticism over the years because of the potentially unreliable method he used and the fact that the findings have rarely been accurately replicated. Nevertheless, his factors are consistent with the other theoretical contributions to motivation at work.

As McGregor noted, low-level needs (survival, safety or existence needs) are no longer operative in a work situation. Moreover, social needs are not relevant as motivators at work, though they may be hygiene factors as Herzberg suggested. So growth needs are the only ones likely to be operative as a basis for rewards in an expectancy model of motivation as described above. A practical approach to motivation has to take account both of individuals with strong growth needs, i.e. those who have a cooperative psychological contract with the organization, and also those with low growth needs, i.e. individuals who may have, or desire to have, a calculative contract. Management needs to design rewards (outcomes for achieved performance) that would be prized by both groups of individuals.

16.4 Rewards for work

Individuals with strong growth needs are most productive in jobs that generate high levels of internal work motivation. Hackman and Oldham in their 'job characteristics' model (Hackman and Oldham 1980) suggested that such jobs need to enable individuals to feel:

- that the work itself is meaningful (i.e. *meaningfulness*);
- that they are responsible for the outcomes of the work (i.e. *autonomy*); and
- that they are fully aware of the results of the work activities (i.e. *feedback*).

By meaningfulness was meant that the job embodied variety, identity and significance. Variety meant that the job comprised a variety of tasks requiring a number of different skills and talents. Identity meant that the job required completion of a whole, identifiable piece of work. By significance was meant that the job was perceived as having a substantial impact on the lives of other people (Hackman and Oldham 1980:78–9). By autonomy was meant the degree to which the job provides substantial freedom, independence and discretion to the individual in scheduling the work and in determining the procedures to be used in carrying it out (Hackman and Oldham 1980:79). By feedback was meant the degree to which carrying out the work gave the individual direct and clear information about the effectivenes of his or her performance (Hackman and Oldham 1980:80).

So long as the social needs/hygiene factors are satisfactory, and so long as the individual has the required knowledge and skill to do the job, then the outcomes for an individual with high growth needs performing a job which provides meaningfulness, autonomy and feedback are:

- high internal work motivation
- high 'growth' satisfaction
- high general job satisfaction
- high work effectiveness

The resulting intrinsic rewards for an individual with high growth needs are feelings of personal competence, personal accomplishment, personal growth and development, personal responsibility and autonomy. Thus a virtuous cycle is achieved. It is important to note that, in these happy circumstances, the addition of extrinsic rewards such as pay through a payment-by-results scheme, or explicit praise for a job well done, may have a negative impact on the motivational power of intrinsic rewards (Staw 1975). For example, praising an individual who is intrinsically motivated may be perceived as patronizing and be wholly counterproductive. Care must therefore be taken in the provision of extrinsic rewards that they are compatible with the intrinsic rewards and do not undermine the meaningfulness, autonomy or feedback embodied in the work.

Those with weak growth needs, who may have, or desire to have, a calculative psychological contract, are likely to be more effectively motivated through extrinsic rewards such as pay, promotion, fringe benefits, recognition and praise by status symbols, special awards and certificates. Extrinsic reward systems are required first to satisfy basic *hygiene* requirements. For example, they should satisfy an individual's existence needs, i.e. provide for food, shelter, safety and security; second, basic rewards should compare satisfactorily with rewards obtainable in other comparable organizations; and, third, rewards should be seen to be distributed equitably within the organization. These basic requirements do not serve to motivate, but their absence would serve to inhibit the motivational power of extrinsic rewards.

Beyond this, reward systems also serve to attract and retain the members required and also to motivate their work performance. A review of reward systems is beyond the present scope, but the expectancy model already described shows how rewards can facilitate effective performance when organization members perceive that effective performance results in the receipt of valued rewards within a reasonable period of time.

16.5 Ownership

Participation in ownership combines the possibility of both intrinsic and extrinsic rewards. Thus, an organization that offers employees participation in ownership may gain the commitment of individuals whether they have strong or weak growth needs. A slice of the action, no matter how small, provides an identification with the strategic interests of the organization that is difficult to create in any other way. Ownership is not only a way of motivating by combining intrinsic and extrinsic rewards, but it also gets back to the heart of entrepreneurialism. The entrepreneur's motivation is not simply to make a quick fortune, but to build a business of substance. Personal ownership is an important underpinning but the problem remains, as suggested in Chapter 1, 'how to recreate this personal "ownership", which is embedded in the entrepreneurial situation, within a multi-product business or multi-business corporation'.

Making arrangements for participation in the results of ownership can be done through schemes for profit sharing or share options or bonuses. These can be highly valued by members. For example, about 35 000 Marks & Spencer staff own shares in their company and hardly any of them sell their shares. Some 4000 Allied-Lyons employees have taken up share options in their company and when their options mature the majority of employees hold on to at least some of their shares. Many thousands of Sainsbury's employees are shareholders and some shop-floor staff have holdings worth more than £15 000. The private shoe manufacturers and retailers, Clark's, opened an employee share scheme in the late 1970s with the idea that anyone who spends their career with the firm would end up with shares 'roughly worth the house they are living in' (Goldsmith and Clutterbuck 1985).

Participation in ownership can, of course, go much further than this to the point where employees may own a controlling share of the company or even 100 per cent. Some of these have been highly successful, though there have also been some notable failures. Some of the most noteworthy failures, however, were fundamentally insolvent companies that were floated for party political reasons. Nevertheless, it is apparent that co-ownership schemes are by no means guaranteed success. Formal participation in ownership, without the other aspects of entrepreneurial organization, will be unlikely to motivate people to a commitment to the organization's strategic aims. However, it may be an extremely powerful final piece in the entrepreneurial organization that has already defined a winning strategy and an achievement culture.

16.6 Summary

- Theory X and Theory Y are not necessarily mutually exclusive, but may coexist in the same organization as crude approximations to the way people may actually behave at work.
- Management's job is to try to ensure that all the people contribute to organizational aims as fully as is feasible.
- Motivation is based on a person's expectations, first that their actions will have certain anticipated outcomes and, second, that certain anticipated levels of satisfaction or dissatisfaction will be experienced as a result of these outcomes. This is called the expectancy model.
- The practical application of an expectancy model can be completely invalidated if it is done in a way that is perceived as unfair.
- The critical management roles in motivation are: providing subordinates with just rewards; making the rewards contingent on achieving certain performance goals; and helping subordinates obtain the rewards.
- Highly prized outcomes are those which satisfy intrinsic human needs.
- There are three relevant groups of human needs that might motivate behaviour – basic needs, social needs and growth needs – but growth needs are the only ones likely to be operative at work as a basis for rewards.
- Those with strong growth needs are most productive in jobs that generate high levels of internal work motivation. Such jobs need to

enable individuals to experience *meaningfulness*, *autonomy* and *feedback*.
- The resulting intrinsic rewards for an individual with high growth needs are feelings of personal competence, personal accomplishment, personal growth and development, personal responsibility and autonomy.
- Those with weak growth needs are likely to be more effectively motivated through extrinsic rewards such as pay, promotion, fringe benefits, recognition and praise by status symbols, special awards and certificates.
- Participation in ownership combines the possibility of both intrinsic and extrinsic rewards. It can have a powerful influence although it will be unlikely to motivate people without the other aspects of the competitive organization.

References

Adams, J. S., 'Injustice in Social Exchange' in L. Berkowitz (ed.) *Advances in Experimental Social Psychology*, Vol. 2, Academic Press, New York, 1965:265–99.

Alderfer, C. P., *Existence, Relatedness and Growth*, Free Press, New York, 1972.

Atkinson, J. W., *An Introduction to Motivation*, Van Nostrand, New York, 1964.

Campbell, J. P. and R. D. Pritchard, 'Motivation Theory in Industrial and Organizational Psychology' in M. D. Dunnette (ed.) *Handbook of Industrial and Organizational Psychology*, Rand McNally, Chicago, 1976.

Goldsmith, W. and D. Clutterbuck, *The Winning Streak*, Penguin, Harmondsworth, 1985:123.

Hackman J. R. and G. R. Oldham, *Work Redesign*, Addison Wesley, Reading, Mass., 1980.

Herzberg, F., B. Mausner and B. B. Snyderman, *The Motivation to Work*, Wiley, New York, 1959.

House, R. J. and T. R. Mitchell, 'Path goal theory of leadership', *Journal of Contemporary Business*, Autumn 1974, 3:91–8.

Lawler, E. E. III, *Motivation in Work Organizations*, Brooks/Cole, Monterey, Calif., 1973.

McClelland, D. C., J. W. Atkinson, R. A. Clark and E. L. Lowell, *The Achievement Motive*, Van Nostrand, New York, 1953.

McGregor, D. M., *The Human Side of Enterprise*, McGraw-Hill, New York, 1960.

Maslow, A., 'A theory of human motivation', *Psychological Review*, Vol. 50, 1943.

Mitchell, T. R., 'Expectancy models of job satisfaction, occupational preference, and effort: a theoretical, methodological and empirical appraisal', *Psychological Bulletin*, 1974, 81:1096–112.

Murray, H. A., *Explorations in Personality*, Oxford University Press, New York, 1938.

Staw, B. M., *Intrinsic and Extrinsic Motivation*, General Learning Press, Morristown, NJ., 1975.

Vroom, V. H., *Work and Motivation*, Wiley, New York, 1964.

17
Plotting the culture profile

17.1 Introduction

This chapter draws together the four main components of culture, which is the second dimension of the competitive model. The different elements of culture have been discussed as though they were quite separate and discrete. However, just as with the components of strategy, it is clear that they intertwine and overlap to form a more or less seamless web. The empowerment of people, integrity, involvement and commitment to the organization cannot be separated in the work situation, but are just different aspects of the organization's character or culture.

The foundation of culture is the management philosophy, which may be oriented, on the one hand, to empowerment or, on the other, to control. It is not simply a style of management that can be put on or discarded as the situation demands, but is bone deep and constant. An empowering philosophy is one of the fundamental beliefs by which the organization is managed. Also permeating every aspect of the organization's activities, and particularly its various relations with the outside world, is the level of corporate integrity. That too is bone deep, not simply a tool that can be used when needed and disposed of when inconvenient. These two, empowerment and integrity, influence every aspect of organizational life and activity. Involvement in leadership and motivation to commitment are the two main ways of engaging the intelligence, talents, knowledge and skills of the people who are empowered, so that they make the best feasible contribution to the achievement of strategic aims.

These various culture components complement each other and develop into a business orientation that forms the basis of strategy. If any factor is weak, it may result in weakness in others. Similarly, a strength in one would serve to reinforce the other, complementary, factors. While each factor is discussed separately, this interdependence and relatedness should be recognized.

The questionnaire at the end of this chapter enables a business to

186 THE COMPETITIVE ORGANIZATION

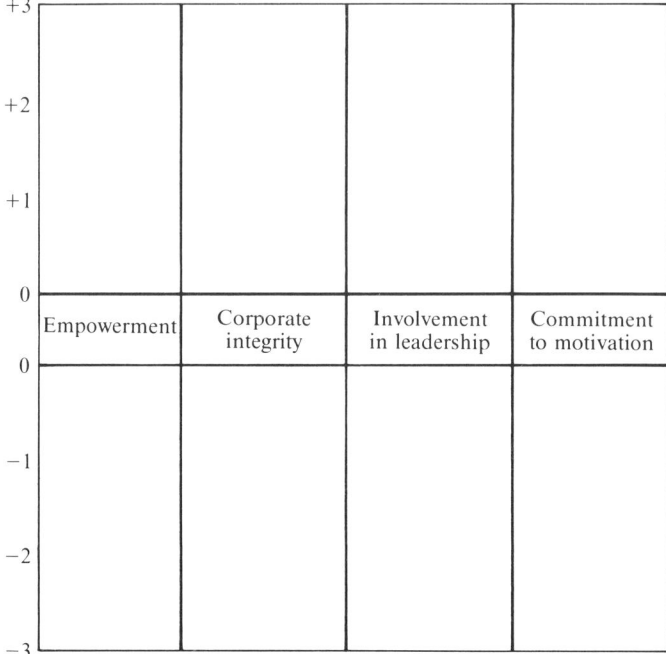

Figure 17.1 The culture profile

identify its relative strength on each factor and so identify its culture profile. As with the strategy profile described in Chapter 12, this serves two purposes: It helps the business to identify particular problems that are highlighted directly from analysing the responses to the various factors; and it enables a business to locate its position on this second dimension of the competitive matrix. Both these purposes are explained below.

17.2 The components of culture

The four components of culture have been identified as:

1. Empowerment
2. Corporate integrity
3. Involvement in leadership
4. Motivation to commitment

Completion of the culture profile questionnaire in Section 17.4 below will generate average scores of between -3 and $+3$ which can then be plotted on the culture profile chart (see Figure 17.1). In addition, an overall average culture score can be calculated which is used to locate the business in the competitive matrix as outlined in Part Four.

A competitive organization should achieve a culture profile that is fairly even across all four characteristics, just as with the strategy profile already discussed. A profile with one or more scores substantially out of line with the others, i.e. an uneven profile, suggests areas for management attention. Investigation of such inconsistent results should begin with a detailed examination of answers to the assessments to determine which aspects have produced the low score. In most industries, a competitive organization should expect to score around +1.5 or more on the culture profile. Significantly lower scores may be the norm in mature industries, or in firms that appear to be operating in a quiet competition-free area and are less affected by the rapid rate of technological development, but such organizations will be extremely vulnerable to change when it occurs. Few sectors will escape the impacts of the current revolution in technology.

17.3 Assessing the culture profile of your business

To assess how effective your organization is in terms of its culture, members should be asked to consider the truth of statements 13.1 to 16.10 as they apply to your organization. The statements are numbered according to the chapters containing the subject matter to which they refer, i.e. statements 13.1 to 13.10 are concerned with empowerment; statements 14.1 to 14.10 refer to corporate integrity, and so on.

The truth of the statements is scored in the range from -3 to $+3$ as indicated below each statement. This quantitative scaling of responses enables scores to be aggregated and averaged. Again, as with the treatment of strategy, responding members should be grouped hierarchically and functionally and their answers analysed accordingly, so that differences in the perceptions of different groups can be identified.

If the overall average score for any of the culture components is negative, then the organization management clearly needs to consider a programme of remedial action. The starting point for this would be an analysis of scores for the individual statements. These should be examined and those with the most negative scores considered in detail. For example, an overall negative score on 'involvement in leadership' may arise even though the organization is managed on the basis of an empowering philosophy and with high corporate integrity, because there are no explicit structures that directly involve members in any leadership situations. Being well intentioned is not enough. Management must take overt, sometimes courageous, steps that lead to organization through teams that directly involve the widest number of members in leadership experience.

A negative overall score may arise because organization members perceive that team working is more a matter of lip service than reality, and that the freedom to make mistakes, for example, does not really exist. This perception may be the result of a particular instance of a mistake being punished in a way that has become symbolically important. A management action plan would therefore be appropriate, to instigate teams with real decision-making power, and to highlight their functions in some symbolically suitable fashion.

Any individual statement that attracts a negative average score needs further investigation into the causes and the possible remedies.

The comparison of perceptions of different groups, particularly hierarchical groups, may be particularly pertinent to the culture profile of an organization. There are often fundamental differences that become apparent when comparing a top management group with a group of sharp end operatives. What may be regarded as highly positive by senior people, may be the source of great frustration, even alienation, at lower levels. Such differences may immediately suggest possible remedial actions. However, the indications should not be regarded as definitive. They suggest areas and aspects that may be problematic and warrant further investigation. The strengths and weaknesses in the profile that the survey highlights may support or confirm prior suspicions and, thus, appear to confirm the need for immediate management action. This may be correct, but it is nevertheless sensible to proceed with caution, investigate further where necessary, and then confirm and agree the proposed management action.

The interpretation of scores mirrors the approach already described for the strategy profile. The simple distinction between positive and negative scores locates the organization on one side of the matrix or the other, but the assessment needs to be much more detailed than this. A competitive organization with a thoroughly progressive culture will score around +1.5 or more and in the newer, high technology and professional service industries, but this may not be a sufficiently high score to ensure they remain competitive. A score well in excess of 2 may be required.

The scores achieved need to be examined at various levels in order to recognize the full implications. The subject matter of each individual question clearly identifies particular issues. The scores for each factor as a whole are important because they carry implications for management action that may be expressed in terms of improvements to management systems, required training and education, etc. The overall profile score identifies the organization's position on the competitive matrix as described in Part Four. At each of these levels, the data extracted from the questionnaire can be used to identify the management action required to improve the score on the individual question and factor, the overall profile and matrix position.

17.4 Culture profile questionnaire

Read the following statements and score each one according to how true you feel it is of your organization. Answer according to the following 7-stage rating scale:

1. completely true
2. mainly true
3. slightly true
4. 50% true : 50% untrue
5. slightly untrue
6. mainly untrue
7. completely untrue

Score by ringing your answer, totalling the scores for all questions and calculating your average score.

Empowerment

13.1. Management generally regard employees as responsible and treat them with respect.
Completely true +3 +2 +1 0 −1 −2 −3 Completely untrue
13.2. Management and work-force cooperate well and work as a team.
Completely true +3 +2 +1 0 −1 −2 −3 Completely untrue
13.3. The company is always prepared to pay for an employee's further training.
Completely true +3 +2 +1 0 1 −2 −3 Completely untrue
13.4. Management puts great effort into communicating with employees so that everyone knows what is going on.
Completely true +3 +2 +1 0 −1 −2 −3 Completely untrue
13.5. Top management's main task is to keep control over how people do their work.
Completely true −3 −2 −1 0 +1 +2 +3 Completely untrue
13.6. If a member of the organization performed badly on any aspect of their job, they would be genuinely helped to improve their performance.
Completely true +3 +2 +1 0 −1 −2 −3 Completely untrue
13.7. Management realize the future of the organization depends on its people, so employees are helped to realize their full potential.
Completely true +3 +2 +1 0 −1 −2 −3 Completely untrue
13.8. Senior people always address employees by their first name and expect to be addressed in the same way in return.
Completely true +3 +2 +1 0 −1 −2 −3 Completely untrue

190 THE COMPETITIVE ORGANIZATION

13.9. Great importance is attached to seniority and many special privileges are enjoyed by the top people.
Completely true −3 −2 −1 0 +1 +2 +3 Completely untrue
13.10. Different departments (e.g. sales and production) communicate closely with each other, not just through department managers.
Completely true +3 +2 +1 0 −1 −2 −3 Completely untrue

Total score: _____   *Average score*: _____

Corporate integrity

14.1. Everyone has an equal opportunity to get on – there is no favouritism.
Completely true +3 +2 +1 0 −1 −2 −3 Completely untrue
14.2. The company is always honest and fair with its customers and suppliers.
Completely true +3 +2 +1 0 −1 −2 −3 Completely untrue
14.3. The company's products are the best in their field.
Completely true +3 +2 +1 0 −1 −2 −3 Completely untrue
14.4. The company takes great care to make sure it does not damage the environment.
Completely true +3 +2 +1 0 −1 −2 −3 Completely untrue
14.5. The company makes a deliberate and positive contribution to the local community.
Completely true +3 +2 +1 0 −1 −2 −3 Completely untrue
14.6. The company is a good and fair employer.
Completely true +3 +2 +1 0 −1 −2 −3 Completely untrue
14.7. We have a formal arrangement (e.g. a regularly meeting committee, working party, formal report, etc.) for the explicit review and reporting of ethical performance.
Completely true +3 +2 +1 0 −1 −2 −3 Completely untrue
14.8. We have a reputation for being the leader in terms of quality.
Completely true +3 +2 +1 0 −1 −2 −3 Completely untrue
14.9. The company would never get involved in any dubious financial dealings with the City (e.g. as Guinness did).
Completely true +3 +2 +1 0 −1 −2 −3 Completely untrue
14.10. The organization has an excellent reputation for ethical behaviour and is very careful to ensure that this reputation is upheld at all times.
Completely true +3 +2 +1 0 −1 −2 −3 Completely untrue

Total score: _____   *Average score*: _____

Involvement in leadership

15.1. Employees have a real opportunity to influence decisions that affect them personally.
Completely true +3 +2 +1 0 −1 −2 −3 Completely untrue

15.2. Staff development is clearly regarded as one of management's main responsibilities.
Completely true +3 +2 +1 0 −1 −2 −3 Completely untrue

15.3. People are encouraged to use their own initiative.
Completely true +3 +2 +1 0 −1 −2 −3 Completely untrue

15.4. People other than just the chief executive are involved in taking important decisions.
Completely true +3 +2 +1 0 −1 −2 −3 Completely untrue

15.5. An employee who had made an expensive mistake would be encouraged to try again, rather than being reprimanded.
Completely true +3 +2 +1 0 −1 −2 −3 Completely untrue

15.6. People in offices and on the shop floor often voice their ideas and suggestions for improving the business directly to top management.
Completely true +3 +2 +1 0 −1 −2 −3 Completely untrue

15.7. Management delegate significant decisions as far down the organizations as possible.
Completely true +3 +2 +1 0 −1 −2 −3 Completely untrue

15.8. There is plenty of opportunity to talk informally to senior management, no matter how junior you are.
Completely true +3 +2 +1 0 −1 −2 −3 Completely untrue

15.9. As much as half or more of most people's time is spent working in a special project team rather than on routine departmental work.
Completely true +3 +2 +1 0 −1 −2 −3 Completely untrue

15.10. People from the lowest levels of the organization may be involved in projects where they contribute to major decisions.
Completely true +3 +2 +1 0 −1 −2 −3 Completely untrue

Total score: _____   *Average score*: _____

Motivation to commitment

16.1. Employees' achievements are always recognized.
Completely true +3 +2 +1 0 −1 −2 −3 Completely untrue

16.2. Most employees do work which is itself satisfying.
Completely true +3 +2 +1 0 −1 −2 −3 Completely untrue

16.3. Employees are regularly given the chance of taking on significant responsibility.
Completely true +3 +2 +1 0 −1 −2 −3 Completely untrue

16.4. Management ensures that members' efforts are always rewarded.
Completely true +3 +2 +1 0 −1 −2 −3 Completely untrue
16.5. Promotions are made on merit, according to skills and effort.
Completely true +3 +2 +1 0 −1 −2 −3 Completely untrue
16.6. The company's salaries and wages are as good as any in the industry/locality.
Completely true +3 +2 +1 0 −1 −2 −3 Completely untrue
16.7. Employees generally enjoy their work and make good friends among their colleagues.
Completely true +3 +2 +1 0 −1 −2 −3 Completely untrue
16.8. Employees are made aware of how they are performing whether it's good or bad.
Completely true +3 +2 +1 0 −1 −2 −3 Completely untrue
16.9. Management's main role is helping and supporting others.
Completely true +3 +2 +1 0 −1 −2 −3 Completely untrue
16.10. We operate a scheme (e.g. profit sharing, share options, etc.) that allows members to participate in ownership of the organization.
Completely true +3 +2 +1 0 −1 −2 −3 Completely untrue

Total score: _____   *Average score*: _____

Overall average culture score: _____

PART FOUR
ACHIEVING THE COMPETITIVE ORGANIZATION

The five components of strategy are concerned with knowing what you want to achieve and how to achieve it. This is the first requirement of the competitive organization. Converting the strategy into action is concerned with people and their work in a progressive culture. The four components of culture are concerned with engaging the intelligence, expertise and commitment of people in achieving the organization's strategic aims. This is the second requirement of the competitive organization. A winning strategy will not be successful without an appropriate culture. One without the other is unlikely to be successful for long, but a lot of research, already quoted, has indicated that the two in combination are extremely powerful.

The questionnaires at the end of Parts Two and Three provide a simple way of seeing how your organization measures up in terms of the most important aspects of the strategy and culture profiles as outlined in Chapters 12 and 17. These two profiles are now brought together as the two dimensions of the competitive matrix outlined in the opening chapter. The matrix, which is repeated in Figure 18.1 on page 199, was developed from the British research programme briefly described in Appendix I. During that programme a number of organizations were studied and positioned on the matrix. From this work it was possible to give a thumb-nail description of the characteristic organization for each quadrant of the matrix. These descriptions reveal some readily recognizable organizational types. Having identified an organization's position on the matrix it is then possible to plan the management action necessary to reposition the organization more advantageously, so that it may be more effectively competitive.

The actions taken to achieve a repositioning may involve any or all of the factors encompassed in the two dimensions. There are all sorts of ways, partial and holistic, of achieving some aspects of competitive organization. It is possible to seek ways round the existing structures, by setting up additional specialized units where a new flexible culture may flourish. New venture departments and divisions or companies are responses of this kind. These limited approaches are not considered at length in this volume, because they merely represent a predictable attempt to protect the *status quo* and avoid, or minimize, change. The alternative is a melt-down of existing structures, systems and ways of managing, so that the whole organization is made not only responsive to the new, but eager to be quick to grasp the opportunities.

Chapter 18 explains the competitive matrix and the significance of the various positions on it. Chapter 19 explains how to reposition your organization on the matrix.

While aspects of the model are new and distinctive, each of the factors that define the two dimensions of the model are derived from a solid basis of published research and practice, referenced in the appropriate parts of the text. There may be different views as to the precise content of the model, but there is already a substantial degree of consensus over its general shape and the nature of the issues that determine competitive success in this era of turbulence and change.

18
The competitive matrix

18.1 Introduction

This chapter describes the competitive matrix (see Figure 18.1), the significance of the various positions on the matrix and how it can be used as an indicator for management action.

The interpretation of the two dimensions of the matrix has been described. The components of strategy have been described in some depth and are measured along a continuum from focused to dispersed. A focused strategy is where everyone in the organization knows what they are trying to achieve and how to achieve it. Similarly, the components of the culture dimension have also been described and they are measured along a continuum from traditional to progressive. A progressive culture is one based on a philosophy of empowerment and integrity where people are involved in leadership according to their skills and capabilities and where they are motivated to a commitment to achieving the strategic aims.

An organization's position on the matrix can be established simply by calculating the overall average strategy and culture scores which resulted from the questionnaires in Chapters 12 and 17. The responses of organization members to these 90 statements comprise a strategy and culture survey, the main purpose of which is to position an organization on the matrix. The various locations on the matrix indicate the need for specific management action, which is discussed later. Apart from this direct benefit derived from administering the survey, there is also the less tangible benefit of putting management closer in touch with other members of the organization. This can be a particularly important advantage for a top management which, as a result of the survey finds, to its surprise, that it is less in touch with its people than it had thought. Such a management may be capable of deluding itself about its own actual and potential attitudes and contributions, and those of its employees.

Like any other management tool, the competitive matrix is open to misuse. Its potential weaknesses or ambiguities can be ignored and its prescriptions applied too literally or mechanistically. So, before using the matrix, it is essential to understand its limitations.

18.2 Caveats and limitations

First, it should be noted that strategy and culture are matters that affect every member of the organization and every member can affect both culture and strategy. An organization's position on either strategy or culture cannot therefore be established with any validity by obtaining responses only from the chief executive. In many respects the chief executive is in the worst position to generate a response to the questionnaires that reflects a true picture of the organization as a whole. With the best intentions, the chief executive is likely either to respond to the various statements by giving a picture of the organization as he or she would like it to be, or, being aware of that risk, they may overcompensate and give a picture of the organization that reflects their worst fears. Even conducting the survey among the top management group may also give a highly biased picture and consequently a wrong location on the matrix. In small to medium-sized organizations it may be possible to conduct the survey with every member. Where this is not practical, a representative sample of the organization should be surveyed, reflecting all layers in the organization and all functions.

A second potential difficulty is that the significance of the position of an organization is, to some extent, situation-dependant. One aspect of the situation, the industry in which the organization operates, has already been considered. The questionnaire in Chapter 6 was intended to help to identify this aspect and show how differences might be accommodated by redrawing the axes of the matrix. A further aspect of the situation that also needs to be considered is the competitive environment. An organization's competitive status can only be defined in relative terms, i.e. relative to its major competitors.

This comparative picture is used continually in ordinary day-to-day managerial situations, but usually the comparison is only implicit. The competitive matrix makes it possible to make the comparisons explicit. This can be done by administering the survey with regard to the major competitors as well as your own organization. There are very obvious difficulties in doing this since you are unlikely to have access to competitors' people to respond to the survey. However, an approximation can be made to establishing relative positions. First, it could be done among your own personnel, whose knowledge will be far from complete, but will be a substantial improvement on no knowledge. Additionally, it could be done by conducting the survey among customers and other 'industry experts', obtaining their responses in the form of rankings of your own organization and the leading competitors. This relative positioning could be a substantial aid to interpreting positions on the matrix. For example, it could be that your organization appears to be positioned in the focused–progressive quadrant. However, the main competitors may all be even better positioned, thus suggesting that further management action is still required to reposition the business effectively.

A third potential problem with this sort of survey is the likelihood that the responses will change over time. A one-off survey will provide interesting and practically useful information, but a series of surveys which plot the movement of the organization over time would provide much more information, especially if they are conducted to monitor the changes that occur following the management action which the survey has prompted. It is always possible that extraneous factors, such as a major economic slump, or the immediate impact of a particular technological innovation, may unduly influence responses to the survey and give a possibly misleading position. These factors, which would not be apparent in a one-off survey, would be more likely to be revealed as part of a series.

Finally, though the survey questionnaire has been used extensively, its results are not beyond the possibility of error. Such a survey should not therefore be regarded as a technique to be applied in any way mechanically. It is concerned with tendencies, and identifying possible areas for management action to improve the situation. These need to be considered against the background of the material presented in the relevant chapter. The prescriptions from the model are not definitive, but indicative.

Further guidance on conducting a survey in your organization is included in Appendix II.

18.3 The two dimensions

Strategy is knowledge-intensive. To score high, i.e. to have a winning strategy, suggests having knowledge about customers, suppliers, competitors and technology, about the economy, government regulation, demographic and social trends, and about what is going to happen to all these in the medium and long term. It requires detailed understanding of customers' needs and perceptions and what is required to satisfy these needs. It requires the identification and acquisition of the requisite core competences and their application in the pursuit of a strategic intent which everyone in the organization can understand and identify with. A competitive organization will have this knowledge and achieve this focus in its strategy. Many organizations may be strong on some areas, but few achieve consistency over all five aspects of strategy.

One of the sometimes misunderstood areas is that of strategic direction. In many organizations top management is clear about the organization's strategic direction, but few of the other members of the organization share that clarity. As a consequence, the few big one-off investments are made in a consistent way that reinforces top management's avowed direction, but other decisions are made randomly. All the daily, mini-resource allocation decisions, the efforts and enthusiasms of people throughout the organization, are pragmatic with no coherent strategic focus. As a consequence resources tend to get misallocated.

For example, a firm aiming to be a leader in quality nevertheless operates its whole management ethos on the basis of strict budgetary control. The reward systems within the organization serve to reinforce low costs as the organizational paradigm, rather than the stated aim of high quality. As a result, when an employee is confronted with a minor decision which trades off between cost and quality, he or she decides wrongly in favour of reducing costs.

Thus it is vital that the entrepreneurial organization's strategy is focused so that *everyone* knows and agrees what the organization is trying to achieve. Similarly, the strategy profile also has to be consistent – a focused direction has to be supported by focused knowledge, competence and customer orientation.

Similar considerations apply with the culture dimension. The profile has to be held by all members of the organization and held consistently across all four factors. Inconsistency in one factor leads to dissonance with the other factors and the loss of a progressive culture. This is most easily exampled by considering the impact of low integrity on the other aspects of culture and particularly its potentially corrosive effects on the involvement and commitment of organization members. A management which is seen not to practise what it preaches in terms of integrity is likely not only to lose the commitment of its members, but actively to encourage their disillusion.

18.4 The matrix

The competitive organization will be positioned in the focused–progressive quadrant of the matrix. To achieve this position the questionnaire survey will have produced a positive score on both strategy and culture. In Figure 18.1 this position has been annotated 'innovative teams', a term which, like the other labels shown, was applied by respondents in the original research to their own organization. This is the quadrant of the matrix that accommodates those organizations which are best adapted to today's environment of rapid technological development, change and global competition. The other three quadrants are less well adapted.

The management actions implied by the model are those that would achieve a repositioning of an organization into the 'innovative teams' quadrant of the matrix. The matrix positions are important, but the individual factors that make up an organization's strategy and culture profiles are, in terms of management action, even more important. Two

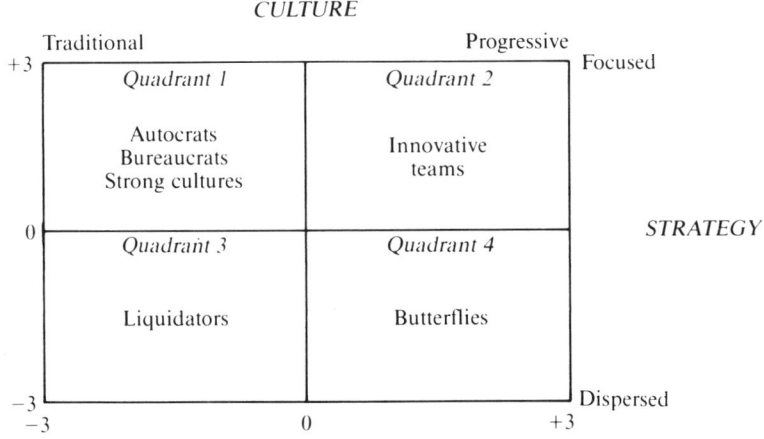

Figure 18.1 The competitive matrix

companies with identical overall culture scores may well have quite different scores at the level of the individual components and therefore require different management initiatives to change the overall position in regard to culture. The matrix positions are summary measures which, while important in themselves, do not reveal the more detailed factor scores that are amenable to management action. The matrix is an aggregate presentation and it would clearly be inappropriate to ascribe the same prescriptions to firms simply because they occupied the same quadrant, or even the same position within that quadrant.

Before considering repositioning actions we will first look at the sorts of organizations which are located in the various quadrants.

The 'innovative team' concept seems to encapsulate the essence of the progressive focused quadrant 2, the teamwork being facilitated by the progressive culture and the target for innovation by the focused strategy. Typically, the management of such an organization takes very deliberate steps to achieve their progressive culture. For example, such firms will generally take explicit initiatives in their corporate communications strategy, involving both regular consultation meetings with employees and formal briefings involving every member of the organization. In addition, all members of the organization are likely to receive communications training. In all quadrant 2 organizations there is strong evidence of effective two-way communications up and down the management line.

A high-scoring quadrant 2 organization may well not have a recognizable management line or chain of command that extends from the top of the organization to the bottom; or at least not one that matters very much to organization members. Many such firms are adopting a project-team approach to management of all but the most routine problems. Even firms in the motor industry – the spiritual home of standardization, mass production, scientific management and the machine bureaucracy – have achieved some success by organization through work teams.

Such progressive management practices are becoming more widely used, not merely in terms of the organization of routine work, but, as has been noted, more particularly in the improvement and development of business organization, with a direct and consequential result in terms of member involvement and commitment to strategic aims.

Firms in the traditional concentrated quadrant appear to fall into three broad categories: autocrats, bureaucrats and strong cultures. A firm that tends towards the autocratic form of traditional culture, dominated by a single top manager, can certainly be an effective innovator and competitor. A bureaucracy, on the other hand, is the antithesis of innovative. Being competitive through the exercise of bureaucratic rules is a contradiction in terms, even if the rules have been drawn up in a way that is designed to ensure a high degree of strategic focus. In contrast, the autocracy does not necessarily contain this fundamental contradiction of innovativeness. It may be extremely inhibiting to members of the organization and make it very difficult for them to be innovative and competitive in the face of change, but the autocrat himself has maximum freedom. He (or she) can make the rules, take instant and personal decisions, pass instructions to his subordinates and anticipate rapid and total compliance.

The effectiveness of an autocracy as a competitor and innovator depends more or less entirely on the effectiveness of the autocrat. It is possible, in certain circumstances, that they can provide the organization with the strategic focus required to be innovative. However, such circumstances are specific and limited, first, to small organizations (which are frequently the creation of a single person who presides over every aspect during the early phase of growth) and second, to organizations in crisis, where quick decisive action is the key to survival. Either situation is unstable and cannot be counted on to last for long.

Autocracy may be an unattractive position even for the autocrat. In the original research (see Appendix I) one such autocrat described his business ruefully – 'in terms of senior management it's a bit of a one-man band!' He was clearly aware of the potential difficulties the organization was vulnerable to as a consequence. If he was successful the company would rapidly become too big for the present structure and management arrangements to cope with. He was also aware of his own mortality. Not only was the chief executive aware of these problems but he was also trying to address them as best he could. He had become very interested in the subject of organizational culture and saw the possibility of creating a 'strong culture' as the best solution. The precise meaning of 'strong 'culture' in this context was not completely clear, though it appeared to be a deliberate attempt to create the effect of infrastructure and order without the problems associated with the traditional bureaucratic approach. Strong culture was certainly seen in some way as inducing a high degree of motivation among organization members to become involved in decision making and committed to the aims identified by the chief executive.

In the traditional–focused quadrant it seems apparent that the autocracy could be competitive and innovative, depending on the nature of the autocrat. Bureaucracies would be largely incapable of the flexibility to compete and innovate. Strong cultures, though not fully defined, would seem to accumulate essentially the same characteristics as bureaucracies and thus to be ill-equipped for competing in a fast-changing environment.

Organizations positioned in the dispersed half of the matrix appear unlikely to be effective innovators whatever their culture profile. This is because they have either espoused strategic aims which are incapable of concentrating resources and efforts, or they appear to have no consistent set of strategic aims at all. In the former category were firms driven by purely financial targets such as returns on capital employed, asset growth, profit margins, etc. These firms invariably fall into the traditional–dispersed quadrant. Dominated by financial considerations, they are likely to have a rigid, though not necessarily autocratic, culture. According to Hayes and Garvin (1982), a company driven by financially stated aims tends to be a liquidator, going down what they identified as 'the disinvestment spiral'. They might espouse a strategy of cost leadership, which becomes a mindset and as a consequence leads down the liquidator's path.

The quadrant may also include relatively new start-ups still struggling to get past the stage of vulnerability to infant mortality. The concepts of liquidation and disinvestment are all too pressing to such firms if they experience any adverse movements in their environment (e.g. economic slump or high interest rates) and it is vital that these young businesses make full use of such financial criteria if they are to survive. At this early stage of their evolution, however, entrepreneurs are still very clear about their business purpose and have a personal commitment to the strategic direction on which they were set when the business was created. Thus, although such firms are in the liquidator quadrant of the competitive matrix, a more focused strategy is 'on hold', pending successful negotiation of the minefield of infancy. Some of these firms will therefore progress to the traditional–focused quadrant in due course. Others, and in this particular period a sadly high proportion, will be forced to follow the liquidator route.

Other types of organization falling into the dispersed half of the matrix may have progressive cultures but less clear and consistent strategies.

Organizations in the progressive-dispersed quadrant might sometimes appear to have clearly stated aims, but still change 'from day to day', with the consequence that members would be unaware of the strategic aims, or at least the current ones, and consequently the organization would be unable to concentrate action and resources consistently in order to achieve the strategic aims.

A respondent from one such organization in the original research described the company's management as 'nice guys, but . . .' and went on to suggest that in his view they were insufficiently decisive and unprepared to be ruthless. A stereotypical example of this quadrant was described as a 'butterfly – always flitting from one project to another, with no consistency over time'. In this company it seemed clear that innovativeness was enabled through a progressive culture but, in the absence of focused strategy, the company failed to be innovative. Not only that but, over time, members of the organization became progressively more disillusioned and even alienated, and an increasingly high management turnover rate resulted.

While it is again emphasized that the matrix is an aggregate device, the annotations serve as shorthand for certain intuitively recognizable organizational types representative of the four quadrants.

In the original research there was no evidence of entrepreneurial organizations being positioned in the dispersed strategy half of the matrix. It seems that a focused strategy is a prerequisite of the competitive organization. For an organization positioned in the dispersed area, the required management action would be to achieve a focused strategy.

A progressive culture, on the other hand, was not necessarily a prerequisite of innovativeness, but the autocratic innovator is less robust and reliable, for the reasons already identified, than the innovating team. The traditional-focused quadrant is thus less desirable than the progressive-focused quadrant. Management action for any traditional-concentrated company should therefore focus on achieving a progressive style in order to achieve a more reliable and robust performance as a competitor and innovator.

18.5 Natural tendencies and management responses

In Chapter 5 it was noted that an organization is subject to a number of apparently natural tendencies as it matures. They are not inevitable, and most of them certainly not desirable, but sufficient firms appear to succumb to them for them to have given rise to an orthodox wisdom about the likely characteristics of a mature organization.

A young organization, in a rapidly developing industry, is likely to be entrepreneurial, flexible and highly innovative. In terms of the competitive matrix, such a firm would seem likely to fall either into quadrant 1, if run by a single invidivual, or more likely into quadrant 2 – an innovative team. As it grows up and its innovation slows down, it begins typically to surround itself with various institutional practices, rules and regulations, pecking orders and so on, in other words to become bureaucratic. There is thus an apparently natural tendency to migrate from the innovating team of quadrant 2 to the bureaucrats in quadrant 1. Moreover, as the organization becomes even more mature, it becomes less and less flexible; it starts to ration investment strictly to cost-cutting items in order to remain competitive. Thus there is a natural tendency for the quadrant 1 firm to migrate to quadrant 3 where the focus is strictly on short-term financial performance. In due course, management of a quadrant 3 firm almost inevitably becomes the responsibility of financial specialists who, when results decline, may feel they can make better use of the assets elsewhere. The business therefore starts down the disinvestment spiral, which leads ultimately off the matrix altogether. Thus there is a natural tendency, as businesses mature, to migrate from quadrant 2 to quadrant 1 to quadrant 3 and, finally, to extinction.

It also seems clear that firms in quadrant 4 cannot stay there for long – their waste of corporate assets is too prolific. They are likely to run out of funds and be forced into a financial strait-jacket simply in order to survive. Thus there is a natural tendency for quadrant 4 firms, if they survive long enough, to migrate to quadrant 3.

The direction of these natural tendencies is indicated in Figure 18.2, together with the directions of management thrusts required to counteract these tendencies and to achieve the most advantageous positioning for effective competition and innovation. The direction of these natural tendencies is widely accepted and understood. However, the appropriate management responses may be less well understood. This is the subject matter of the final chapter.

18.6 Conclusion

In managing a competitive organization there is no substitute for knowing what you are doing and why you are doing it, whether it is coming to an international technology collaboration agreement, embarking on a new employee training scheme or simply reviewing ethical performance. Everything has to have a purpose which is related to the achievement of strategic aims.

Similarly with the application of the competitive matrix: there is nothing clever in the matrix and nothing in it that has to be taken on trust. It is simply a way of viewing the strategic management of your organization and using it to highlight some areas for improvement and development

204 THE COMPETITIVE ORGANIZATION

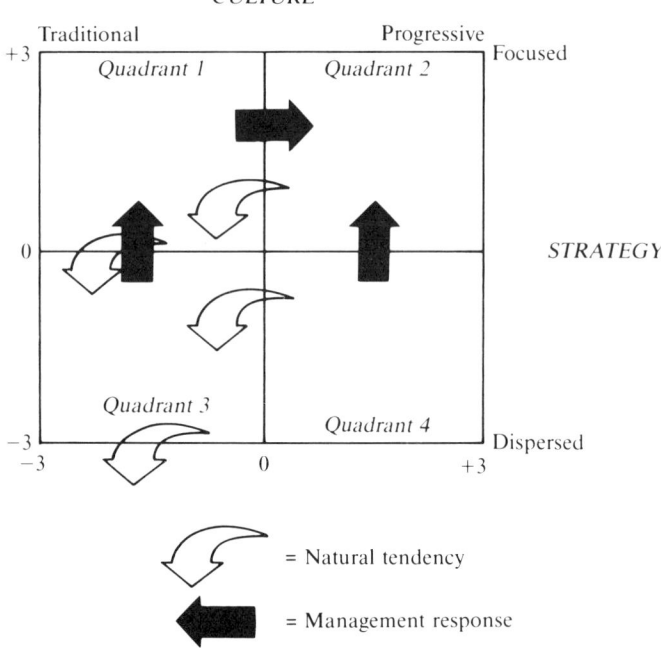

Figure 18.2 The competitive matrix: natural tendencies and management responses

which may not have become apparent by any other means. However, the diagnosis that the competitive model provides is not definitive and its prescriptions are only indicative. An uncompetitive position arising from the questionnaire survey suggests a broad directional thrust for management action. More detailed analysis of the strategy and culture profiles will suggest specific areas where the broad thrust is most likely to be effective. Considering the scores for individual questions within the profile components may suggest quite detailed management initiatives.

These indications for management action are not intended to be used mechanistically as, for example, the early Boston matrix was often interpreted. In the Boston matrix, if the market growth or relative market share were both 'low' then the prescription was simply to withdraw from the business as cost-effectively as possible. With the competitive matrix there are no such simple prescriptions. A position on the matrix suggests, in some considerable detail, where you may look for the problems. Moreover, consideration of the sections of this book that deal with the problem areas identified may also suggest possible solutions. However, both problems and solutions are essentially matters for managerial judgement. This book and the questionnaire survey will have increased the knowledge base from which that judgement can be exercised, as suggested in the final chapter.

Reference

Hayes, R. H. and D. Garvin, 'Managing as if tomorrow mattered', *Harvard Business Review*, May–June 1982:71–9.

19
Repositioning your business

19.1 Introduction

The first chapter of this book briefly outlined the competitive matrix so that subsequent chapters could be understood in the context of the overall model. The rest of Part One included a review of much of the research work that has been carried out in the field of innovation and innovativeness, which in this current period are the dominant issues in competitive business. The firm that cannot create and cope with change will fail to be competitive in an era of change.

Thus, in terms of the competitive matrix, the position to be aimed for is high up in the progressive–focused quadrant, which is labelled 'innovative teams'.

The competitive model suggests how organizations falling outside that quadrant may take action to reposition themselves. Some of these actions are relatively straightforward, although the sort of management action required to modify structural and cultural characteristics may be problematic. It is these factors which appear to impact directly on the way people in organizations behave. In general, the required action is most often intended to create new fluid structures to replace older, more rigid systems.

For firms that appear relatively stable it may be sufficient to adopt ways round the existing organization. There are a number of permanent and temporary structures that can be adopted to achieve an innovative sub-part of the organization while not interfering with the control orientation of the main business. For most firms, however, these partial approaches will not be enough. What is required is to make the whole organization entrepreneurial.

This chapter discusses the main repositioning moves, focusing in particular on the problem of melting down traditional structures and replacing them with an organic organization suited to the 1990s.

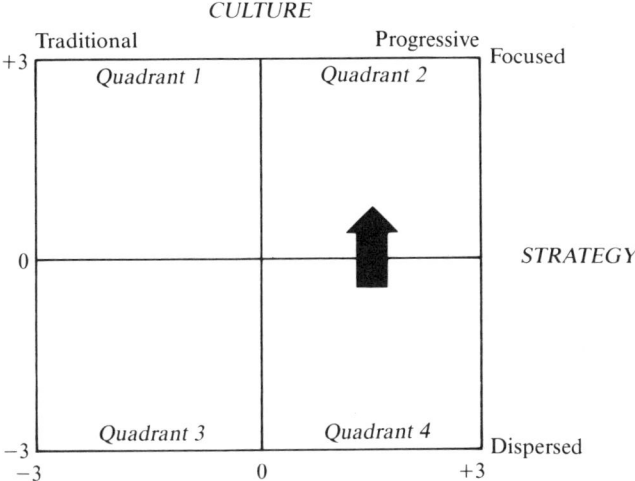

Figure 19.1 Repositioning 'butterflies'

19.2 Repositioning 'butterflies'

'Butterflies' are quadrant 4 organizations. They enjoy a progressive culture, but lack a focused strategy. Top management in these organizations are often extremely intelligent and well educated, but sometimes too idealistic. Their basic philosophy is based on the seemingly enlightened ideas of recruiting the right people and giving them the freedom and resources to do the job. The assumption is that satisfactory results will automatically follow. It rarely seems to work out like that. The difficulty is that the organization needs to know what it is trying to achieve and the strategic intent needs to be understood and supported by the people in the organization. Obvious though this may seem, there are many butterfly organizations where skilled, intelligent, motivated people are progressively reduced to alienation by a lack of coherent direction.

The difficulty is that people will be unlikely, spontaneously, to agree and work to a focused strategy. The establishment of a strategic focus can be a long and painstaking process. It may involve the development of formal planning systems in order to establish strategic direction, together with some formal monitoring system to maintain a measure of how effectively resources, efforts and enthusiasm are being concentrated and how consistently over time. It may involve the formal setting up of external communications, as well as a formal means of identifying and acquiring core competences, all focused on the satisfaction of customer needs, which again require formally identifying and linking with the other initiatives.

Setting up these explicitly formal systems is the main task in repositioning a 'butterfly' into the 'innovative teams' quadrant. The systems have to be formal. Otherwise, in a 'butterfly' they simply will not happen. Formality is a characteristic of bureaucracy, not of progressive cultures. The sort of creative, intelligent people who are likely to be found in butterfly organizations may well be temperamentally unsuited to formal systems, or anything that smells of bureaucracy. This is the main difficulty in effecting any repositioning moves. The imposition of bureaucratic systems is likely to be met with strong resistance.

The alternative, retaining a dispersed strategy, is, however, not a long-term option. The inevitable lack of financial performance is bound, in due course, to force a change on the organization. More often than not, this will be the imposition of strict financial controls. Thus, rather than frittering resources away in a random scatter, the organization will cease to invest altogether except where essential to survival. This natural tendency to migrate towards quadrant 3 does nothing to solve the underlying problem of the butterfly organization, but may disguise the fact that lack of a focused strategy is the real problem.

Formal systems must therefore be introduced but without bureaucratic excess. The formal systems must focus the strategy, but not create a monster that would consume inordinate amounts of paper, time and enthusiasm. A light and simple approach is required that quickly gets to the nub of the strategic issues involved, without stifling initiative and creativity. But the approach has to be formal and timetabled because, if it isn't, it won't happen. Such an approach might include one or more of the following initiatives:

1. Form small teams (3 or 4 members each) to identify and prepare concise written reports on the items listed below. These reports to be circulated prior to the away day workshop.
   – customer needs
   – core competences
   – competitor product strengths
   – new technology
   – long-term industry trends and changes
2. Set up an away day workshop to:
   – receive reports from the above teams – 30 minutes presentation + a maximum 30 minutes discussion on each; discussion to include renewed briefs for each team;
   – discuss options for strategic direction;
   – consider options for a challenging strategic intent in terms of competitors to beat;
   – consume a high-class dinner.

3. Form a 'strategic direction' team to propose a one-sentence statement of strategic direction, supported by operational detail not to exceed a single side of A4 in total.
4. Form a 'strategic planning' team to create a planning timetable and minimum planning standards, including paperwork requirements and monitoring arrangements.
5. Agree a rotation of members (from all the above teams) to report on strategic issues to the board or executive committee each month.
6. Agree rotation of members of board or executive committee (excluding chairman or chief executive) to have responsibility for strategic issues.
7. Set up a second away day workshop to agree the following items:
   – statement of strategic direction
   – statement of competitive strategic intent
   – milestones along the route to the strategic intent
   – annual strategy planning timetable and process
   – regular monitoring and reporting arrangements.

These actions would start off the strategy process in a way that would involve a large number of organization members. Team memberships and other roles can and should be rotated from time to time so that the expertise of individuals is fully exploited, but at the same time their experience and knowledge is broadened. A programme as outlined above gives a number of ideas, but still leaves a lot of room for shaping to the needs of the individual organization. Care should be taken to introduce an element of formality and time commitment, without introducing the sort of fruitless paper chase which many large mature bureaucratic organizations have succumbed to.

Not all the factors referred to above will be lacking in most butterfly organizations, but those that the survey responses suggest are weak need to be rectified before a coherent strategic direction can be concentrated on with any consistency. Recognition of the 'butterfly' before it becomes a liquidator may provide a sufficient opportunity for management to reposition the organization in quadrant 2.

19.3 Repositioning liquidators

In the case of liquidators, it is clear that both culture and strategy need to be changed in order to achieve a position in quadrant 2. There are few successful examples of firms that have achieved this double change simultaneously.

Within quadrant 3 are organizations that are managed entirely through the imposition of short-term financial controls. There are organizations that may be unwitting liquidators – in order to reduce costs to remain

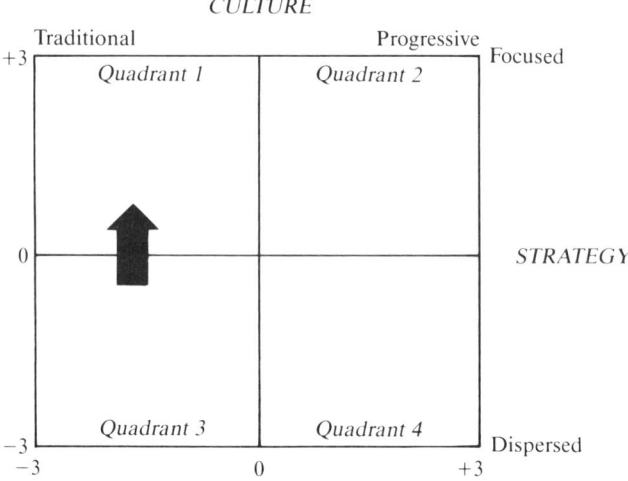

Figure 19.2 Repositioning liquidators

competitive they relinquish the possibility of ever regaining real competitive capability. They are the firms that have developed a cost leadership mindset, that are sliding down the disinvestment spiral, that have not foreseen the logical conclusion of their short-term decisions.

In addition there are those organizations which are clearly in crisis and for which either turnaround, or closure, are the obvious alternatives. With these firms there is nothing unwitting about the imposition of short-term financial controls. The intended outcome is simply survival. Without that there is no long term, and so long-term considerations are deliberately put on the back burner. Some of the organizations do not survive. Those that do, either struggle on under continuous threat of extinction, or are enabled to raise their sights above survival and embark on a programme that could ultimately reposition them in the 'innovating teams' quadrant.

The difficulty of achieving a double change in both strategy and culture is usually overcome by approaching them sequentially, as was done at Jaguar.

When John Egan took over at Jaguar Cars, survival was the issue. His immediate response was to impose an authoritarian control, taking decisions unilaterally, simply informing the unions and work-force what had to happen. Later, when the survival crisis was over, Jaguar focused its strategy on quality, moving from the liquidator quadrant to autocrat. Total quality management programmes were initiated, just as the fight for survival had been, by the autocrat at the top, but they could only be implemented by involving all the people in the process. Thus began a system of management through teams, starting at the bottom with quality circles.

The change from the autocrat quadrant to 'innovating team' achieved some obvious successes, as Jaguar's quality and productivity were revolutionized. Nevertheless, the change is extremely difficult and Sir John Egan clearly did not complete the task at Jaguar.

For the firm that has come back from the brink of extinction, the first change that is made is to identify an appropriate strategic focus. Only subsequently does the management turn its attention to the cultural issue, if at all.

Slatter (1984) identified four phases in corporate recovery:

- *The analysis phase*: problem identification and initial decision as to immediate actions;
- *The emergency phase*: actions necessary to ensure survival . . . emphasis on cash flow and tight central financial control;
- *The strategic change phase*: focus on product market segments where the organization has greatest competitive advantage; study of long-term viability of business;
- *The growth phase*: growth organically, by new product development or by acquisition, on the back of a recovered balance sheet.

This progression is probably fairly representative of successful turnarounds. Not surprisingly, it focuses on the first phase of change, which takes the organization from the liquidator quadrant to quadrant 1. The cultural change that has to follow if the organization is to become truly entrepreneurial goes far beyond Slatter's turnaround programme.

19.4 Repositioning autocrats, bureaucrats and strong cultures

Both of the repositioning moves described above are relatively simple. In both cases the organizations concerned are in crisis. The butterfly organization will typically find itself unable to retain good people, and if it does then it will be uncomfortably aware that they are demotivated. This is the best butterfly position. Most probably they will also perceive the lack of financial results and recognize the inevitable consequences. The liquidator, on the other hand, is an organization already on the brink of disaster. In both cases, the necessity for action is apparent to all. And in both cases the aim of the action should be to take the organization away from the brink, so that it can stop liquidating and start to invest in its long-term future.

Repositioning a quadrant 1 organization is much more difficult. The need for action is not immediately apparent. The organization may be

212 THE COMPETITIVE ORGANIZATION

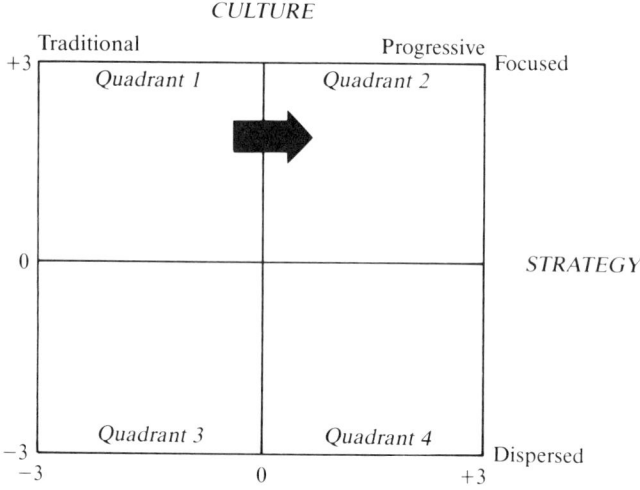

Figure 19.3 Repositioning autocrats, bureaucrats and strong cultures

extremely successful. It may have achieved good financial results and see a good future for its core business. Why then should it change?

Traditional organizational structures still seem to have some attractions: you surely have to know who does what, who reports to whom and who is responsible if things go wrong. Fayol first laid down the laws of classical organization structure based on his experience of the nineteenth-century French mining industry (Fayol 1916). Urwick embellished the rules, adding such concepts as the 'span of control' (Urwick 1947). Pugh and colleagues at Aston University added further precision to the structural concept (Pugh *et al.* 1969) and Mintzberg sought to develop the structural idea to modern forms of bureaucracy and what he called 'adhocracy' (Mintzberg 1983).

These are all models of how established organizations operated in environments which have, in most cases, now long gone. For today's environment, they are really measures of how not to do it; they define the form of organization that inhibits innovation and frustrates competitive endeavour. In order to move from quadrant 1 to the 'innovative teams' quadrant, structure has therefore to be circumvented by one means or another and its inhibiting pressures avoided. Many organizations take the view that the difficulty with innovation can be accommodated by setting up a separate structure within the main organization where the normal control-oriented rules can be relaxed. This is one approach. Alternatively, the whole organization could be melted down and turned into an innovative team. The following sections look briefly at these two options.

Ways round the organization

Most organizations try to adjust to change by a limited approach to structural adjustment, by setting up a separate structure within the main structure that adopts different organizational rules and norms and is specifically charged with the task of 'entrepreneuring'. The main organization continues to be managed on a more or less bureaucratic basis in order to maintain tight control, while the separate structures are deliberately created to handle innovation. Such arrangements can be temporary or permanent:

Permanent designs
New venture group or department (radical)
Standing new product committee (incremental)
New product department (incremental)
Technical department (incremental)
Marketing department (incremental)

Temporary designs
New ventures team (radical)
Temporary new product committee (incremental)
Marketing department-led project team (incremental)
Technical department-led project team (incremental)
Interdepartmental project team

Modular matrix organization
Individuals report up the formal line for existing business management, but report functionally, or through special groups, for purposes of managing innovation. (Based on Johne 1985)

This approach was further popularized by Peters and Waterman (1982) who suggest that company performance could be aided by simultaneously 'loose-tight' organizational structures. The approach was repeated by Kanter (1983) who suggested parallel structures – a 'mechanistic' organization for maintaining the existing business and an organic organization, in parallel, for initiating change. Such organization structures are widely held to be important determinants of the company's innovative role and performance.

The idea of parallel, or matrix, structures was further developed by Johne (1985) who defined the span of feasible organization designs that could be used for product innovation. The critical variations relate to the degree of centralization or decentralization of control and the degree of permanence of organizational arrangements. For example, in a multi-division company with centralized control, responsibility for product innovation might be held within the central corporate planning function. By contrast, responsibility might be decentralized so that each division controls its own product innovation with no involvement from the centre. Alternatively, it would be feasible to have dual control with involvement both by the divisions and central planning. The potential advantages and disadvantages of these different arrangements are not hard to envisage and Johne identifies what he considers to be the main ones.

As well as these rather rigid approaches, there is a whole battery of management writers in the Tom Peters mould who advocate setting up unofficial 'skunkworks', which work on time and resources hi-jacked, or boot-legged, from the company, in the knowledge that if they go through official channels they will get nothing done. Dixon described a German study of 73 industrial innovations, most of which had been progressed in this way: 'the originators kept their idea to themselves until their feasibility could no longer be questioned, often working on refinements secretly . . .' (Dixon 1990). The idea of project champions has also gained some favour for similar reasons – they help the innovative project circumvent the rigid structure of the existing organization.

These approaches are all symptoms of a malaise at the heart of the organization. The fact that they may be beneficial to an innovative project merely highlights the fact that the existing organization is incapable of handling innovation and change. In an era of rapid change this is the problem that needs to be overcome.

Melting down the organization

For most firms the partial solution will not be sufficient. These firms will need to achieve a root and branch change in the way they work if they are to become competitive. Classical structures need to be deliberately broken down and replaced by more fluid organic matrices. However, there are few examples in the literature of change being made to the structure of the *whole* organization. Such cases that are recorded are, in the main, changes towards bureaucracy, by imposing order on chaos, for example Alfred Sloan at General Motors (Sloan 1965). Deliberate whole organizational change in the opposite direction is less common, though an increasing number of such attempts are being made.

Work design has attracted much attention since the turn of the century with figures like Taylor and the Gilbreths who concentrated on the simplification, specialization and standardization of work so that the then new mass-production technologies could be exploited. Much of the subsequent work on organization development has aimed to reverse these tendencies to bureaucratize. However, as Leitko and Szczerbacki put it,

> Organisational development (OD) has yet to escape from its past – from its origins within humanistic psychology, in part as a reaction to the restrictive and

authoritarian conditions characteristic of the machine bureaucracies found in many manufacturing organisations. However, the limitations that this past has created for OD are becoming more apparent as . . . machine bureaucracies give way to more open systems within the manufacturing sector, and as OD experts study organisations outside the manufacturing sector.

(Leitko and Szczerbacki 1987)

Work design has thus tended to move organizations away from bureaucratic structures through such processes as job enlargement, job rotation, job enrichment, various exercises in group technology and the Quality of Working Life movement, which is currently experiencing a revival of interest (Heller 1988). These approaches all address the problem of bureaucratic structures by changing the design of work in the organization, but it does not necessarily impact on all jobs. In particular, job design has tended to focus attention on non-managerial work, whereas management itself must also be freed from rigid structure if involvement and commitment are to be achieved.

The problem presented by an autocratic chief executive is even more difficult to melt down than bureaucratic structures. British industry has been overburdened with bullies and petty dictators at the top of management trees. Ironically, this was one of the problems found by Michael Edwardes when he moved into British Leyland, despite the fact that the overwhelming problem was that management had largely lost the will to manage (Edwardes 1982). The reason there are so many autocrats is probably that they are motivated by the need for power, without having the talent to exercise it effectively when it has been achieved. The only solution to the repositioning of most autocrat organizations may rest simply on a palace revolution, or other mode of getting rid of the autocrat. Reluctant autocrats are rare, though they do exist, and may themselves seek to reposition their own organization, as exampled in Appendix I.

Strong culture organizations are to all intents and purposes similar to bureaucracies in the problems they present for repositioning. The difficulties are, however, likely to be even greater since not only will the strong culture have been built up deliberately and painstakingly, it will also be based on the invisible, but robust and long-lasting foundation of the naturally evolving culture. Moreover, recognition of strong culture as a flexibility problem is not yet widespread and the will to change a strong culture may be distinctly absent.

There are two approaches to melting down rigid structures. In some circumstances it may be possible to create a major change with an almost immediate effect. For example, the removal of an autocratic chief executive would present such an opportunity. The fact of his removal will clearly have major symbolic impact. It announces to every member in the organization that the world has changed; everything may be different from now on. Immediately, every member is sensitized to look for clues to the new state of affairs. They are receptive to change and eager to seek improvements.

In these special circumstances it is possible to make the change from the 'dictator' quadrant to the 'innovative teams' quickly and efficiently. However, it does not happen automatically. If the old dictator is simply replaced by a new appointee with no planning of how the change to 'innovative team' will be made, then the organizational customs and practices that reinforced the previous incumbent as autocrat will quickly envelope the replacement and merely create a new autocracy. The change has to be planned, with the various components of a progressive culture being designed and implemented at the time of the change so that the new incumbent is associated with the new culture.

Other than in these special circumstances the move from traditional to progressive cultures is a long, slow process. There are no quick fixes or magic formulae. A carefully designed programme of initiatives is needed to establish the four main components of culture: empowerment, integrity, involvement and commitment. Detailed analysis of the culture profile and of responses to individual statements will indicate the sort of management action that may be required. It might include one or more of the following initiatives:

- A programme to improve internal corporate communications, both formal and informal. Opening up informal communications, i.e. between departments and individuals across the organization, may be best attacked through communications and interpersonal skills training programmes. Formal communications may be improved by written media such as house journals, news sheets, employee financial reports and *ad hoc* noticeboard statements, as well as verbal communications using communications and consultation committees formed across the organization, regular team briefings, and occasional business-wide short 'conferences' where top management speak directly to all members. The creation of project teams for a wide variety of purposes can also play a key role in opening internal communications. Open communications are only part of the story; the other part is the message being communicated. This needs to be concerned with matters which in many quadrant 1 organizations would be regarded as confidential and incorporate as much of the content of strategy as possible, including strategic direction and intent, any milestones towards a competitive challenge (critical stages towards 'beating Xerox'), issues arising from external communications and long-term orientation, competitor analysis, technological developments and targets, core competences and customer information.

- A programme of people development including training and education, job enrichment and job rotation, and involvement in project teams designed to broaden individual experience and responsibility.

- A programme to involve people in cooperative psychological contracts may also play a key part in culture change where groups operate strictly on a calculative basis. How this can be done is very situation-dependant and may involve changes to legal contractual arrangements; the initiative will have to be made by the organization giving more to the cooperative contract than members have previously enjoyed.

- Corporate integrity initiatives may need to be taken explicitly, for example, the setting up of an 'ethics committee' and the development of an ethics clause within a mission statement. The establishment of a high level of corporate integrity is essentially a slow process. Lip service needs to be confirmed by continuous and painstaking practice which must be seen to be done. Thus the opening moves must be overt and explicit.

- A programme of recognition of individual contributions by making valued awards for individual performance.

- A programme to involve groups normally excluded from the processes of strategic development and improvement of the business. In unionized units this might include member representatives meeting customers, technology suppliers, shareholders and competitors. It would almost certainly include inviting member representatives to join key project teams with roles beyond their normal scope.

- Ensuring that all members are provided with just rewards that are related to performance as far as possible, and seeing that members receive all help and encouragement to achieve performance and consequent rewards.

- A programme to encourage members to grow and develop, not only by training and promotion but also by ensuring as far as possible that jobs are meaningful, that people enjoy a maximum practical degree of autonomy and that all job holders receive feedback on their performance.

- A programme to identify possible means of involving members in ownership of the business, either directly through a share scheme or indirectly through participation in the benefits of ownership in the form of profits or growth.

A number of the items included above use terminology (e.g. autonomy) which has a particular meaning that is fully defined in the relevant chapter of this book. When considering initiatives like these it is important to consider them not only in the light of the detailed questionnaire responses but also in the context of the material in this volume. Clearly, the initiatives above are not exhaustive, but serve to indicate some of the management actions that would contribute to repositioning a quadrant 1 organization into quadrant 2. Other initiatives are suggested in the text of Part Three.

The repeated references to the formation of project teams for various initiatives is crucial to the melting-down option, not merely because they offer a sound operational means of achieving change, but more importantly because they provide an alternative means of organization to the traditional line structure. The need is for task-oriented teams that progressively take on more and more responsibility for organization operations. The teams themselves need to involve everyone in the organization; they should be non-hierarchical and led on the basis of expertise. For example, the chief executive of the organization should participate as a member of one or more of the project teams, and should not necessarily lead any team of which he or she is a member. In some organizations this may seem perfectly natural; in others, less well fitted for survival, it would represent an utterly incredible arrangement.

The tasks for which team operations take responsibility as outlined in this chapter are specifically related to the improvement and development of the business, for dealing with specific initiatives that may be temporary or permanent. But the role of teams should progressively be increased. Routine line management, in a modern organization, is a relatively routine task, but even in this there are some opportunities for the use of group working to improve the quality of working life. However, the strength of team operations lies in their organizational development possibilities. Solving new problems that arise from the work situation is work for problem-solving teams, some of which will be short-lived and simple; others will be almost permanent and fulfilling tasks of extreme complexity.

Team membership and participation in leadership can provide inexperienced people with direct learning opportunities in a way which orthodox line management structures would take a lifetime to provide. Management by project teams is the subject of a sister volume by J. Rodney Turner in the Henley Management Series and is therefore not dwelt on at length here. However, in the evolving literature on new forms of organization there are some provocative generalizations that are suggested as rules of thumb:

– Communications should be totally open in all directions.
– There should be minimum hierarchical layers in any organization – some suggest a maximum of four:

entrepreneurs
  managers
  leaders
  operators
- The job of leaders is to engage the intelligence and talents of those with low growth needs (i.e. with calculative psychological contracts, mainly operators) in the pursuit of the organization's strategic aims.
- Managers should spend at least 60 per cent of their time on project team work rather than on line matters.

The essential message is effectiveness. Not just empowerment, but empowerment for a purpose; not just involvement, but involvement in leadership to a strategic end; not just communications, but communication of a particular message about strategic intent; not just motivation, but motivation to a commitment to the organization's strategic aims.

19.5 Conclusion

The competitive model which this book has described is based on many thousands of different works of research into organizational effectiveness, innovation, competition and strategy. As such it is in the broad stream of management thinking, even though the precise structure and components of the matrix were derived from one particular piece of research.

The purpose of the model is to help managers make their businesses more effective competitors in an era when technological change has created instability and volatility in all business environments and the ability to cope with and indeed create change has become the key competitive tool.

In terms of the model, the essential prerequisite for success is to be in the top half of the matrix, i.e. to have a focused strategy. Such an organization will have a clear strategic direction, and will concentrate its resources and efforts on progressing in that direction, consistently over time. Such a well-founded strategy will be based on effective external communications, a long-term orientation, relevant core competences and a careful customer focus. With such a strategic profile the organization is potentially competitive.

To ensure that it is truly competitive the organization must also have a progressive culture that engages the intelligence, skills and commitment of all its people.

Turning your organization into a successful competitor, an 'innovative team', may not be easy, but it is hoped that the competitive model helps. Tomorrow's organizations must achieve this position.

References

Dixon, M., 'On the receiving end', *Business*, June 1990:153.
Edwardes, M., *Back from the Brink*, Collins, London, 1982.
Fayol, H. *General and Industrial Management*, Pitman, London, 1949. (Translated by C. Storrs from the original French *Administration Industrielle et Générale* (1916).)
Heller, F. A., 'Working models on the shop floor', *Times Higher Education Supplement*, 29 January 1988:15.
Johne, F. A., *Industrial Produce Innovation: Organisation and Management*, Croom Helm, 1985.
Kanter, R. M., *The Change Masters: Corporate Entrepreneurs at Work*, Unwin Hyman, London, 1983.
Leitko, T. A. and D. Szczerbacki, 'Why traditional OD strategies fail in professional bureaucracies', *Organizational Dynamics*, Winter 1987.
Mintzberg, H., *Structure in Fives: Designing Effective Organizations*, Prentice-Hall, Englewood Cliffs, 1983.
Peters, T. and R. H. Waterman, *In Search of Excellence*, Harper & Row, New York, 1982.
Pugh, D. S., D. J. Hickson, C. R. Hinings and C. Turner, 'The context of organisation structure', *Administrative Science Quarterly*, Vol. 14, 1969:91–114.
Slatter, S., *Corporate Recovery: successful turnaround strategies and their implementation*, Penguin, Harmondsworth, 1984.
Sloan, A. P., *My Years with General Motors*, Sidgwick & Jackson, London, 1965.
Urwick, L. F., *The Elements of Administration*, Pitman, London, 1947.

Appendix I
A note on the original research project

In the preface to the third edition of *Diffusion of Innovations*, published in 1983, Rogers refers to 3085 diffusion publications, of which 2297 were empirical research reports. 'I think there is almost no other field of behaviour research that represents more effort by more scholars in more nations' (Rogers 1983). This apparently ever-increasing volume of work on innovation has continued over the past few years, additional interest being stimulated perhaps by an awareness of the potential impacts of the technological innovations now being made possible because of basic developments primarily in the field of electronics.

Consequently, it might be assumed that new research into innovation is based on more solid foundations than previously. However, this is not necessarily the case. Rogers and Shoemaker illustrated the point nicely in the appendix to the second edition of *Diffusion of Innovations* by categorizing empirical studies and highlighting the surprising lack of consensus. For example, several hundred studies support the hypothesis that organization size is positively related to innovativeness. At the same time, several hundred other studies reject the same hypothesis. All the empirical and theoretical work that has been done has not yet resolved into a single accepted theory of innovation. Every situation is unique, and the best way forward seems likely always to be contingent on situational circumstances. So it is necessary for new research to be very specifically related to the research that has previously been published.

As well as the diffusion literature there is another area of work on innovation that focuses on new product or process development. Diffusion is concerned with the pattern of innovation through an industry so that the pace and shape of new product acceptance can be better predicted. Such studies often have a marketing or economics based motive. The new product development literature is concerned with the process of innovation *within* an organization. Research concerned with the process of innovation has focused on three sets of factors:

1. those relating to the external environment in which innovation occurs;
2. those related to the individual innovator or adopter who may be a key person within an innovating or adopting group;
3. those relating to the innovating organization itself.

Rogers pointed out that there has been much more research in the first two categories than there has been in the third and there is a need for more research into the organizational characteristics of the innovating group. The present research seeks to contribute to satisfying this need.

Managers are rarely empowered to effect change in the environments in which their organizations operate. Neither do they have much control over the personal characteristics of an innovator, other than in the context of selection and dismissal decisions. However, managers do have the power and responsibility to influence organizational characteristics. If the present research adds to our understanding of the influence of organizational characteristics on innovation, then it might be both practically useful and also possibly satisfy Rogers' identified need for further research in the area.

Many researches may have focused on individual characteristics because it is quicker and cheaper to do so. A research programme based on interviews just with chief executives, for example, would be a much easier enterprise than an investigation of organization factors based on studies of many individuals from various levels in the organization. However, the perceptions of one individual, no matter how senior, are likely to be different from the perceptions of other organization members. Chief executives may, for example, find it difficult to distinguish between how they actually perceive things to be and how they would like them to be. This difference may be crucial.

Studying organizational factors would, it was hoped, identify influencing variables over which managers can establish some control.

The nature of the project required that research be undertaken actually within firms, trying to identify critical factors; it was not a problem that was amenable to analysis of secondary data. An early issue to be considered was which firms should be investigated. In order to focus on organizational characteristics it was decided to eliminate, as far as possible, the environmental differences that might make an impact. Thus it was essential to choose firms from a single industrial sector, which would therefore experience similar environmental turbulence and stimulation.

Much innovation research has focused on the new high-technology industries. Consequently, and for reasons referred to in the preface, it was decided that the sector chosen would be mature. There is of course a problem in defining maturity. Is maturity simply a matter of years, or is it a question of recent growth rate? Or are the essential characteristics of maturity better identified by having regard to the sector's anticipated future? Maturity is an ambiguous concept.

There is an established orthodoxy regarding the way an industry, or product, develops. The product life cycle starts with a period of very slow growth while development of the product is still proceeding. After this initial phase, while the product is gaining limited acceptance, successful products enjoy a period of high growth, the unsuccessful being generally withdrawn. During this high-growth phase, the product is developed rapidly, encouraged by its increasingly widespread use. Gradually standards of performance become established and product development slows down as market growth slows. The two coincide because, it is suggested, the two are interdependent. Thus the product enters a mature low-growth phase. Initially, this is characterized by fierce competition while producers fight for shares of the market, which now appears not to be as large as previously projected. During this period of change from growth to maturity, profit margins are reduced, many participants are 'shaken out' or withdraw, and the emphasis of innovation turns decisively from product development to cost-reducing process developments. Thus the emphasis of innovation in a mature industry is, according to the orthodox wisdom, likely to be on process rather than product.

For the purposes of this research, therefore, maturity was assumed to refer simply to the stage in the sector's development where it has already progressed through the highly volatile stage from high growth to more or less stable low growth.

It was also decided to choose a sector that could be defined by its process. In seeking to eliminate as far as possible variables arising from the environment it would clearly be convenient if the firms to be studied had all had available to them the same opportunities for innovation. In a mature sector with innovations being related mainly to process, it would clearly be convenient if the firms shared the same process and thus had available to them the same innovative developments.

A number of potential sectors were considered initially, mainly within engineering, for reasons of personal familiarity. For example, pumps and valves seemed likely candidates. However, in these areas there are a number of different technical solutions to basically similar problems. Thus there are firms with fundamentally different technological backgrounds and expertise competing in essentially the same (though not exactly) product market. The ideal sector would be one that did not exhibit this ambiguity.

The textile industry was also considered. This can be divided in a number of ways: by raw material (wool, cotton, etc.), by end market (apparel, household, industrial, etc.) or by process (weaving, knitting, non-woven, etc.). One such textile sector, warp knitting, had a number of features which made it attractive. It was undoubtedly mature – it had been in existence for over 200 years, had experienced two periods of growth and shake-out since the Second World War, and had shown little growth over the past decade. It was also an easily distinguished sector, with few apparent ambiguous edges to it – firms either use warp knitting machines or not. It was also a small sector, making it feasible within the limits of the research to make contact with all participants. Finally, it was geographically convenient, being centred mainly around Nottingham and the East Midlands.

Warp knitting was selected for the research and as the programme progressed it became clear that, mature or not, warp knitting contained some highly innovative participants. The sector had benefited from many pervasive electronic innovations and their applications in automation and information technology. These, as the orthodox wisdom suggests is likely, were mainly deployed in the *process* of warp knitting. However, the impact has been so great on warp knitting economics that many new products have also been made possible as a result.

In recent years the sector has seen many important innovations become available. Not surprisingly, some firms have adopted them rapidly while others have been slower or even appear to have avoided them altogether. The aim of the research was to discover which, if any, organizational characteristics differentiated the leading innovators from the laggards and thus might facilitate or hinder innovation.

Outline of the empirical study

The first phase of the research was to identify firms in the warp knitting sector and conduct a survey in order to rank them in terms of innovativeness. The approach used followed precedents set in a number of diffusion studies (e.g. Allen and Hayward 1972). A total of 17 innovations were identified that had been available to the warp knitting industry, some related to the production process, some to product developments and some to new administrative and management systems. Participants were asked simply if and when they had invested in each of the innovations. Thus a picture was built up of how innovations had been adopted and which firms were the leaders and which the laggards.

This objective approach was then corroborated by reference to the opinions of industry experts as to which firms were most and least innovative. This permitted a rank ordering in terms of innovativeness to be made of participants in the industry. While the accuracy of this ranking must be open to some doubt, there was considerable coincidence of results from the two methods and the general picture of innovativeness in the sector, from leaders to laggards, appeared unambiguous.

A methodology pilot study was carried out to assess the validity and practicality of various research approaches in assessing the organizational characteristics of potential interest. The approaches that were used included participant observation, unstructured and semi-structured interviews, as well as the progressive development of structured interviews.

The next phase of the project was to select a subset of warp knitters to investigate in greater depth in order to establish which were the organizational characteristics that effectively distinguished the innovative firms from the less innovative. This was done by comparing some of the most innovative firms and some of the less innovative, initially using primarily observation and semi-structured interviews, the interviews being conducted with several individuals in each firm drawn from different levels of the organization. A most important aspect of this part of the project was establishing a suitable methodology for measuring the characteristics in each firm.

The project followed the approach espoused by Glaser and Strauss in *The Discovery of Grounded Theory* in that the hypothesis was developed progressively out of the research and was then, as far as possible in a project of this limited scale, verified. The research followed an iterative process from theory to pilot study to theory to preliminary interviews to theory to main interview programme.

During the main phase of research the nature of the various factors that appeared critical to a firm's innovativeness became progressively clearer. These were found to form two clusters of factors, one related to the strategic focus of the business and the other related to the organizational style or culture.

A tightly structured interview schedule was progressively developed using the semantic differential scaling method, which permitted the hypothesis to be represented as a perceptual map and also for some preliminary statistical testing to be carried out. This interview schedule was the basis of the questionnaires provided at the end of Parts Two and Three.

Each cluster of characteristics was seen as being measurable along a single dimension. The characteristics associated with strategy were measurable along a continuum from dispersed to focused, while those related to culture were measurable along a continuum from traditional to progressive. The derivation of these terms was largely as explained in the present text.

Thus the competitive matrix described in this book is derived directly from the above research programme with subsequent amendments as suggested by further usage.

References

Allen, D. H. and G. Hayward, 'Innovations in the capital equipment area: their effect on diffusion', *Business Graduate*, Vol. 2, No. 3, 1972.

Glaser, B. G. and A. L. Strauss, *The Discovery of Grounded Theory*, Weidenfeld & Nicolson, London, 1967.

Rogers, E. M., *Diffusion of Innovations* 3rd edn, Free Press, New York, 1983.

Appendix II
A note on using the questionnaires

These notes provide some additional guidance in assessing the competitive position of an organization, by identifying the strategy and culture profiles using the questionnaires at the end of Chapters 12 and 17.

As emphasized in the text, the position of any organization cannot be established simply by reference to the chief executive and his or her response to the survey questions. The chief executive is at a particular disadvantage when it comes to assessing the status of the organization. The chief executive will be able to indicate the desired or intended position but, as the original research revealed, the difference between the intended position and the actual can be both extreme and extremely important.

The survey must be carried out with a cross-section of the organization, ideally with every member, but failing that with a sample representing the different levels and functions within the organization. Administering the survey among groups of people from widely different backgrounds requires care and special attention should be paid to the points below.

The wording of the statements may need to be amended according to the organization and the interviewee. The statements quoted in the text, though using essentially simple language, were prepared for use with the management team in a high-technology manufacturing organization. The language and terminology used needs to be appropriate to your organization.

Where terminology is inappropriate, the question should be amended accordingly. Questions relating specifically to manufacturing, for example, should be modified for service and public sector organizations. References to profitability can be changed to refer to efficiency where profits do not apply. Similarly, a number of questions included contain vocabulary which is appropriate to management groups, but which may be misunderstood by other groups. These can also be modified. Such changes, and other similar ones which may be necessary to meet particular circumstances, will not change the essence of the survey, so long as the point at issue raised in the question and explained in the relevant chapter, is understood and retained in the reworded statement. The essential point is to ensure that interviewees understand the question they are being asked.

The questions should be asked face to face and respondents' immediate answers recorded. It is respondents' perceptions that are being assessed, because it is perceptions of reality, rather than the reality itself, which affect behaviour. Where respondents don't know the truth of any statement, it is still their perception that matters. Where they have no idea, or feel, for the truth of a statement, the response should be left blank and that question omitted from the averaging and percentage calculations.

Although the statements included in Chapters 12 and 17 are grouped according to the profile component being assessed, when the questionnaire is actually being administered the statements should be mixed so that they are delivered in random order. This reduces the risk of the response to one statement influencing the response to a related statement.

It is also advisable for the survey to be conducted by a 'neutral' individual rather than a member of the management team or an employee representative. Using a third party – consultant, academic or student – would provide this degree of neutrality, so that responses to the statements are not biased by the perceived role of the interviewer.

Some of the statements may be regarded as sensitive and confidentiality of individual responses has to be guaranteed if truthful answers are to be obtained.

In the original research interviews took place in neutral territory wherever possible, such as canteens, rest rooms or reception areas, rather than managerial offices. The only requirement was that the process should not be interrupted by personal interventions or the phone.

Interviewees were put at their ease, given a brief and neutral explanation of the purpose of the interview and assured of confidentiality. The process was then briefly explained including the requirement to provide their responses immediately rather than after deep thought or consideration. The interviewee was then given an answer card with the rating scale on it so that they could respond either in words (completely true, mainly true, etc.) or in numbers (1 to 7). In practice, most interviewees quickly find numbers the most convenient way of answering.

Before starting the process, respondents can be given one or two dummy questions to respond to, just to make sure they understand the process.

The full interview process can generally be completed within half an hour. If it takes much longer than this it is probably because the respondent is taking too long to think the answers through, rather than giving an immediate perception.

One of the great virtues of the process is its simplicity and practicality, both in administering the interviews and analysing the responses. However, simplicity and practicality are bought at a price. A more sophisticated instrument may be able to achieve greater validity and reliability, though the practicality of using such a process on any scale would be extremely limited on grounds of time and cost. Nevertheless, it is worth re-emphasizing the point made in the text that the model is not definitive, but indicative. It does not directly prescribe management action, but rather indicates areas for management consideration. It does not give complete answers, but it does highlight potential problem areas and possible solutions that would not be recognized otherwise.

Bibliography

Adair, J., *Effective Leadership*, Gower, London, 1983.
Adams, J. S., 'Injustice in Social Exchange' in L. Berkowitz (ed.) *Advances in Experimental Social Psychology* Vol. 2, Academic Press, New York, 1965:265–99.
Adler, N. J. and F. Chador, 'Strategic Human Resource Management – a global perspective' in Pieper Rudiger (ed.), *Human Resource Management in International Comparison*, de Gruyter, Berlin, 1989.
Alberts, W. W., 'The experience curve doctrine revisited', *Journal of Marketing* July 1989.
Alderfer, C. P., *Existence, Relatedness and Growth*, Free Press, New York, 1972.
Allen, D. H. and G. Hayward, 'Innovations in the capital equipment area: their effect on diffusion', *Business Graduate*, Vol. 2, No. 3, 1972.
Atkinson, J. W., *An Introduction to Motivation*, Van Nostrand, New York, 1964.
Bailey, J., *Job Design and Work Organization*, Prentice-Hall, Englewood Cliffs, 1983.
Barham, K., J. Fraser and L. Heath, 'Management for the Future' – a research project sponsored by the Foundation for Management Education and Ashridge Management College, 1988.
Bass, B. M., 'From transactional to transformational leadership: learning to share the vision', *Organizational Dynamics*, Winter 1990.
Baumol, W. J., 'Entrepreneurship and a century of economic growth', *Journal of Business Venturing* No. 1, 1986.
Best, W. J., 'Japanese logistics', *Strategic Direction*, June 1990:14–15.
Bentham, J., *Introduction to the Principles of Morals and Legislation*, 1789.
Blake, R. R. and J. S. Mouton, *Managing Group Conflict in Industry*, Gulf Publishing Company, 1964.
Boston Consulting Group, 'Perspectives on Experience', Boston Consulting Group, Boston, 1968a.
Boston Consulting Group, 'Growth and Financial Strategies', Boston Consulting Group, Boston, 1968b.
Bower, J. L. and M. Hout, 'Fast cycle capability for competitive power', *Harvard Business Review*, Nov–Dec 1988:110–18.
Brech, E. F. L., *Organization: the Framework of Management*, Longman, Harlow, 1957.
Burgelman, R. A., 'Managing the internal corporate venturing process', *Sloan Management Review*, Winter 1984:23–48.
Burgoyne, J., 'Management development for the individual and the organisation', *Personnel Management*, June 1988.
Burns, T. and G. M. Stalker, *The Management of Innovation*, Tavistock Institute, London, 1961.
Campbell, A. and M. Devine, *A Sense of Mission*, Economist Publications, 1990.

Campbell, J. P. and R. D. Pritchard, 'Motivation Theory in Industrial and Organizational Psychology' in M. D. Dunnette (ed.) *Handbook of Industrial and Organizational Psychology*, Rand McNally, Chicago, 1976.

Carnall, C. A., *Managing Change in Organisations*, Prentice-Hall, Hemel Hempstead, 1990.

Carter, C. F. and B. R. Williams, *Industry and Technical Progress – factors governing the speed of application of science*, Oxford University Press, Oxford, 1956.

Centre for the Study of Industrial Innovation, survey of shelved R&D projects – 'On the Shelf', 1971.

Chandler, A. D., 'The enduring logic of industrial success', *Harvard Business Review*, March–April 1990:130–40.

Chase, R. B. and D. A. Garvin, 'The service factory', *Harvard Business Review* July–Aug 1989:61–9.

Child, J., H.-D. Ganter and A. Lieser, 'Technological Innovation and Organizational Conservatism' in J. M. Pennings and D. Buitendam (eds) *New Technology as Organizational Innovation*, Ballinger, Cambridge, Mass., 1987.

Chisnall, P. M., *Strategic Industrial Marketing*, Prentice-Hall, Hemel Hempstead, 1985a.

Chisnall, P. M., *Marketing: a behavioural analysis* 2nd edn, McGraw-Hill, Maidenhead, 1985b.

Clark, K. B., 'What strategy can do for technology', *Harvard Business Review*, Nov–Dec 1989.

Cooper, A. C., G. E. Willard and C. Y. Wood, 'Strategies of new and small firms: a re-examination of the niche concept', *Journal of Business Venturing*, Vol. 1, No. 3, 1986:247–60.

Cooper, R. G., 'How to identify potential new product winners', *Research Management*, Vol. 23, No. 9, 1980.

Croome, H., 'Human Problems of Innovation', Department of Scientific and Industrial Research pamphlet, Problems of Progress in Industry, No. 5, 1960.

Deschampes, J. P., 'Market driven product development', *Strategic Direction*, June 1990:8–11.

Devlin, G., and M. Blackley, 'Strategic alliances – guidelines for success', *Long Range Planning*, Vol. 21/5, No. 111, October 1988:18–23.

Dixon, M., 'On the receiving end', *Business*, June 1990:153.

Donaldson, J., *Key Issues in Business Ethics*, Academic Press, London, 1989.

Drucker, P. F., *Managing for Results*, Harper & Row, New York, 1964. (Currently available from Heinemann Professional Publishing, Oxford, 1989.)

Drucker, P. F., *Innovation and Entrepreneurship*, Heinemann, London, 1985.

Drucker, P. F., 'The coming of the new organization', *Harvard Business Review*, Jan–Feb 1988.

Edwardes, M., *Back from the Brink*, Collins, London, 1982.

Evans, M. G., 'The effects of supervisory behaviour on the path goal relationship', *Organisational Behaviour and Human Performance*, No. 5, 1970.

Evans, M. G., 'Extensions of a path goal theory of motivation', *Journal of Applied Psychology*, 59, 1974.

Fayol, H., *General and Industrial Management*, Pitman, London, 1949. (Translated by C. Storrs from the original French *Administration Industrielle et Générale* (1916).)

Ferguson, A., 'The myth of leadership dismantled', *The Independent on Sunday*, 10 June 1990.

Fiedler, F. E., *A Theory of Leadership Effectiveness*, McGraw-Hill, New York, 1967.
Foster, W. K. and A. K. Pryor, 'The strategic management of innovation', *The Journal of Business Strategy*, 1985.
Fox, A., 'Industrial Sociology and Industrial Relations', Royal Commission on Trade Unions and Employers' Associations, Research Paper 3, HMSO, 1966.
Garvin, D. A., 'Competing on the eight dimensions of quality', *Harvard Business Review*, Nov–Dec 1987.
Gilbert, X. and P. Strebel, 'Developing Competitive Advantage' in J. B. Quinn, H. Mintzberg and R. M. James, *The Strategic Process*, Prentice-Hall, Englewood Cliffs, 1988.
Gilder, G., *The Spirit of Enterprise*, Penguin Books, Harmondsworth, 1986.
Glaser, B. G. and A. L. Strauss, *The Discovery of Grounded Theory*, Weidenfeld & Nicolson, London, 1967.
Gluck, F. W., 'A fresh look at strategic management', *The Journal of Business Strategy*, Fall 1985.
Goldsmith, W. and D. Clutterbuck, *The Winning Streak*, Penguin, Harmondsworth 1985:123.
Green, D., 'Learning from losing a customer', *Harvard Business Review*, May–June 1989:54–8.
Green, P. and D. S. Tull, *Research for Marketing Decisions*, Prentice-Hall, Englewood Cliffs, 1970.
Hackman, J. R. and G. R. Oldham, *Work Redesign*, Addison Wesley, Reading, Mass. 1980.
Hall, W. K., 'Survival strategies in a hostile environment', *Harvard Business Review*, Sept–Oct 1980.
Hamel, G., 'Corporate Strategies and Technological Cooperation', paper presented to a UACES Conference on European Technological Collaboration, Brunel University, 14 May 1987.
Hamel, G., Y. L. Doz and C. K. Pralahad, 'Collaborate with your competitors – and win', *Harvard Business Review*, Jan–Feb 1989.
Hamel, G. and C. K. Pralahad, 'Strategic intent', *Harvard Business Review*, May–June 1989.
Handy, C. B., *Understanding Organizations*, Penguin, Harmondsworth, 1981.
Hayes, R. H. and W. J. Abernathy, 'Managing our way to economic decline', *Harvard Business Review*, May–June 1980.
Hayes, R. H. and D. Garvin, 'Managing as if tomorrow mattered', *Harvard Business Review*, May–June 1982:71–9.
Heller, F. A., 'Working models on the shop floor', *Times Higher Education Supplement*, 29 January 1988:15.
Herzberg, F., B. Mausner and B. B. Snyderman, *The Motivation to Work*, Wiley, New York, 1959.
HMSO, Central Advisory Council of Science and Technology, *Technological Innovation in Britain*, HMSO, 1968.
Hodder, J. E., 'Evaluation of manufacturing investments: a comparison of US and Japanese practices', *Financial Management*, Spring 1986:17–24.
Holloman, J. H., 'Innovation and Profitability', Science of Science Foundation, 1967.
Hopkins, D. S., 'New product winners and losers', *R&D Management*, May 1981.
House, R. J. and M. L. Baetz, 'Leadership: some generalisations and new research directions' in B. M. Staw (ed.) *Research in Organisational Behaviour*, JAI, 1979.

House, R. J. and G. Dessler, 'The path goal theory of leadership: some post hoc and a priori tests' in J. G. Hunt and L. L. Larson (eds) *Contingency Approaches to Leadership*, Southern Illinois University Press, 1974.

House, R. J. and T. R. Mitchell, 'Path goal theory of leadership', *Journal of Contemporary Business*, Autumn 1974, 3:91–8.

Hutton, W., 'Short-changed by short-termism', *The Guardian*, 20 June, 1990.

Jaeger, A. M. and B. R. Baliga, 'Control systems and strategic adaption: lessons from the Japanese experience', *Strategic Management Journal*, Vol. 6, 1985:115–34.

Johne, F. A., *Industrial Product Innovation: Organisation and Management*, Croom Helm, London, 1985.

Kanter, R. M., *The Change Masters: Corporate Entrepreneurs at Work*, Unwin Hyman, London, 1983.

Kanter, R. M., *When Giants Learn to Dance*, Unwin Hyman, London, 1990.

Kobayashi, N., 'Strategic alliances with Japanese firms', *Long Range Planning*, Vol. 21/2, No. 108, April 1988.

Kotter, J. P., *A Force for Change: How Leadership Differs from Management*, Macmillan, New York, 1990.

Kuhn, R. L., 'Japanese-American strategic alliances', *Journal of Business Strategy*, March–April 1989.

Lawler, E. E., III, *Motivation in Work Organizations*, Brooks/Cole, Monterey, Calif., 1973.

Lei, D., 'Strategies for global competition', *Long Range Planning*, Vol. 22, No. 1, February 1989:102–9.

Leitko, T. A. and D. Szczerbacki, 'Why traditional OD strategies fail in professional bureaucracies', *Organizational Dynamics*, Winter 1987.

Lewin, K., R. Lippitt, and R. K. White, 'Patterns of aggressive behaviour in experimentally created "social climates"', *Journal of Social Psychology*, No. 10, 1939.

Lorsch, J. W., 'Managing culture: the invisible barrier to strategic change, *California Management Review*, Vol. xxviii, No. 2, Winter 1986.

McClelland, D. C., J. W. Atkinson, R. A. Clark and E. L. Lowell, *The Achievement Motive*, Van Nostrand, New York, 1953.

McGregor, D. M., *The Human Side of Enterprise*, McGraw-Hill, New York, 1960.

Maddison, A., *Phases of Capitalist Development*, Oxford University Press, Oxford, 1982.

Madia, W. J., 'EC technology partnerships', *Strategic Direction*, February 1990.

Mansfield, E., *Industrial Research and Technological Innovation: an econometric analysis*, Longman, London, 1969.

Maslow, A., 'A theory of human motivation', *Psychological Review*, Vol. 50, 1943.

Miller, W. F., 'Technology and global strategy', *Strategic Direction*, January 1990.

Mintzberg, H., *Structure in Fives: Designing Effective Organizations*, Prentice-Hall, Engelwood Cliffs, 1983.

Mintzberg, H., 'The strategy concept', *California Management Review*, Fall 1987:11–32.

Mitchell, T. R., 'Expectancy models of job satisfaction, occupational preference, and effort: a theoretical, methodological and empirical appraisal', *Psychological Bulletin*, 1974, 81:1096–112.

Mohr, L. B., 'Innovation Theory: an assessment from the vantage point of the new electronic technology in organizations' in J. M. Pennings and D. Buitendam

(eds) *New Technology as Organizational Innovation*, Ballinger, Cambridge, Mass., 1987.
Morone, J., 'Strategic use of technology', *California Management Review*, Vol. 31, No. 4, 1989:91–112.
Mueller, R. K., *Corporate Networking – Building Channels for Information and Influence*, Free Press, New York, 1986.
Murray, H. A., *Explorations in Personality*, Oxford University Press, New York, 1938.
Myers, S. and D. G., Marquis, 'Successful Industrial Innovations: a study of factors underlying innovations in selected firms', National Science Foundation, 1969.
Ohmae, K., 'Getting back to strategy', *Harvard Business Review*, Nov–Dec 1988.
Ohmae, K., 'Companyism and do more better', *Harvard Business Review*, Jan–Feb 1989a.
Ohmae, K., 'Managing in a borderless world,' *Harvard Business Review*, May–June 1989b.
Ouchi, W. G. and M. Kremen Bolton, 'The logic of joint research and development', *California Management Review*, Vol. xxx, No. 3, Spring 1988.
Pascale, R., 'The paradox of "corporate culture": reconciling ourselves to socialization', *California Management Review*, Vol. xxvii, No. 2, 1985:26–41.
Patton, A. and J. C. Baker, 'Why don't directors rock the boat?', *Harvard Business Review*, Nov–Dec 1987.
Pearson, G. J., *The Strategic Discount*, Wiley, Chichester, 1985.
Pearson, G. J., 'Factors which facilitate and inhibit innovation in a mature industry', Unpublished doctoral thesis, Manchester Business School, University of Manchester, 1989.
Pearson, G. J., *Strategic Thinking*, Prentice-Hall, Hemel Hempstead, 1990.
Pearson, G. J., A. W. Pearson, and D. F. Ball, 'Innovation in a mature industry: a case study of warp knitting in the UK', *Technovation*, Vol. 9, 1989:657–79.
Pedler, M., T. Boydell and J. Burgoyne, 'Learning Company Project Report', Training Agency, 1988.
Pedler, M., T. Boydell and J. Burgoyne, 'Towards the learning company', *Management Education & Development.*, Vol. 20, Part 1, 1989.
Peters, T and R. H. Waterman, *In Search of Excellence*, Harper & Row, New York, 1982.
Piatier, A., *Barriers to Innovation* (a study carried out for the Commission of the European Communities Directorate), Francis Pinter, London, 1984.
Pinchot, G., *Intrapreneuring*, Harper & Row, New York, 1985.
Porter, M. E., *Competitive Strategy: Techniques for Analyzing Industries and Competitors*, Free Press, New York, 1980.
Porter, M. E., Video film and pamphlet: 'Michael Porter on Competitive Strategy', Harvard Business School Video Series, 1988.
Pralahad, C. K. and G. Hamel, 'The core competence of the corporation', *Harvard Business Review*, May–June 1990.
Project SAPPHO, 'Success and Failure in Industrial Innovation', Science Policy Research Unit, University of Sussex, 1972.
Pugh, D. S., D. J. Hickson., C. R. Hinings and C. Turner, 'The context of organisation structure', *Administrative Science Quarterly*, Vol. 14, 1969:91–114.
Purcell, J., 'Mapping management styles in employee relations', *Journal of Management Studies*, September 1987.
Quinn, J. B., T. L. Doorley and P. C. Paquette, 'Beyond products: services-based strategy', *Harvard Business Review*, March–April 1990:58–68.

Rabstejavek, G., 'Let's get back to the basics of strategy', *The Journal of Business Strategy*, Sept/Oct 1989:32–5.
Ramo, S., 'National security and our technology edge', *Harvard Business Review*, Nov–Dec 1989.
Ray, G. F., 'The diffusion of mature technologies', *National Institute Economic Review*, No. 106, November 1983.
Reichheld, F. F. and W. E. Sasser Jr., 'Zero defects: quality comes to services', *Harvard Business Review*, Sept–Oct 1990.
Reynolds, P. C., 'Corporate culture on the rocks', *Across the Board*, October 1986.
Robertson, A., 'The marketing factor in successful industrial innovation', *Industrial Marketing Management*, Vol. 2, 1973.
Roberston, T. S., 'The process of innovation and the diffusion of innovations', *Journal of Marketing*, Vol. 3, January 1967.
Rogers, C. R., *Freedom to Learn*, Charles Merrill, Columbus, Ohio, 1969.
Rogers, E. M., *Diffusion of Innovations* 3rd edn, Free Press, New York, 1983.
Rothwell, R., 'Successful and unsuccessful innovators', *Planned Innovation*, April 1979.
Selznick, P., *Leadership and Administration*, Harper & Row, New York, 1957.
Simon, H. A., 'How managers express their creativity', *Across the Board*, No. 3, 1986.
Skinner, W., 'The productivity paradox', *Harvard Business Review*, July–Aug 1986:55–9.
Slatter, S., *Corporate Recovery: successful turnaround strategies and their implementation*, Penguin, Harmondsworth, 1984.
Sloan, A. P., *My Years with General Motors*, Sidgwick & Jackson, London, 1965.
Spekman, R. E., 'Buyer–seller relations', *Strategic Direction*, February 1990.
Staw, B. M., *Intrinsic and Extrinsic Motivation*, General Learning Press, Morristown, NJ, 1975.
Stogdill, R. M., 'Personal factors associated with leadership: a survey of the literature', *Journal of Psychology*, No. 25, 1948.
Stogdill, R. M., *Handbook of Leadership: a survey of theory and research*, Free Press, New York, 1974.
Taylor, F. W., *Scientific Management*, Harper & Row, New York, 1947.
Telser, L. G., *A Theory of Efficient Cooperation and Competition*, Cambridge University Press, Cambridge, 1987.
Urwick, L. F., *The Elements of Administration*, Pitman, London, 1947.
Utterback, J. M. and W. J. Abernathy, 'A dynamic model of process and product innovation', *OMEGA*, Vol. 3, No. 6, 1975:639–56.
Vroom, V. H., *Work and Motivation*, Wiley, New York, 1964.
White, I., 'The Perception of Value in Products' in J. W. Newman (ed.), *On Knowing the Consumer*, Wiley, New York, 1966.
Yip, G. S., P. M. Loewe and M. Y. Yoshino, 'How to take your company to the global market', *Columbia Journal of World Business*, Vol. 23, No. 4, Winter 1988:37–48.

Index

Accounting philosophy, 164
Achievement-oriented leadership, 169
Adair, J., 166, 171–172
Adams, J. S., 177
Alberts, W. W., 5
Alderfer, C. P., 179
Atkinson, J. W., 178
Authoritarian leadership, 167
Authority decisions, 32
Autocrats, 16–18, 32, 63, 199–200, 211–219
Autonomy, 156–157, 181, 182

Bailey, J., 160
Barham, K., J. Fraser and L. Heath, 141–142
Baumol, W. J., 20
Behavioural inertia, 46
Benneton, 106–107
Bentham, J., 155–156
Best, W. J., 111
Blake, R. R. and J. S. Mouton, 168
Boards of directors, 73, 171
Body Shop, 154
Boston's matrix/portfolio model, 4, 23, 72, 99
Bower, J. L. and M. Hout, 106
Brainstorming, 33
Brech, E. F. L., 170
Burgelman, R. A., 95
Burgoyne, J., 142
Bureaucratic organizations, 32
Bureaucrats, 16–18, 199–200, 211–219
Burns, T. and G. M. Stalker, 43, 45–46, 137, 146
Business Assessment Array (BAA), 5, 6
Business ethics, 149, 155–157
Business life cycle, 52–54
Business maturity, 52–62

Business strength, 6
Butterflies, 16–18, 63, 64, 78, 199, 202, 207–209

Campbell, J. P. and R. D. Pritchard, 176
Canon, 102–103, 106, 107
Carter's Gold Medal Soft Drinks, 12, 100, 101
Carter, C. F. and B. R. Williams, 39–40, 42–43, 81
Categorical imperative, 156
Centre for the Study of Industrial Innovation, 43
Chandler, A. D., 103
Change agents, 32–33
Change:
  avoidance, 33
  evaluating, 34–37
  implementing, 372
  initiating, 33–34
Chase, R. B. and D. A. Gavin, 116
Child, J., H.-D. Ganter and A. Lieser, 41, 47, 127–128
Chisnall, P. M., 40, 44
Clark, K. B., 100
Coca-Cola, 107
Collaboration, 103–105
Collectivism, 163
Commitment, 45–46, 48, 73, 169, 185, 186, 191–192
Communications, 45, 103, 169, 216, 218
Communications networks, 86–87
Compatibility (of innovations), 41
Competence gaps, 107–108
Competitive advantage, 34, 102
Competitive challenges, 107–108
Competitive specialism, 13–14
Competitive matrix/model, 15–17, 63–66, 195–205

Competitor analysis, 119–120
Complexity (of innovations), 41
Concentration, 75, 79, 80
Consideration leadership, 168
Consistency, 75, 80
Consumption, 21
Continuous innovations, 40
Control of the environment, 52, 57
Control (of the organization), 143–145
Conversion process, 21
Cooper, A. C., G. E. Willard and C. Y. Wood, 79
Cooper, R. G., 44
Core competences, 99–109, 120, 125, 132–133
Core (generic) products, 100, 120
Corporate integrity, 149–158, 185, 186, 190, 217
Corporate networks, 86–87
Corporate recovery, 211
Cost leadership, 9–11, 72, 201
Creativity, 33–34
Croome, H., 45–46
Culture, 15–17, 72, 79, 99, 135–136, 140, 185–188, 198 (*see also* Strong cultures)
Culture profile questionnaire, 189–192
Customer focus (orientation), 110–121, 125, 133–134
Customer needs (and perceptions), 115–118)

DCF (Discounted cash flow), 36, 164
Decision making, 164–166
Declining industries, 65
Defensive innovation, 42
Demand–pull, 30
Democratic leadership, 167
Deschampes, J. P., 116
Devlin, G. and M. Blackley, 105
Differentiation, 9–11, 72
Diffusion effect, 41–42
Diffusion (of innovations), 103
Direction, 75 (*see also* Strategic direction)
Directional Policy Matrix (DPM), 6
Directive leadership, 168
Discontinuous innovations, 40
Discovery–push, 30
Disinvestment spiral, 97, 105, 201
Distinctive competence, 99

Distribution, 21
Diversification, 55
Dixon, M., 214
Double standards, 154
Drucker, P. F., 9, 25, 61, 99, 170
Dynamically continuous innovations, 40

Economic environment, 84–86
Edwardes, M., 215
Employee-oriented leadership, 168
Empowerment, 137–147, 185, 186, 189–190, 216
Entrepreneur, 13
Entrepreneurial, 72
Entrepreneurialism, 12–15
Equity (theory of motivation), 177
Evans, M. G., 168
Evolutionary innovations, 40
Expectancy (theory of motivation), 176, 182
Experience (curve), 4
External communications, 71–72, 81–89, 124, 131–132

Facilitation, 139
Falcon Computer, 153
Fashion leaders, 32
Fayol H., 170, 212
Feedback, 181, 182
Ferguson, A., 166–177, 169
Fiedler, F.E., 167
Financial evaluation, 35–37
Focus, 11
Focused strategy, 16–17
Fox, A., 160–161
Freedom to learn, 138

Garvin, D. A., 111–114
Gatekeepers, 32
Generic (core) products, 100, 120
Generic strategies, 7–11, 72
Gilbert, X. and P. Strebel, 9
Gilder, G., 14, 102
Global competition, 12
Global leadership, 101
Globalization, 100
Gluck, F. W., 6
Going concern, 36
Golden rule, 156–157

INDEX

Goldsmith, W. and D. Clutterbuck, 149, 150, 183
Green, D., 83, 115
Green, P. and D. S. Tull, 117–118
GWRK file, 86–87

Hackman, J. R. and G. W. Oldham, 181
Hall, W. K., 9
Hamel, G., 105
Hamel, G., Y. L. Doz and C. K. Pralahad, 105
Hamel, G. and C. K. Pralahad, 81, 102
Handy, C. B., 145–146
Hayes, R. H. and W. J. Abernathy, 96
Hayes, R. H. and D. Garvin, 96–97, 201
Heller, F. A., 215
Herzberg, F., B. Mausner and B. B. Snyderman, 178, 179, 180
Hewlett Packard, 106, 111
Hodder, J. E., 35
Holloman, J. H., 44
Honda, 26, 101–102, 105, 114
Hopkins, D. S., 44
House, R. J. and G. Dessler, 168
House, R. J. and T. R. Mitchell, 168, 178
Hutton, W, 96

Individualism, 162–163
Industry assessment, 63–68
Industry analysis, 7–8
Industrial revolution(s), 22–24
Ingredient 'X', 114
Inertia, 33
Initiating structure leadership, 168
Innovation, 13, 15
 and business evolution, 58–61
 and competitive advantage, 24–27
 and economic growth, 20–24
 and living standards, 20
 categories, 40–42
 evaluation, 31
 implementation, 31
 initiation, 31
 leaders and laggards, 24
 process, 29–37
 research, 39–48
 roles, 31–33
 waves, 23

Innovative teams, 16–18, 63, 198–201, 206–219
Integrity of top management, 151–153, 185
Intrapreneur, 13
Intrinsic human needs, 178–180
Involvement, 160–171, 175, 185, 186, 191
IRR (Internal rate of return), 36

Jaeger, A. M. and B. R. Bakiga, 144
Johne, F. A., 213–214

Kanter, R. M., 81, 213
Key communicators, 32
Kotter, J. P., 74, 166, 167, 169

Laissez-faire leadership, 167
Lawler, E. E., 176
Leadership (market), 25, 55, 99–100, 101, 102, 103
Leadership (management), 166–170, 175, 185, 186, 191
Learning company, 142–143
Learning organization, 141–143
Legitimation, of ideas, 32
Leitko, T. A. and D. Szczerbacki, 214–215
Lewin, K., R. Lippitt and R. K. White, 167
Limits (of development), 25–26
Liquidators, 17–18, 63–65, 199, 201, 209–211
Long-term investment, 94–95
Long-term orientation, 72, 91–98, 124–125, 132
Lorsch, J. W., 140
Losing a customer, 115–116

McClelland, D. C., J. W. Atkinson, R. A. Clark and E. L. Lowell, 178–179
McGregor, D. M., 138–140, 180
Maddison, A., 20
Madia, W. J., 104
Management philosophy, 137–141, 145, 185
Management responses (to natural tendencies), 64, 202-2-3
Managerial discretion, 55–578
Mansfield, E., 44
Market attractiveness, 6
Maslow, A., 178–179

Matrix management, 170, 213
Meaningfulness, 181, 182
Mechanistic organization, 45–46, 146, 213
Miller, W. F., 100
Mintzberg, H., 79, 101, 212
Mitchell, T. R., 176
Mohr, L. B., 46
Monopoly, 57
Morone, J., 95
Motivation, 169, 175–183, 185, 186, 192–193
Mueller, R. K., 86–87
Murray, H. A., 178
Myers, S. and D. G. Marquis, 30–31, 42, 43

Natural tendencies, 64, 202–203
Neales Ltd, 56–57
NEC, 106, 107, 171

Objectives, 77–79, 92–94
Observability (of innovations), 41
Offensive innovation, 42
Ohmae, K., 77, 100, 110
Openness, 157–158
Opinion leaders, 32
Organic organization, 45–46, 213, 214
Organismic organization, 45–46, 146
Organizational conservatism, 47–48
Organizational slack, 55–57
Ouchi, W. G. and M. K. Bolton, 103
Outcomes of strategy, 75–77
Ownership, 14–15, 182–183

Participation, 164–166
Participative leadership, 169
Pascale, R., 56, 144–145
Path–goal theory, 168–169
Patton, A. and J. C. Baker, 73–74
Pearson, G. J., 5, 36, 60–61
Pedler, M., T. Boydell and J. Burgoyne, 141, 142, 143
Penney, Wilf, 54
Peters, T. and R. H. Waterman, 110, 117, 170, 213, 214
Philip Morris, 9, 26
Piatier, A., 22
PIMS database, 99
Pinchot, G., 13
Pluralism, 156–157

Pluralist view, 160–162, 175
Political environment, 84–85
Porter, M. E., 7–11, 75
   competitive strategy, 23
   five forces, 7
   generic strategies, 7–11, 119
   implied matrix, 7
   stuck in the middle, 9
Power, 47
Pralahad, C. K. and G. Hamel, 93, 99, 105, 106
Preference mapping, 117–118
Process innovation, 58–61
Product champion, 44
Product innovation, 58–61
Production-oriented leadership, 168
Productivity paradox, 96, 97
Progressive culture, 15–17, 185–188
Progressive management, 138–141
Project champion, 33
Psychological contracts, 145–146, 161, 162
Psychological investment, 47, 55
Pugh, D. S., D. J. Hickson, C. R. Hinings and C. Turner, 212
Purcell, J., 140–141, 162, 163
Purpose (of business), 13
Purpose (of strategy), 74–75, 80

Quality, 110–115
Quinn, J. B., T. L. Doorley and P. C. Paquette, 102

Ramo, S., 104
Ray, G. F., 44
Reciprocity, 156
Reichfield, F. F. & W. E. Sasser, 116
Relative advantage (of innovations), 41
Revolutionary innovations, 40
Rewards (in relation to motivation), 181–183
Reynolds, P. C., 153
Risk premium, 36, 164–165
Robertson, T. S., 40, 44
Rogers, C., 38–141
Rogers, E. M., 13, 15, 24, 32
Rothwell, R., 39

SAPPHO, 43, 44
S-curve, 25–26

Secondary sources (of information), 87–89
Selznick, P., 99
Short-term pressures, 96–97
Simon, H. A., 33, 34
Skinner, W., 59, 96
Slatter, S., 211
Sloan, A., 214
Social environment, 85–86
Social responsibility, 149
Socialization, 144–145
Spekman, R. E., 103
Standardization, 127
Status quo (maintenance), 57
Staw, B. M., 181
Stimulation, of ideas, 32
Stogdill, R. M., 166
Stuck in the middle, 9, 48, 79
Strategic:
  alliances, 104–105
  direction, 48, 72–80, 93, 95, 124, 130–131
  discount, 36
  innovation, 61
  intent, 102
  objectives, 92–94
  position, 76, 79–80
Strategy profile questionnaire, 130–134
Strategic responsibility, 72–74
Strategy, 15–17, 71–80, 123–129, 197–198
Strong cultures, 17–18, 63, 144–145, 199, 200–201, 211–219
Structural change (of industries), 95
Structural designs (ways round the organization), 213

Supportive leadership, 169
Survival, 52–53
SWOT analysis, 75
Synectics, 33
System goals, 52

TAC Construction Materials Ltd, 54–55
Tastemakers, 32
Teams, 170, 217–218
Technological competence, 93, 95, 97
Technological competition, 11–12
Technological environment, 85–86
Technology gap, 35
Telser, L. G., 103
Theories X and Y, 138–140, 145, 175
Traditional management, 138–141
Transactions (as communications), 82–84
Trialability (of innovations), 41

Universalism, 156
Utilitarianism, 155–156
Urwick, L. F., 212
Utterback, J. M. and W. J. Abernathy, 59

Value, 111–115, 119
Value chain, 82
Vroom, V. H., 176

Warp knitting industry, 60–61
White, I., 39

Xerography, 26
Xerox, 102, 103, 106, 107